Internet 101

⇨ Other Glossbrenner computer books

The Complete Modem Handbook, 1995

Online Resources for Business, 1995

Making Money on the Internet, 1995

Finding a Job On the Internet, 1995

The Little Online Book, 1995

The Information Broker's Handbook, Second Edition, 1995

Internet Slick Tricks, 1994

DOS 6, 1993

Power DOS!, 1993

File & Disk Management: From Chaos to Control, 1993

Glossbrenner's Guide to Shareware for Small Businesses, 1992

The Information Broker's Handbook, 1992

DOS 5, 1992

Glossbrenner's Master Guide to GEnie, 1991

Glossbrenner's Complete Hard Disk Handbook, 1990

The Complete Handbook of Personal Computer Communications—3rd Edition, 1990

Glossbrenner's Master Guide to FREE Software for IBMs and Compatible Computers, 1989

Glossbrenner's Master Guide to CompuServe, 1987

How to Look It Up Online, 1987

The Complete Handbook of Personal Computer Communications—Second Edition, 1985

How to Get FREE Software, 1984

How to Buy Software, 1984

The Complete Handbook of Personal Computer Communications—First Edition, 1983

Word Processing for Executives, Managers, and Professionals, 1983

Internet 101
A College Student's Guide
2nd Edition

Alfred Glossbrenner

McGraw-Hill

New York   San Francisco   Washington, D.C.   Auckland   Bogotá
Caracas   Lisbon   London   Madrid   Mexico City   Milan
Montreal   New Delhi   San Juan   Singapore
Sydney   Tokyo   Toronto

pbk   1 2 3 4 5 6 7 8 9 0 DOC/DOC 9 9 8 7 6 5

Library of Congress Cataloging-in-Publication Data
Glossbrenner, Alfred.
     Internet 101 : a college student's guide / by Alfred Glossbrenner.
     —2nd ed.
        p.   cm.
     Includes index.
     ISBN 0-07-024207-0
     1. Internet (Computer network)—Handbooks, manuals, etc.
  I. Title.
  TK5105.875.I57G58   1995b
  004.6'7—dc20   95-9198
                                                                              CIP

Acquisitions editor: Brad Schepp
Editorial team: Joanne Slike, Executive Editor
              David M. McCandless, Managing Editor
              Emily Glossbrenner, Book Editor
              Joann Woy, Indexer
Production team: Katherine G. Brown, Director
              Donna Harlacher, Coding
              Jan Fisher, Layout
Design team: Jaclyn J. Boone, Designer
              Katherine Lukaszewicz, Associate Designer   WK2
                                                                       0242070

Contents

Part 3
Working the Net

Part 4
Campus & academic life

Part 5
Summer vacation, spring break, & study abroad

Part 6
Fun & games

Introduction

WARNING: The Dean of Academic Affairs has determined that accessing the Internet can be hazardous to your grades. In extensive tests, the GPA of laboratory animals was *severely* affected by repeated exposure to the Internet. Their IQs, on the other hand, showed a marked rise.

"They don't tell us *anything*!" That's what my friend Will said. He was working at a local computer store for the summer, and I was in buying four megabytes of memory for one of my systems. Will goes to a good school, and he's got an Internet account on the campus system. But he and his friends are basically flying blind on the Net because the system administrators either aren't around or are too busy or don't know much about the Internet themselves.

"If only there were a course I could take," Will said as he put the memory modules in an anti-static bag. I smiled. Because at the time I had already begun writing this book.

An incredible resource!

It would be a real tragedy these days to go through school without ever learning to use the Internet. Sure it's a hot topic. Sure it has been on the covers of *Time* magazine and *Business Week*. No question about it—the Internet is fashionable.

But it's also the most incredible storehouse of knowledge and information in human history. And for you, as a college student, it is almost certainly *free*! Learning to use the Net will not only help you with your research papers and coursework, it will also help you in your career after you graduate. For not only is the Net *everywhere*, it covers *everything*.

Of course, you can also have a lot of fun on the Internet—way too much fun, probably. It shouldn't be too long now before Internet addiction is officially recognized as a syndrome and treatments and various 12-step programs are created to cure it. Then magazines will do cover stories on *that*.

Teach a person to fish . . .

Meantime, this book is specifically designed to get you plugged in and up to speed fast. It begins with "The Internet 5-Minute University," a chapter that gives you instant Internet skills. That's followed by "Top 10 Cool Things You Can Do Right Now!," a chapter that will have you doing some pretty amazing stuff in seconds.

You can always use a computer or terminal at the campus computer center to tap the Internet. But since that's not always convenient, the next chapters in Part 1 cover the hardware and software you'll need to tap your campus computer system, and thus the Internet, from your dorm room or any other location.

Then there are the basic skills chapters that show you how to find and get things, and how to deal with the many types of compressed and other files on the Net. There are also chapters that teach you how to

capture, process, and view graphics and sound files from Internet newsgroups, and how to create your own home page on the World Wide Web.

The Internet is not a simple place. It is largely the creation of computer programmers and others with minds that thrive on complexity and originality. The result is a veritable jungle of differing procedures and options and ways of doing things. The chapters in Part 1 of this book will guide you through. They're designed to do three things: make it clear, keep it simple, and teach you to survive on your own.

Are we having fun yet?

The rest of the book—Parts 2 through 6—shows you how to use those skills to mine Internet goodies. You'll learn how to make the most of Internet e-mail and how to put your parents online so you can correspond with them (assuming you want to). You'll learn how to locate—and then get your hands on—books you find in the Library of Congress online catalogue.

Foreign language practice, reference works online, music, the full text of hundreds of classic works of fiction and poetry—it's all just a few keystrokes away. You'll find that you aren't the only one with a "roommate from Hell," and you'll learn about resources like the recipe database that can help you find something creative to do with those eggs that are about to expire.

Then you'll see how the Internet adds a new twist to the mating and dating rituals we all go through. As if communicating by computer weren't insulation enough, you can also post messages and engage in discussions anonymously. You'll also learn how to get the inside scoop on a school before transferring, and how to locate sources of grants, funding, and scholarships for grad school.

The chapters in Part 5 show you how to use the Net to find a job (summer or otherwise) in the location of your choice, how to make the

most of online travel information, and how to identify and investigate opportunities to study abroad.

If the first part of the book is the meat and potatoes (or the tofu and tomatoes), Part 6 is the dessert. You'll learn all about the games you can play or download, movie information, television, jokes without end, and other stuff that's just plain fun.

Finally, there's the Appendix, where you'll find information about a set of disks called Glossbrenner's Choice. Throughout the book, I've identified all sorts of great text files and programs that you can find on the Internet and download to your computer. I encourage you to use the skills you'll learn in the book to get these files for yourself. But for those readers (or their parents!) who would rather not do the legwork, Glossbrenner's Choice is the answer—all the good stuff conveniently organized and offered on 3.5-inch DOS-formatted disks.

I could go on and on—like some professors I know—but you're holding the book. Give it a good going over. Pick a page at random and read a couple of paragraphs. I think you'll like what you find. And there's just the possibility that you'll be amazed. I certainly hope so. And I hope you enjoy reading this book as much as I enjoyed writing it.

Final notes

The elements that helped get this book done: The most important element was Emily Glossbrenner, my uncredited co-author. This is no mushy dedication. She did the research and editing. I did the writing. Videos watched included *Much Ado about Nothing* (12 times; still in love with it), *The Adventures of Baron Munchausen*, *Henry V* directed by Kenneth Branagh, and *Last of the Mohicans*. O.J. trial coverage was limited to one half hour per day. Music: Enya (assorted CDs), Diva (Annie Lennox), The Future (Leonard Cohen), Mozart's Serenade in D (K185) performed by the Academy of Ancient Music (Jaap Schroder/Christopher Hogwood), and Respighi's Ancient Airs and Dances (Neville Marriner/Los Angeles Chamber Orchestra). Radio/tapes: "Whadayaknow?" with Michael Feldman, "Car Talk,"

and 21 hours of Herman Melville's *Moby Dick*, read by the incredible Frank Muller.

Drugs of choice: Rolling Rock, St. Pauli Girl, and Becks. Blenheim Old Fashioned Ginger Ale (#3, The Hot One). Grandma Utz's Handcooked Potato Chips. Blue Diamond Smokehouse Almonds. Herr's Extra Thin Pretzels. General Tso's chicken, cheesesteaks, and assorted fast foods. Futurebiotics Relax & Sleep (Secret Ingredient: Catnip). Fruits and vegetables were consumed in medicinal quantities only.

1
The Internet 5-Minute University

ONE of the best characters ever to appear on the TV show *Saturday Night Live* was Don Novello's Father Guido Sarducci. With his clerical getup and ever-present cigarette, Father Guido would appear as a commentator on "Weekend Update." One of his best bits was his proposal for the 5-Minute University.

It makes a lot of sense, when you think about it. At the 5-Minute University, you are taught only those key points most college students remember about major subjects five years after graduation. For example, the economics course at FMU consists of three words: Supply and Demand. Physics consists of a single formula: $E=MC^2$ In Theology you learn that the key question is "Where is God?"—and the answer is "God is everywhere." On to the next course.

Thanks to the 5-Minute University, everyone is saved a great deal of time, trouble, and money. And the results are the same. (Tuition is only $20, including cap and gown rental, snack, and Polaroid graduation photo.)

That's what we're going to do here with the Internet, though you'll have to supply your own cap and gown, Polaroid photo, and snack.

 # The Net & its features

Although it's only slightly less complicated than organic chemistry, the Internet really can be boiled down to a set of major features and step-by-step instructions for using each. This is what you need to know about the Internet or "the Net" in general:

➤ It grew out of a U.S. Defense Department project in the 1960s that was designed to link the Pentagon, military bases, defense contractors, and universities in a network that could not be destroyed by a single—or even multiple—atomic blasts.

➤ As time went on, more and more institutions and businesses hooked themselves up to the Internet. And, with the end of the Cold War and the opening of the Net to the general public, the number of hookups has skyrocketed.

➤ Physically, the Internet consists of high-speed digital links and the networking software running on the computers that are connected by them.

➤ No one controls or owns the Net. The Internet simply *is*.

 # The Internet as a "cloud"

The Internet connects thousands of computers and computer networks all over the world. But the speed of communications is so high (most of the time) that in a single online session, you might connect to systems in Switzerland, India, Japan, and the U.S. and not notice any delays or differences.

The geographical location of a given system and the physical connection that links it and you are thus largely irrelevant. If someone says "Go to this address and get this really great file," all that matters is the address and the filename.

This means you can think of the Internet as a sort of cloud. Shoot an arrow bearing a particular address into the cloud, and you'll get a certain response. Use a different arrow with a different address, and you'll get a different response. The stuff going on behind the scenes simply does not matter.

The one exception is when your target system is available to outside users only after local business hours. Then locations and time zones are indeed relevant. But, you know what? So many things on the Net are duplicated—or "mirrored"—on many different systems that if one system is closed to you when you call, you can almost certainly find another that has the same file or feature.

Establishing your own connection

The first step, of course, is to get connected to the Internet. If you're a student or are otherwise associated with a college or university, this probably won't be much of a problem since most such institutions are already on the Net. In most cases, it's a simple matter of contacting the right person at the computer center to ask about setting up an account. There is rarely a charge for this, and you can usually use your account both from a terminal at the computer center and by phone and modem from your own personal computer.

At many schools these days, every student automatically has an account or "address" on the campus system. If you're in doubt, your best bet is probably to contact Student Services or some similar organization. Tell them you want to be able to send and receive mail on the Internet and ask them what steps you should follow to make that possible. Policies vary with the college or university, but these days, the Internet is so hot that they're sure to know what you're talking about. (If they don't, tell them you want to transfer!)

NET TIP

Ask a hacker!

The word hacker has gotten a bad rap in recent years. Its true meaning is someone who is completely immersed in computers and computing—often to the point where they forget about bathing and other components of personal hygiene. But they know their stuff, and they do tend to hang around university computer centers. Find one, befriend him or her, and ask the person to be your guru and guide. You'll be amazed at how much you can learn. Technically, it's the cracker who makes breaking into systems illegally a major life's goal, not the hacker.

 # The main Internet features

One of the biggest conceptual mistakes any new Net user can make is to assume that the Internet is somehow like a much bigger version of CompuServe, America Online, or some other commercial system. It's not. Instead, it is wild and woolly, delightful and disorganized, eclectic and anarchistic, and anything else you can imagine. Yet through it all, a reasonably coherent set of features has developed. We'll explore Veronica and Archie and Jughead and the other leading Internet characters later. Right now, I want you to zero in on these features:

> E-mail. Send a message anywhere on the planet in seconds.

> Finger. Instantly retrieve information about an individual or organization. You can only be "Fingered" if you take steps to make this possible, and only then if you're on a certain kind of system.

> Newsgroups. Read and contribute questions, answers, and information on any topic you can imagine. (Newsgroups are sometimes referred to as *Usenet newsgroups* or the *Net news*.)

> Mailing lists. Like newsgroups in breadth of topic, but everyone on the list gets *every* contribution.

> FTP. Transfer files to your location, once you find them.

> Telnet. The basic method of logging on to a computer connected to the Internet. What you see once you get there depends on the Telnet address you have used and the program that has been set to run when people enter at that location. A good example is Telnetting to a location and being able to search a college library's card catalogue.

> Gopher. A Gopher is a menu system that someone has created to make it easier for you to locate and use Internet resources. The two things to remember are that each Gopher menu at each Gopher site is unique and that Gopher menus typically embrace all the other features of the Internet. You can use a Gopher to Telnet to a location or to FTP a file or to do just about anything else—as long as it's on the Gopher menu.

➤ World Wide Web. The World Wide Web is designed to turn your computer screen into a magazine page, complete with fancy text fonts, photos, and graphics. You will also find hypertext "hot buttons" that link you to other pages, features, or information. If you have the right software and (preferably) a high-speed Internet connection, all you have to do is click.

How to use Internet e-mail

Sending and receiving Internet mail could hardly be simpler. All you need to know are a few commands and, most important of all, the correct address of your correspondent. Don't worry about what the various parts of the address mean right now. To send electronic mail, you log onto your college computer and key in mail userid@domain. For example, if someone told you that his address was **John57@AOL.com**, that's the address you would use. (Addresses like this are pronounced "john57 at AOL dot com.")

You will almost certainly be prompted for a "Subject:" line, which you can key in or not as you please. On most college systems, you can probably just type in your message one line at a time and key in Ctrl-D (the EOF or End of File command) to automatically send your letter.

Naturally, there are all kinds of other, more elaborate commands you can use, but what I've told you here is really all you need. Reading mail is usually a matter of keying in mail. Key in a question mark (?) to get a command summary at any time.

Other mail programs exist, as do user-friendly front-end programs to shield you from the command line. But there are so many of them that your best bet is to ask someone at the computer center or some fellow student who is adept at using computers and mail.

How to use the Finger program

All UNIX-based computers (ask your hacker friends or the computer center system administrator about UNIX) support the Finger

command. On your own system, you may thus be able to key in finger john57 and automatically be told some information (full name, voice phone, whether the person is logged on right now, last time on the system, etc.) about the person. Different versions of the Finger program provide different kinds of information. To enter your own Finger profile on your system, key in chfn to "change Finger information," and follow the prompts that will appear.

So Finger is useful on your local college system. But it is also useful on the Net. You can key in finger user@domain at your UNIX system prompt. Assuming that *user@domain* is a valid Internet mail address, your system will connect to the Net and to the system specified by the domain name and Finger the user.

And just why would you care? The answer is that some users and companies have created quite elaborate profiles containing information of interest, and these profiles will be returned to you when you Finger the addresses.

Making the most of Internet newsgroups

A *newsgroup* is basically a "player-piano roll" of messages, each one tacked onto the next. Each newsgroup is devoted to a particular topic—whether it's the correct pronunciation of Chaucer's Middle English or the latest sex techniques from the Internet sex wizards. By some estimates, the total number of newsgroups has topped the 12,000 mark, and new ones are created all the time.

There are just two things you need to know about Internet newsgroups at this point:

> ➢ A *newsreader program* of some sort is used to read the messages posted to newsgroups. The lowest common denominator here is the **nn** program, but many other newsreaders exist. As a suggestion, see if your campus system offers the **tin** newsreader. You will find it much easier to use than **nn**. All newsreaders let you read an initial message and then follow the *thread* of messages it generated. You do not have to scan every message on the "piano roll."

➤ The system administrator at each site determines which newsgroups the site will subscribe to. Some sites get all newsgroups, some are selective. Since the actual newsgroup articles you read are stored on your site's system, the administrator also determines how long the messages in each group will continue to be available for reading before they are erased to conserve storage space.

Making the most of mailing lists

Yet another Internet feature is the *mailing list*. These are similar to newsgroups in that each is devoted to a particular topic. But the mechanics are different. Reading the messages in a newsgroup is like perusing a cork and thumbtack bulletin board. You can pick and choose which messages you want to read. Once you put yourself on a mailing list, every article anyone contributes to the list ends up in your mailbox.

You should also know the following:

➤ Some lists are moderated; some are mechanized. With a moderated list, all uploads go to a single individual who then decides what material will be sent to the list as a whole. Unmoderated lists are handled by software that automatically mails articles without human intervention.

➤ To subscribe to a given list, you normally send a message to the subscription address. If subscriptions are handled by *list-server software*, all you have to do is put some specified word in your letter or in its subject line.

➤ Most lists use different addresses for subscription requests and article postings. Don't make the classic new-user mistake of posting your subscription request to the main list address.

Getting files by FTP

The way you transfer files from one location on the Internet to another is via the Internet File Transfer Protocol (FTP). Fortunately, the details of how the transfer takes place don't need to concern us.

The most important point to bear in mind is where the file ends up when you get it using FTP. More than likely, it will end up in your own, personal filing area or workspace on your college system.

On a UNIX system this is called your *Home Directory*. This is where the system "puts" you when you log on with your ID. Non-UNIX systems handle things slightly differently, but one way or another, you will have some area on your college system that you "own." That's where the files you FTP from Internet sites will end up, and it is from there that you must copy the file or download it to your personal desktop or notebook system over the phone.

The three things you need to easily get a file from a remote system are the address of the system, the directory path on that system where the target file is stored, and the name of the file itself. To FTP a file, do this:

❶ Log onto your campus system or other Internet connection and key in ftp systemname, where *systemname* is something like **rtfm.mit.edu**.

❷ When you are prompted for a username, key in anonymous and hit your Enter key. That tells the system that you are entering anonymously, meaning you are not expected to have a previously prepared account name or password. At some sites, "anonymous" is the default, so all you have to do is hit your Enter key.

❸ Next you'll be prompted for a password. Respond to this prompt by keying in your e-mail address. Once again, this may be the default, in which case all you have to do is hit your Enter key.

❹ You will now be logged onto the remote system, and some welcoming text will almost certainly appear. Your mission is to move to the path location containing the file you want. Presumably you have gotten the path and filename information from a book like this or from a friend. Let's assume you've been told the path to enter is doc/gutenberg/novels.

❺ Key in the command cd "doc/gutenberg/novels" to change to the directory with that name. The quotes may or may not be necessary, depending on the system you're using, but they never hurt. It's a good idea to get in the habit of using them. (DOS users, notice that the slash is the forward slash, not the backslash you're used to for pathnames.)

❻ Key in dir to get a list of files in that directory and thus verify that the target file is there and called by the name you are expecting.

❼ Key in binary to set the transfer mode from ASCII text to binary. (You can skip this step if the file you want is a plain ASCII text file. But if it's a binary file you're after, or you're not sure, specify binary.)

❽ Then key in a command like get "moby_dick.z" moby.z. This tells the system to transfer the file to you, renaming it "moby.z" in the process. Renaming is not crucial, but if you are a DOS user, you will find that the long filenames used in the UNIX system will automatically be truncated to no more than 11 characters.

❾ The file will now be in your Home Directory or equivalent on your campus system. If the file ends in a character or series of characters that look strange to you, it's a sure indication that it is a *compressed, archived* file. That means you'll have to uncompress and unarchive it before you can read or use it.

You can almost certainly do so from your Home Directory on the campus system. But, with the proper free, public domain software program, you can also do so on your own PC, Macintosh, or other personal computer. Basically, if you plan to download the file into your own personal computer via modem, leave it compressed and process it after you get it. Otherwise, process it on your campus host system.

Don't worry if none of this makes any sense right now. Focus on the general concept. You will find much more detail on file compression and the software tools you need later in this book.

Telnet: the simplest command of all

The Telnet protocol makes it possible for you to log onto a remote system—after you've logged onto the Internet yourself. Telnet is how you "move" from place to place on the Net. The key concept is this: Just as the FTP command gives you access to and lets you transfer files from only a portion of a remote computer, the Telnet command

gives you access to a remote system and lets you run a specific program on that system.

A good example would be Telnetting to another college's system to search its library card catalogue. Or Telnetting to a location that lets you use its campus-wide information system to discover what's happening, where, and when.

The command to enter, once you have logged onto your college computer is telnet followed by a valid address. For example, if you want an instant weather report, key in telnet downwind.sprl.umich. edu 3000. The "3000" at the end of the address is the *port number* you've got to specify in order to tell the remote system which program to run.

Telnetting to various locations is a lot of fun. And it's easy. The only twist is that some locations expect to be "talking to" a DEC VT-100 terminal. That shouldn't be a problem if you Telnet directly from a computer center terminal. But if you are connecting via modem with your own computer, check your communications software to see what you must do to *emulate* a VT-100. If you can, make this emulation your permanent setting, since it normally will not interfere with most other, non-VT-100 online sessions.

 # Go for it with Gopher!

A Gopher is a menu system that someone has created to make it easier for you to locate and use Internet resources. The software that makes this possible was developed by some real computer geniuses at the University of Minnesota. Gopher software is available free of charge to any site requesting it, but it arrives as an empty shell. The system administrators at each Gopher site are the ones responsible for creating the site's Gopher menu.

That menu can embrace all aspects of the Net—from Telnet to FTP to newsgroups and more. And, of course, there are menus and submenus and sub-submenus. The two key points to remember are these:

❶ Each Gopher menu is unique. So, naturally, the Gophers at some sites are more complete and comprehensive than at others.

❷ Gopher menu items don't just tell you about some item or feature—they go get it! Thus, if you select an item like "Shakespeare's Complete Works" on the Gopher you are using, you will be connected to the Internet location that has those files. Indeed, you might pick that item and then be shown a list of plays. Choose one and the Gopher might actually connect to the remote site and get the file containing the play for you.

NET TIP

Gopher, Gopher, who's got a Gopher?

Gopher software is so popular that there's a very good chance your campus system already has at least one Gopher menu installed. If so, you can almost certainly use it to access "all the Gophers in the world."

*If this is not the case, however, there are publicly available Gopher sites. You will find the most recent list in the Gopher FAQ (Frequently Asked Questions) file available by FTP from **rtfm.mit.edu**, Path: /pub/usenet/news.answers/gopher-faq.*

*Or you might check the following newsgroups, where the Gopher FAQ is posted every two weeks: **comp.answers**, **comp.infosystems.gopher**, or **news.answers**.*

Here are some of the publicly available Gopher sites you can Telnet to (sample command: telnet panda.uiowa.edu*). Use the site nearest you to minimize network lag and traffic. If you are prompted for a "login" and the site doesn't specify what to enter, try keying in* gopher.

Hostname	Area
consultant.micro.umn.edu	*North America*
ux1.cso.uiuc.edu	*North America*
panda.uiowa.edu	*North America*
gopher.msu.edu	*North America*
gopher.ebone.net	*Europe*
gopher.sunet.se	*Sweden*
info.anu.edu.au	*Australia*
tolten.puc.cl	*South America*
ecnet.ec	*South America*
gan.ncc.go.jp	*Japan*

 # Browsing the World Wide Web

Now let's turn to the World Wide Web. This is generally considered to be the hottest (or coolest—take your pick!) spot on the Internet. And no wonder—with special fonts, graphics, and sounds, these screens make the rest of the Internet look downright dull by comparison.

Also, the concept of *hypertext links* is enthralling. Imagine starting from a World Wide Web *home page* (or opening screen) devoted to the TV show *Seinfeld*. You click on an icon for one of the show's characters and are taken to a site offering career highlights and a list of episodes featuring that character.

Click on a particular episode and you're presented with a full-color image of a scene from the show. Then click on a Sound icon and play an audio clip through your computer's speakers. Or click on "Vandelay Industries" to be taken to a totally different site where you'll find out how to subscribe to a mailing list devoted exclusively to *Seinfeld*.

You could go on like this for hours, hopscotching around from one Web site to another, clicking on whatever item interests you and letting your curiosity be your guide.

That's the good news. The bad news is that transmitting those graphic images can take a lot of time. Unless you have endless amounts of patience and a great deal of time to kill, you won't want to use the Web with anything less than a 28.8 modem. A direct high-speed connection of the sort you are likely to have access to on campus would be even better.

Here are the other key points you need to know about the World Wide Web:

> ➢ To take full advantage of the Web, you need some special software called a *Web browser*, preferably one that supports graphics, sound, and text. You can use a text-only browser, like Lynx. But you won't want to once you've seen what a graphical browser can do. To get an idea, take a look at Fig.1-1, which shows Time Warner's O.J. Central Web site. Then look at Fig. 1-2, the same site as seen through a text-based browser.

Figure 1-1

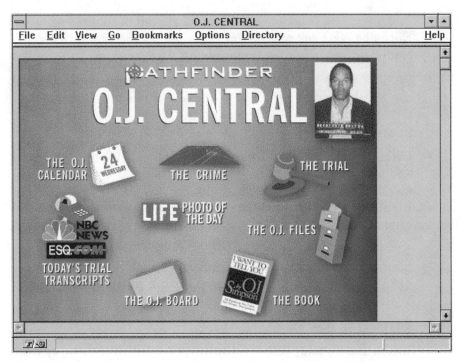

Here's what O.J. Central looks like with a graphical Web browser.

Figure 1-2

```
O.J. CENTRAL
Page 1 of 1

                O.J. CENTRAL
[1][IMAGE]

[2]The O.J. Files    [3]The Crime    [4]The Trial    [5]The Book

[6]Life Photo of the Day    [7]The O.J. Calendar    [8]The O.J. Board

[9]Today's Trial Transcript
```

And here's O.J. Central using a text-based Web browser.

➤ Two of the most widely used graphical Web browsers are Netscape Navigator and NCSA Mosaic. (NCSA stands for National Center for Supercomputing Applications.)

➤ With most graphical Web browsers, you access a particular Web site by pulling down the File menu and choosing "Open URL" or "Open Location." Then key in the Uniform Resource Locator (URL) for the Web site you want to visit.

➤ URLs for sites on the World Wide Web that offer text, graphics, and sound always begin with **http://** followed by a unique identifier for the site. For example, **http://www.pathfinder.com** is the URL for the site that offers O.J. Central and other features relating to Time Warner publications like *Time* and *People* magazines.

➤ You can also use your Web browser to visit FTP, Gopher, and Telnet sites, and to read newsgroups. Just turn the address into a URL by putting the right notation in front of it:

To reach an FTP site: **ftp://**

To reach a Gopher site: **gopher://**

To reach a Telnet site: **telnet://**

To read a newsgroup: **news:**

For example, if someone tells you to "check out the Gopher at **wiretap.spies.com**," pull down your Web browser's File menu, choose "Open URL," and key in gopher://wiretap.spies.com. To read the newsgroup devoted to Barney haters, key in the URL news:alt.barney.die.die.die.

➤ URLs are often long and complicated. And they sometimes include unusual characters like tildes (~) and underlines (_) that must be typed in exactly as shown in order to reach a particular site.

NET TIP

Where to find World Wide Web browsers

Netscape Navigator, NCSA Mosaic, and other Web browsers are widely available on most college campuses. Or you can get the software for free from these and other Internet sites:

Netscape Navigator   *FTP to **ftp.mcom.com/netscape/***

NCSA Mosaic   *FTP to **ftp.ncsa.uiuc.edu***

For the definitive guide to all the latest information on Web browsers—Cello, Lynx, DOSLynx, and many others—see the World Wide Web FAQ. It's posted regularly on many newsgroups, and is available from Glossbrenner's Choice or by FTP at the following location:

*FTP to **rtfm.mit.edu***

Path: /pub/usenet/news.answers/www/faq

 # Post-graduate work

You have now completed all course requirements for graduation from the 5-Minute Internet University. (It took you 10 minutes, you say? Well, then, may I interest you in matriculation at the 5-Minute Speed Reading University?) However long it took you, if you are reading this, you are now ready for post-graduate work. That is, you are ready to instantly apply what you've just learned about the Internet.

That's what the next chapter is all about, done in a way David Letterman would appreciate: "Top 10 cool things you can do right now!"

2

Top 10 cool things you can do right now!

W ELL, with apologies to David Letterman, direct from the home office in Blue Ridge Summit, Pennsylvania, here are 10 really cool things you can do within seconds of logging onto your campus computer or other Internet connection.

"Okay, kiddos—ready to do a little Net cruising?"

⇨ Thing 10: Tap the atomic clock

How? Key in telnet india.colorado.edu 13.

You'll get the exact Mountain Standard Time as determined by a government-run atomic clock in Boulder, Colorado, as well as confirmation of the day, month, and year. Great for establishing alibis. ("Yes, officer, I'm certain it was 9:37 when Kato and I returned from McDonald's because I had just checked the atomic clock from my Bentley's laptop.") Who needs a watch?

⇨ Thing 9: Play Trivia Time

How? Key in finger cyndiw@magnus1.com.

If you love trivia of every sort, and if your system supports the Finger command, you'll get a real charge out of pitting your wits and memory against others with the output of this command. The week's new quiz and the answers to the one from the previous week are available each Monday. Answers are due by noon on Friday. Want to test your knowledge right now? Okay, here are seven questions drawn from a Trivia Time quiz. You'll find the answers at the end of this chapter.

❶ "She Wore A Yellow Ribbon," John Ford's heartfelt tribute to the U.S. Cavalry, starred what actor as Capt. Nathan Brittles?

❷ What former *LA Law* actress had the initial female lead in the series *Love & War*, but was replaced when no sparks flew?

❸ Sparks flew on the series *MoonLighting* when Sam Crawford, played by what actor, turned up to court Maddie?

❹ What chain of commercial retail stores was founded in America on September 16, 1893, and lists among its catalog models John Davidson, Gloria Swanson, Ginger Rogers, and Lauren Bacall?

❺ The number *22* appeared on what star's jersey at West Palm Beach High and Florida State? (Hint: He also wore it in two of his movies.)

❻ While this is the minimum age to become president, it is the maximum age to begin astronaut training.

❼ To what U.S. Marine Corps platoon was Pvt. Gomer Pyle, USMC, assigned?

Thing 8: Explore college tunnel systems

How? Read the newsgroup **alt.college.tunnels**.

Who would have thought you could do a newsgroup about the tunnel systems at various colleges? Typical article titles include "Caltech Steam Tunnels," "UCLA Tunnel Map in TIFF Format," "Tunnelling Tales," and "Rutgers Tunnels."

The UCLA tunnel system would appear to be a particular favorite. And no wonder. The newsgroup postings read like a giant game of Adventure:

```
Has anyone discovered why the huge pit exists? Has anyone found
the old bridge? Have you been in the belltower?
I have found the old bridge often. I love that collection of
toilet bowls! I have yet to go in the belltower, but I have been
into Royce Hall more than once.
Have you found the blueprint room in Royce? It's a room that
contains blueprints for every building on campus.
```

⇨ Thing 7: Get HotWIRED

How? Visit the HotWired Web site (shown in Fig. 2-1) at **http://www.hotwired.com/**.

Figure 2-1

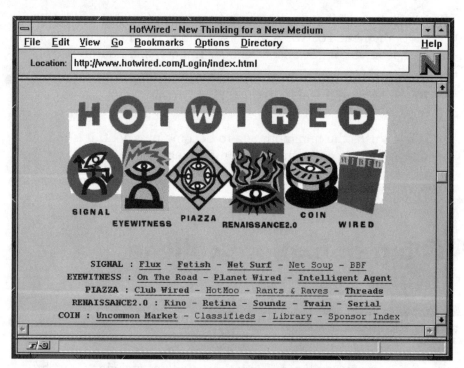

Experience "way cool journalism" at the HotWIRED Web site.

Or send an e-mail message to **hotwired-info@hotwired.com**. You can leave both the subject line and the message area blank. Check your mail a short time later and you'll find a copy of "The Official HotWIRED FAQ" in your mailbox.

As you'll learn from the FAQ, *HotWIRED* is brought to you by the creators of *Wired* magazine. It's the creation of the "best and brightest digital artists, correspondents, musicians, dreamers, and realists," and it will "either blow your mind or crash your computer." This is *not* your parents' Web site.

Thing 6: Become an InfoManiac

How? For starters, send an e-mail message to **infobot@infomania .com**. In the subject line, key in HELP. Leave the message area blank.

Check your mail a short time later and you'll find complete instructions on using the InfoMania "information-by-mail" server. There are more than two dozen offerings. You'll learn, for example, that if you send a message to **infobot@infomania.com** and key in TOPTEN in the subject line, you'll receive the latest version of David Letterman's Top Ten List. Key in GEEK in the subject line to request the complete text of the "Code of the Geeks."

Here's just a sampling of some of the other InfoMania commands:

ACRONYM   Search a database of common acronyms.

ALMANAC   Look up today in history (weather, trivia, etc.).

AREA   Look up area codes and country codes.

CHEF   Translate your message into "Swedish Chef." Bork, Bork, Bork!

FINDCD	Search a CD music catalog for author or title.
JARGON	Check the Hacker's Jargon File for a particular word. (Try PIZZA.)
PI	Get the value of *pi* (several hundred digits).
ROOT2	Get the square root of 2 (several hundred digits).
WEBSTER	Look up any word in the English language.

Thing 5: Get weather & ski reports

How? Key in telnet downwind.sprl.umich.edu 3000

No, you don't need a weatherman to tell which way the wind's blowing. All you need is the University of Michigan Weather Underground. When you log in, you can press Enter for a menu or key in a three-letter city code. Since you won't know the code the first time you do this, go for the menu (shown in Fig. 2-2) and choose the first option, "U.S. forecasts and climate data."

Figure 2-2

```
WEATHER UNDERGROUND MAIN MENU
*********************************
 1) U.S. forecasts and climate data
 2) Canadian forecasts
 3) Current weather observations
 4) Ski conditions
 5) Long-range forecasts
 6) Latest earthquake reports
 7) Severe weather
 8) Hurricane advisories
 9) National Weather Summary
10) International data
11) Marine forecasts and observations
 X) Exit program
 C) Change scrolling to screen
 H) Help and information for new users
 ?) Answers to all your questions
   Selection: 1
```

Welcome to the Weather Underground!

```
CITY FORECAST MENU
------------------------------------------------
1) Print forecast for selected city
2) Print climatic data for selected city
3) Display 3-letter city codes for a selected state
4) Display all 2-letter state codes
M) Return to main menu
X) Exit program
?) Help
   Selection:
```

Once you've got the right state or city code, you can quickly get forecasts for just about anywhere in the country, whether it's the place you're going for a ski weekend or spring break. Forecasts include temperature, humidity, wind, barometric pressure, current weather, forecasts for the rest of the day and several days ahead, special bulletins, the works! There's even a special Ski Reports menu.

Thing 4: Explore the Wiretap Online Library

How? Gopher to **wiretap.spies.com** and choose "Wiretap Online Library" from the main menu. (This is a very popular site, so don't be surprised if you get an "unable to connect" message. Just try again at a different time of day.)

You can also access Wiretap by pointing your Web browser at **http://www.spies.com**.

What you'll find is an incredible collection of useful and entertaining information, organized into the following categories:

Articles	Mass Media
Assorted Documents	Miscellaneous
Civic & Historical	Music
Classics	Questionables
Cyberspace	Religion
Fringes of Reason	Technical Information
Humor	Zines

You'll be amazed at what you'll find in the Wiretap Online Library. I'll leave you to explore on your own, but don't miss "Fringes of Reason" and "Questionables."

Thing 3: Experience Seinfeld fever

How? Read the **alt.tv.seinfeld** newsgroup.

I think *Seinfeld* is one of the two best shows on TV. (The other is *Mad About You*.) So if you're a *Seinfeld* fan, you won't want to miss out on this newsgroup and the "Vandelay Industries" mailing list.

You can access the newsgroup with your favorite newsreader. To subscribe to "Vandelay Industries," send a message with the subject line subscribe to the following e-mail address: **seinfeld-request @cpac.washington.edu**.

For even more Seinfeld fun, try the Gopher at **fir.cic.net**. From the main menu, choose "Quartz," then "Television," then "Seinfeld." Or visit one of these Seinfeld Web sites, where you'll find episode guides, collections of quotes, and even images and sound clips of Jerry, Elaine, and the gang:

http://www.ifi.uio.no/~rubens/seinfeld/

http://www.cs.cmu.edu/afs/cs/user/vernon/www/vandelay/

http://www.yahoo.com/Entertainment/Television/Shows/ Comedies/Seinfeld/

Thing 2: Beavis & Butt-head become electronic

If you're a Beavis and Butt-head fan, you probably shouldn't admit it. But from the privacy of your own terminal, no one will know if you

try the Gopher site at **fir.cic.net**. Choose "Quartz," then "Television," and then "Beavis."

What you'll find is the complete transcript of the "Beavis and Butt-head on What's Cool and What Sucks" interview from *Rolling Stone*, August 19, 1993; summaries of all "BnB" episodes; famous quotes; and more.

If even this is not enough, join one of the discussions in the newsgroup **alt.tv.beavis-n-butthead**. Or visit the Official Beavis Web page at **http://beavis.cba.uiuc.edu/** (shown in Fig. 2-3), where you'll find the Beavis and Butt-head FAQ. Or check out **http://calvin.hsc.colorado.edu/links.html**, where you'll find links to dozens of other Beavis and Butt-head sites. Cool. Heh heh heh.

Figure 2-3

This is cool!

 # Thing 1: Cool Site of the Day

You'll find a new, incredibly cool Web site every day at **http://www.infi.net/cool.html**.

On my first visit, the featured site was "Internet-in-a-Baby" (see Fig. 2-4):

> You probably know about Internet-in-a-Box, one of the earlier attempts to make the Internet more accessible for new users. We now proudly present the next generation, the ultimate user interface, the only Internet product that even a baby could use: Internet-in-a-Baby. Just click on various parts of the baby . . .

But what about all those days you've missed? Not to worry. Several months' worth of cool sites are just a click away on the "Cool Site of the Day!" opening screen. Or go there directly by pointing your Web browser at **http://www.infi.net/oldcool.html**. For a real challenge, you *must* try Find-the-Spam!

Figure 2-4

A recent "Cool Site of the Day!"

 # Conclusion

Working the Net is hours of fun, and these 10 Cool Things are only the beginning. After a brief break for a little hardware and software chalk talk, the adventure continues. In fact, if you're already up to speed on how to connect with your campus computer system via modem, skip the next two chapters and jump ahead to Chapter 5, where you'll learn how to find things on the Net with Archie, Veronica, and friends.

Oh, and by the way, here are the answers to the Trivia Time quiz:

❶ John Wayne

❷ Susan Dey

❸ Mark Harmon

❹ Sears, Roebuck & Company

❺ Burt Reynolds

❻ 35 years old

❼ 318th

3
The hardware you'll need

THE good news is that if you're a college student, you probably won't have to buy any hardware to be able to tap into the Internet. You can simply stroll on down to the computer center or wherever else you have access to a terminal and log on.

The even better news is that if you've already got a computer of some sort, you can almost certainly log onto your campus computer over the telephone. All it takes is a device called a *modem* (short for "modulator/demodulator") and a communications software program. (In fact, if you've got the bucks, you can do without the phone line altogether and use a cellular modem and your account on a cellular phone network to access the Net from *anywhere*.)

If you got your computer in the past few years, there's at least a chance that it is already equipped with a modem and a comm program. If not, you'll be pleased to discover how dirt cheap they are. But let's start at the beginning, with a quick word or two about your computer. Then I'll give you an equally quick bit of advice about getting a modem.

Computers are commodities

These days, it hardly matters what kind of computer you buy. It used to make a difference whether you bought a Macintosh with its

Motorola CPU (Central Processing Unit) or a DOS/Windows machine built around an Intel chip like the 486 or the Pentium.

Today, everything is converging. The latest Macintoshes use the PowerPC chip, a CPU designed and produced by Apple, IBM, and Motorola to try to break Intel's grip on the industry. (Macintosh holds only about 10 percent of the market; everything else belongs to computers built around Intel chips and their clones.) The strategy may just work, for a PowerPC Mac can completely emulate a DOS/Windows machine.

Apple has also finally begun to license its Macintosh operating system software to other computer makers. Although no non-Apple Macintosh computers have appeared at this writing, when they do, it will be possible for an Intel-based computer to completely emulate a Macintosh. And, of course, there will be PowerPC-based machines from IBM and other computer makers.

Computers really have become commodities.

Thus, as a student today, your first consideration is likely to be the size and shape of the machine, not its brand. Do you want a notebook-style portable or a desktop system? Obviously, if you can afford it, it would be great to have both: the notebook to take to the library and lecture halls, and the dorm room desktop system for the big screen, the full-sized keyboard, and the huge hard disk drive. Not to mention the CD-ROM drive and SoundBlaster card with attached speakers. Only you can decide, but to help you in your deliberations, you'll find a few tips nearby.

NET TIP

Tips for buying any computer

It's true that there is a lot to consider when you're buying a computer, even if it's not your first machine. Yet it's also true that books and magazines tend to exaggerate the complexity. If they didn't, they'd have nothing to write about. So here is Alfred's instant guide to buying your first computer—or trading up:

- *You always pay for miniaturization when dealing with computers. Thus notebook computers typically cost several hundred dollars more than desktop systems with the identical features. If it's a hot box, like an IBM ThinkPad or Compaq Contura, you'll pay an even*

greater premium. It's like Father Guido Sarducci said: "Supply and demand."

- *The keyboard and screen are crucial. If you don't like the way the keyboard feels, forget the machine and keep looking. Hold out for an active matrix display when considering a laptop or notebook machine. The extra crispness and clarity will be much easier on your eyes, under all lighting conditions.*

- *Because business travelers are a prime market for notebook computers, battery life is often stressed as a significant feature. But if you are going to be using the computer day-to-day at school, battery life may be less important to you.*

- *Think about service, security, and insurance. If your notebook computer gets jostled the wrong way in your backpack and no longer works, where will you get it repaired? If you leave your machine at your table in the Student Center while you go visit with friends, the computer may not be there when you get back. Desktop systems have been known to disappear from dorm rooms as well. In any case, it's worth checking to see if such things are covered under your parents' homeowner policy.*

- *Buy the most powerful computer you can afford. That means the fastest processor, the biggest hard disk drive, and the most memory your bank account can handle.*

At this writing, for example, you can get an IBM-brand 486SX/33 machine with a color monitor and a 170-megabyte hard drive for $800. For $1,000, you can get a Compaq 486DX2/50 "multimedia PC" with a double-speed CD-ROM drive, and all kinds of other goodies. These are desktop systems offered by Computer Palace in New York City. For mail-order information, call 212-629-8977.

For about $650, you can get a remanufactured Contura Aero 486SX/25 notebook-style computer with an 84-megabyte hard drive and a one-year Compaq warranty. For information, call Excel Computer & Software in New York at 212-684-6930.

Basic, no-frills, HP (Hewlett-Packard)-compatible laser printers can be had for as little as $400. Thus, for $1,400 or less, you should be able to get a laser printer and a desktop or laptop computer with plenty of power.

As you read this, prices will have dropped even more, and you may even be able to get a Pentium-based system for the prices quoted here. It's also a good bet that the kind of configuration I've described will be well on its way to becoming the new entry-level system. Among other things, regardless of what Microsoft claims, this is the kind of system people will need to run Windows 95 when it becomes available.

- *Finally, beginning with MS-DOS 6, Microsoft began including a program that effectively doubles the capacity of your hard drive. (IBM's DOS package includes a similar program.) So you can buy, say, a 170-megabyte drive and "double it" to around 340 megabytes through software. That's important, because the new version of Windows is expected to eat up 35 megabytes of disk space all by itself!*

Wait till you get to school!

If you don't already have a PC to take to school, *wait* till you get there. Two reasons:

❶ You'll have a chance to see what everyone else is using and get user comments on what's good and what's bad.

❷ Many computer makers and mail-order firms give students special discounts and deals. So you may be able to get the same item cheaper at school than buying it at home.

When power matters

We all want "muscle machines." And in general, my advice to anyone interested in buying a computer is this: Get the fastest, most powerful system you can afford.

But in fairness, I have to point out that for plain communications, a decade-old IBM/PC or Apple II works just as well as the hottest Pentium box on the market today. That's because, to communicate with most remote computers, your own computer must pretend to be a "dumb" terminal. An actual dumb terminal is nothing more than a keyboard and a screen, so little or no processing power is required.

There *is* one exception to the rule that "power doesn't matter when you're online." That's when you are online with a highly graphical system like the Internet's World Wide Web. The Web is designed to make your computer screen look like a magazine page, complete with different type sizes and type styles and illustrations.

Unfortunately, photos, graphic images, and other illustrations make significant demands on any computer. That's because displaying such *bit-mapped* images requires your computer to individually turn on or off the tiny dots of color that make up your screen. Depending on the size of the image, hundreds of thousands of dots may be involved. So the faster your computer can work, the faster it will be able to handle this chore, and the faster those images will appear.

Of course, the bits that make up those images must also be transmitted over the phone line, and this, too, can take a long time. Which is to say, three to five minutes or more *per image*, depending on the size of the image and the speed of your modem. The speed and power of your computer have no effect on this part of the process. It's all up to your modem.

If you're beginning to think you'll have to make a major investment in a powerful computer so that you'll be able to use the World Wide Web, I have some good news. First, online graphics make for some very pretty screens, as you will see. But there's a lot you can do on the Internet that has absolutely nothing to do with graphics.

Second, many Web sites give you the option of turning off graphics and receiving just the text they contain. And most Web browser programs (like NCSA Mosaic or Netscape Navigator), let you turn off graphics as well. Instead of taking the time to receive and display an image, they show you a generic icon at the place where the image would normally appear.

All of which is fine. More important, it's fast. And more important still, the power and price of your personal computer have no relevance in this mode because nothing but text is being received and displayed.

Everything you need to know about modems

In the simplest terms, a modem is what lets a computer talk on the telephone. As you may know, computers deal exclusively in pulses that physically consist of two different voltage levels. For convenience, everyone calls them on/off *bits* (short for "binary digits") and symbolizes them as 1 and 0.

 ## Three bit-points

There are three things to remember about computer bits:

➢ There is no in between. Like a light bulb, a bit is either an "on" or an "off." There is no dimmer switch to shade things one way or the other.

➢ Through the magic of the binary numbering system, you can write any number you like using the 1's and 0's of computer bits. (It just takes an awful lot of them to do it.) If you give every letter in the alphabet a number and make sure everyone agrees on these assignments, text can be translated into binary numbers and back again.

➢ The bits whizzing around inside your computer consist of very weak voltage pulses. At least they're weak compared to those in the outside world. Before they can be sent out into the phone system, they must thus be converted into a more rugged form, in this case *sound*.

Enter the modem

The copper cable used in phone lines was designed to carry sound. In technical terms, the telephone is an *analog system* because, as you speak into the handset, the vibrating microphone generates a current that rises and falls in a way that is *analogous to* your voice.

The modem makes it possible for your digital computer to use the analog phone system by translating the computer's two types of bits into two different sound frequencies. When you use your modem to dial up your campus computer system, a modem at the computer center answers the call. You will hear the two modems do a little chatting back and forth—a process called *handshaking*—and then the noise will stop and they'll get down to business.

I've simplified things greatly here. But that's really all you need to know about what a modem is and does.

Modems are commodities

I know. It sounds like a broken record—I wonder how long *that* expression will last in this age of audio CDs—but it's true. After nearly two decades of experience, the modem industry is at a point where almost *every* unit offers comparable quality and features. And so the price-cutting has begun.

Only a few years ago, 9,600 bps modems sold for $1,000. Today, you can pick one up for less than $100. But don't do it! For about $150 you can get a 14,400 bps data/fax modem that can pump data 50 percent faster. And for just a little more, you can get one that tears along at 28,800 bits per second.

How to buy a modem

Sorry about that. I didn't mean to make your head spin. But I started my life online with a 300 bits-per-second acoustic coupler that required me to thrust the telephone handset into a box that had two foam-rubber cups. The availability of affordable modems that operate nearly 100 times faster than that is simply remarkable.

The question of speed

But it also makes it easy to tell you what to look for in a modem, starting with speed. Modem speeds are measured in *bits per second*

or *bps*. You'll hear the term *baud* used, but it is accurately applied only to "300 baud" modems. Stick with bps. Or kbps for *kilobits per second*. Thus 14,400 bps is the same as 14.4 kbps, and 28,800 bps is the same as 28.8 kbps. (The kbps is often left out, since, presumably everyone knows that it is implied.)

The official international standard for 28.8 modems was finally approved in June 1994. It's called V.34 and pronounced "vee dot thirty-four." Prior to this, modem companies made modems based on their best guesses as to what the V.34 standard would consist of. They labelled these units *V.Fast*. Do *not* buy a V.Fast modem, should any still be around as you read this. You simply cannot be sure that one maker's V.Fast modem will work at 28.8 with any other maker's model, or with models implementing the full V.34 standard.

There seems little question but that V.34/28.8 modems will eventually become the standard. However, it's important to note that having a modem capable of such speeds does you no good if the place you want to call doesn't have one of equal power. If your computer center offers only 9,600 bps connections, then that's the top speed you'll be able to use, even if you've got a V.34 modem.

✳ Who you gonna call?

It all depends on what systems you plan to call. The campus computer center is one place. Commercial systems (like CompuServe, Prodigy, and America Online) are another set of places. The commercial systems are only beginning to offer 28.8 access, and only in certain cities.

Bulletin board systems (BBSs) are yet another possibility. The system operators or *sysops* who operate BBSs tend to be early adopters. So you can expect many boards to offer 28.8 access as soon as the sysop can scrape together the money needed to buy such a modem.

This is not fear and trembling and the sickness unto death Kierkegaard writes about. If you make a wrong decision, you're not going to damn your immortal soul. If all you can afford right now is an inexpensive 9,600 bps model, buy that and wait for the prices of 28.8 units to fall.

As for fax capabilities—heck, yes, why not! Silicon is cheap. At this point, it costs a modem maker very little to include the chips needed to let your modem send and receive messages from fax machines, which use a different signalling technique than data modems.

NET TIP

The modem speed/time continuum

The speed of your modem connection to the campus computer system is most relevant when you are transferring files. Typically, you will connect with the computer center and use the Internet FTP function to go get a file. The file will be whooshed into your personal directory or workspace on the campus system at Internet speeds.

Trouble is, you must then get it from your directory on the campus system into your desktop machine in your room, and you must do so at "modem" speeds, not Internet speeds.

To get a handle on this speed thing, you've got to know that computers do almost everything using eight-bit chunks called bytes. Program and graphic files consist of bytes, and so do text files. In fact, one byte is required to represent one character of text. Which is why the terms character and byte are sometimes used interchangeably.

For technical reasons, 10 bits are required to send a single byte via modem. That means that you can divide any modem speed by 10 to come up with the number of characters/bytes transmitted per second.

A speed of 2,400 bps thus transmits 240 characters per second, while at 9,600 bps, you're transmitting 960 characters per second. Once you know the size of a given file, you can quickly figure out how many seconds will be required to download it via modem. (Quick tip: One double-spaced typewritten page contains 28 lines of 65 characters each, for a total of 1,820 characters or bytes per page.)

Here's a quick comparison of how long it takes to transmit a file that occupies 100K (100,000 bytes). These figures assume perfect conditions. Your mileage may vary. To be more accurate, you should probably add about 15 percent to the transmission times shown here:

Speed	Transmission Time
2,400 bps	*7 minutes*
9,600 bps	*1 minute, 45 seconds*
14.4 kbps	*1 minute, 10 seconds*
28.8 kbps	*35 seconds*

⇨ Internal or external or PCMCIA?

There are essentially three modem "profiles." Internal modems are just circuit boards that you plug into a vacant slot on your motherboard (the computer's main circuit board). Once installed, you can plug an internal modem into the phone jack just as if it were a telephone.

External modems are free-standing "boxes" that you connect to the phone line like a phone and to your computer via the system's *serial* or *RS-232C* port.

PCMCIA modems consist of shirtpocket-sized circuit boards that are protected by a plastic case and equipped to be temporarily plugged into a PCMCIA socket. The letters stand for Personal Computer Memory Card International Association, and while any kind of computer can have a PCMCIA socket, they are most often found on notebooks.

❋ Externals: Pros & cons

An external modem offers two main advantages. It can be used with *any* computer. As long as that computer has a serial port, you can plug in your external modem. (You may need to pay attention to the cable, however, since Macintosh computers connect to external modems with a round, 8-pin DIN plug and DOS machines typically use a DB-25 connector. Details, details!)

Second, external modems have little lights to let you know what's going on. The SD (Send Data) light flashes when you hit a key and the RD (Receive Data) light flashes as the remote system sends you information.

On the negative side, they tend to be a bit more expensive than comparable internal models, and they are bulky to carry around. Ideal for a desktop system. Lousy for a portable.

❋ Internals: Pros & cons

The two main advantages of an internal modem are, first, that it saves space on your desktop and causes less clutter. Internal modems

draw their power from your computer, while externals need to be plugged into an electrical outlet. More cords, more cables.

Second, if you have an older PC, you won't have to worry about replacing your old serial card to be able to use a modem that operates faster than 9,600 bps. Techno-gobbledy-gook time, I know. But, if you got your computer sometime prior to about 1992, you may not be able to use a 14.4 or 28.8 *external* modem with your current serial card because such cards have a top speed of 9,600 bps.

The key question is, does the computer have a 16550A UART? The UART is the Universal Asynchronous Receiver/Transmitter chip that is the heart of your serial communications port. If you're in doubt about what you've got, run Microsoft Diagnostics (key in **msd** at the DOS prompt and then choose "COM ports").

Or run the program UARTID.EXE. (This is a shareware program that's widely available on the Internet and elsewhere. If you have trouble finding it, see the appendix for information on ordering it from Glossbrenner's Choice on the disk called System Configuration Tools.) UARTID.EXE will check your serial communications ports and tell you what it finds.

If it finds a 16550A UART chip, then you can indeed operate at 14.4 or 28.8 with the appropriate external modem. If it doesn't, then you will have to either replace the serial port connection or go with an internal modem.

✳ PCMCIA: Pros & cons

Most notebook and other portable computers come with a serial port, so you can plug in a conventional external modem if you want to. You would not want to lug such a unit around, however. Alternatively, you might be able to equip your notebook with an internal modem. No muss, no fuss, just plug in the phone line whenever you want to communicate. It's neat, but then you are always carrying your modem with you as part of your computer.

The PCMCIA modem-on-a-card solution solves both problems. It's light, self-contained, and detachable. You don't have to take the

modem with you unless you want to. And if you do want to, it can be carried someplace else. All of that is to the good.

The downside is the expense: PCMCIA modems tend to cost more than comparable external or internal models. And there's the convenience factor. An internal modem may add a bit of weight to your system, but it eliminates the need to think ahead. Who knows where you'll be before day's end or how many times you will want to be able to go online? If you've got an internal modem, you may not even have to worry about bringing along a phone cord, since you can simply unplug a telephone and plug in your computer at many locations.

Two other considerations. First, you may have to pay a bit more for a notebook equipped with a PCMCIA socket. Second, battery life. Internal modems and PCMCIA modems alike draw the power they need from your computer. If the computer is plugged into an electrical outlet, no problem. Otherwise, they will both drain your battery.

Conclusion

Once again, as when considering a computer, it does not hurt to wait until you've been on campus and checked things out before deciding on the kind of modem you want to buy. Ask around. Get people's advice. Try to use as many different products as you can. Then make your decision.

You may even find a "Student Modem Agency" on campus offering rock-bottom prices. Or you may find folks who want to sell their current equipment so they can upgrade.

In any case, very little money is at risk, regardless of what you do—at least very little when compared to your college tuition or the size of your student loan!

Hardware information on the Net

Not surprisingly, there are many Internet sites devoted to all aspects of computer hardware. For starters, you might try the Internet

Computer Index, where you'll find well-organized collections of resources for PC, Macintosh, and UNIX users. They even offer the latest information on used computer prices from the American Computer Exchange.

To reach the Internet Computer Index, gopher to **proper.com**. Or point your Web browser at **http://ici.proper.com**.

You can also check the Ziff Davis home page at **http://www.ziff.com/** for the latest online editions of *Computer Shopper* and other magazines that offer hardware information, reviews, and prices. See Fig. 3-1 for a sample of what you'll find there.

Figure 3-1

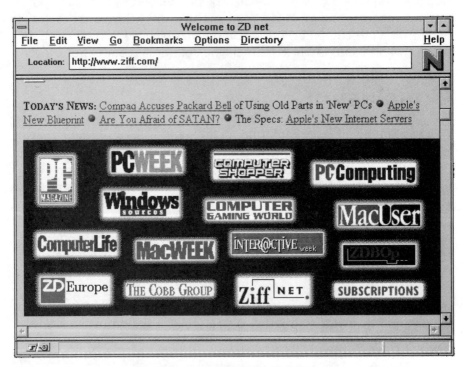

The Ziff Davis home page on the World Wide Web

4
Using communications software

ONCE again: You *don't* need a computer, a modem, or a communications software program to access the Internet if you do so from a terminal at your college computer center. But if you plan to connect to the computer center via personal computer and modem over the telephone, you will most definitely need a comm program.

The good news here is that most modems these days come with a communications program of some sort. If the modem can handle both data and fax, the software supplied with the unit will be able to do so as well. Not that such software is necessarily all that great. It is most likely a watered down version of some commercial program. But you can bet that it will be at least serviceable.

⇨ The shareware alternative

If you are a Windows user, you will find that you've got a basic comm program in the application called Terminal. (Click on the Main program group and then on the Terminal icon.) If you're a Macintosh user (with System 7 Pro or later), see your documentation for instructions on using the PowerTalk communications module that's included as part of the Macintosh operating system.

Alternatively, if you are using any of the leading "works" packages—ClarisWorks, GreatWorks, Microsoft Works, or WordPerfect Works—you will find that you already have a comm program as well. WordPerfect Works for DOS machines also includes a comm program module.

If absolutely *none* of this applies to you, you are still in luck, because there are wonderful public domain and shareware comm programs available for *every* kind of machine. The shareware comm program I like best for DOS machines is Qmodem from Mustang Software. For Windows, my current favorite is a program called CommWin. Both programs are available from Glossbrenner's Choice. Or look for them on the Net in one of these vast shareware archives, which offer programs of all kinds for DOS/Windows, Macintosh, and other systems:

FTP to **archive.umich.edu**

FTP to **oak.oakland.edu**

FTP to **sumex-aim.stanford.edu**

FTP to **wuarchive.wustl.edu**

If you're a Macintosh user, you might also call Educorp, one of the leading distributors of Mac shareware, and request a free catalogue. The number is 800-843-9497. There is simply no need to pay a lot of money for a first-class comm program.

NET TIP

Paying—yes paying!—for shareware

Public domain programs are yours to do with as you like; shareware programs represent "software on the honor system." If you like and use a shareware program, you are duty-bound to register by sending its author the small contribution he or she requests—usually about $10 to $25. In return, you will get all kinds of benefits (like being able to call up the program's author for help), in addition to a clear conscience.

Everyone—you, me, the commercial software industry as a whole—knows that college campuses are hotbeds of software piracy. I won't comment on that. But, as someone who makes his living creating intellectual property, you can probably guess that my sympathy lies with the men and women who have spent their time creating wonderful commercial programs.

But I will say that when someone gives you a fully functional, non-crippled program and all the documentation, as is the case with shareware, asking only a modest contribution in return, you should sit up and listen. I know it's not fashionable to say so, but if you like and regularly use such a program without paying for it, you should feel guilty as hell.

Shareware programmers are not multimillion-dollar corporations. They are artists—men and women who have labored long and hard to create something of elegance and beauty. If you don't like it, fine. Erase it from your disk. No hard feelings. But if you like and regularly use a shareware product, and if you have any honor at all, you should pay for it.

We're all responsible for our own karma. So make your own decision. But even if you can't afford the suggested contribution, at least send something. Even if it is only a note of thanks and appreciation. I've written three books about shareware, and, believe me, shareware programmers are not in it for the money. These are good people and they deserve your support, whether monetary or moral, via a brief note of appreciation. 'Nuff said.

 # What you need to know about any comm program

The commands, keystrokes, and mouse clicks differ. But every comm program for every computer offers the same essential functions. At the most basic level, a comm program opens a channel between your keyboard and your modem, allowing you to "talk" to the modem directly when you are in what's called *terminal mode*. Once you are in terminal mode, you can key in AT or at and the modem should respond by displaying "Okay" or "OK" on your screen. (The AT command essentially says "Attention, modem.")

If you have a modem connected to your machine and you do the AT routine and get no response, check each of the following, if applicable:

> ➤ Your cable connections. Everything plugged in firm and secure?

> ➤ Your power connections, if you're using an external modem.

> The COM port address. DOS/Windows machines can support four or more communications ports—typically COM1 through COM4. If your modem does not appear to work, make sure that your communications software is set to "talk" to the port the modem is connected to.

If you are a new user, set your comm software to talk to COM1 through COM4 in turn. After changing each setting, get into terminal mode and key in AT. If you get no response, tell the comm software to address the next higher COM port. If you try all four and still have no "Okay," call in a computer guru.

Or, if you are not a comm novice, check the modem or software manual for references to *jumpers* or *DIP* (dual-inline-package) *switches*. The key point is that the port your comm software addresses must be the same port to which your modem is attached.

The tools you've got to work with

The most crucial point when communicating with any remote system is that your settings match the settings of the remote system. You don't even need to know what the settings mean. All you need to remember is that there are just two general settings: 7/E/1 and 8/N/1. Translated, that means "7 data bits, Even parity, and 1 stop bit" and "8 data bits, No parity, and 1 stop bit."

Believe me, you do not need to know what these settings mean. All that matters is that your settings match the settings of the system you're calling. Start with 7/E/1 and if it does not work, try 8/N/1. The Help file or printed manuals that came with your software will tell you how to control these settings.

As far as your campus computer center is concerned, ask them "Do you want me to be at seven, even, and one, or at eight, none, and one?" That'll get their attention and possibly save you a lot of hassle.

Now let me take a moment to introduce you to the most important features offered by any comm program:

➤ Capture buffer. In computer talk, a *buffer* is simply an area of memory set aside to serve as a temporary holding tank. When the tank fills up with incoming text, the software dumps it to disk, using a filename you have previously specified. If you don't open your capture buffer or otherwise tell your comm program to "log to disk," all incoming text will simply scroll off the screen, never to be seen again.

Personally, I open a capture buffer each time I go online with any system. That way I don't have to worry about whether I've captured something or not. When I sign off, if there is nothing I want to look at again, I simply delete the capture file.

➤ Dialing directory or phone book. Most comm programs let you record frequently dialed numbers in a *dialing directory* or *phone book*. That means you can key in something like Alt-D and be presented with a list of numbers. Pick a menu item off the list, and the program will automatically dial the number. (You key in a single menu item number, and the software does the rest.)

➤ Scripts. Many comm programs today let you prepare *scripts* that tell them to dial a number, wait for a particular response, and, only when they see such a response, issue some command. With the right comm program and the right script, you could issue a single keyboard command and have the software dial up the campus computer center, download any mail messages in your mailbox, and sign off. And you could arrange to have this done at any hour of the day or night—automatically.

➤ Upload/download protocols. A *protocol* is nothing more than an agreement between two machines on how they will handle the delicate task of transferring an error-free copy of a file from one system to another. A number of protocols—often called *error-checking protocols*—exist. Among them, Xmodem is the lowest common denominator, while Zmodem is unquestionably the best. In between are Kermit, Ymodem, and Xmodem 1K.

Each of these protocols can transfer a binary file from your directory on the campus computer system to your own computer in your room—and do so without errors. Everything depends on which protocols are supported by your college

computer system, because most PC and Mac comm program support them all. The key thing is that the protocol used by one system must match that used by the other system; otherwise, no file transfer can take place.

➤ Terminal emulation. To this day, the vast majority of online, personal computer communications is based on the old mainframe-and-terminal model. That model is simple to understand: You've got a big, expensive, powerful mainframe computer located in a climate-controlled "glass house" somewhere, and you've got any number of dumb terminals scattered about.

The dumb terminals consist largely of a keyboard and a screen and have very little processing power of their own. But each does have certain characteristics. The most common set of characteristics are those embodied by the DEC VT-100 model terminal. Thus, many of the sites you log into on the Internet will expect you to be a VT-100. Your comm software can almost certainly produce a convincing illusion, but you've got to tell it to do so.

➤ If you plan to access the Internet often, I suggest that you make "VT-100 emulation" the default setting for your comm program. This will not interfere with most of your other online activities, but it will simplify things greatly when you Telnet to some location on the Net.

⇨ Conclusion

There are two main things to remember about comm programs and file transfers. First, for one computer of any sort to talk to another, both have got to agree on their communications settings. If you're set for 7/E/1 and the system you're calling is expecting 8/N/1, you will see garbage characters on your screen. Solution: Change your settings to 8/N/1 and call back. Or vice versa, if you called in set for 8/N/1 and the host was expecting 7/E/1.

Second is the difference between ASCII text files and binary files. ASCII, the American Standard Code for Information Interchange and

pronounced "ask-ee", is the internationally agreed-upon code that assigns a specific number to each upper- and lowercase letter of the alphabet. An ASCII file is a text file, and text files need no special treatment when being transferred from one spot to another.

Why? Because if one or more text characters are garbled in transmission, the entire file is not ruined. You can puzzle out the correct letters or call the sender and ask for clarification. But if even a single byte in a program or archive file is corrupted, the entire file may be useless. That's why an error-checking protocol like Zmodem must be used to guarantee that a perfect copy of the file arrives on your disk.

You will find many people on campus who will happily discourse on the ins and outs of communications and file transfer protocols. Listen to them with interest. But remember that *both* sides of a connection must support the same protocol if you want to be able to use it. Otherwise, you will have to find the highest common denominator between you.

5

How to *find* things on the Net

IN the most general sense, the Internet offers two things: features and files. A feature is something like e-mail, mailing lists, and the opportunity to search the *CIA World Factbook* for information and statistics on every country. Files are things like the full text of the U.S. Constitution, the plays of Shakespeare, or some nifty shareware game or utility program.

As you already know, the Internet is rich in both files and features. But since the Net links thousands of networks, many of which in themselves link thousands of computers, just *finding* the file or feature you want can be a major challenge.

NET TIP

The wild & woolly Internet

Finding specific information on the Internet is a challenge, even for longtime Internet users. Take Clifford Stoll, whose best-selling book The Cuckoo's Egg recounted how he tracked down the "Hanover Hacker" through the Net—a trail that led to a KGB-backed spy ring. Mr. Stoll's most recent book is Silicon Snake Oil—Second Thoughts on the Information Highway.

Here's what this experienced Internaut had to say in Newsweek (February 27, 1995) about the frustration of trying to locate a particular fact on the Internet.

What the Internet hucksters won't tell you is that the Internet is an ocean of unedited data, without any pretense of

completeness. Lacking editors, reviewers, or critics, the Internet has become a wasteland of unfiltered data. You don't know what to ignore and what's worth reading.

Logged onto the World Wide Web, I hunt for the date of the Battle of Trafalgar. Hundreds of files show up, and it takes 15 minutes to unravel them—one's a biography written by an eighth grader, the second is a computer game that doesn't work, and the third is an image of a London monument. None answers my question, and my search is periodically interrupted by messages like "Too many connections, try again later."

The Internet's major "finding" tools

Fortunately, numerous good-hearted souls on the Net have developed an entire range of tools to help you. Not all of them work equally well, and many attempt to burden you with more computeristic commands and features than you will ever need. But, with a little practice, these tools can have you cruising around the Net as if it was your old neighborhood.

Two general classes of tools are involved. There are interactive programs like Archie and Veronica and InfoSeek. And there are crucial files, like the famous Yanoff List and John December's Internet resource guides. In this chapter, I'll show you how to use the tools. In Chapter 6, I'll show you how to get files, starting with some of the most useful "tool" files.

Here, then, are the main tools you need to know about:

> Archie. The Archie database is made up of the file directories from hundreds of systems. When you search this database on the basis of a file's name, Archie can thus tell you which directory paths on which systems hold a copy of the file you want.

> Gopher. Gopher software makes it possible for the system administrator at any Internet site to prepare a customized menu of files, features, and Internet resources. When you use the Gopher, all you have to do is select the item you want from the menu.

> ➤ Veronica. The Veronica database is a collection of menus from most Gopher sites. Thus, when you do a Veronica search, you are searching menu items. In the course of the search, Veronica builds an on-the-spot menu consisting of just the items that match your request. When the search is finished, Veronica will present you with your own, customized Gopher menu, which you can use as you would any Gopher.

> ➤ Jughead. Available at some Gopher sites, Jughead is like Veronica—except that it uses the menu items on a *single* Gopher menu as its database.

> ➤ WAIS, the World Wide Web, and InfoSeek. All of the other tools on this list help you search for files and features. These three are designed to let you search the *contents* of one or more files.

All about Archie

The Archie solution to locating files on the net was created by Alan Emtage, Bill Heelan, and Peter Deutsch when they were students at McGill University in Montreal. They called the system Archie because of that word's similarity to *archive*. The name has nothing to do with the hatch-headed boy of comic-strip fame.

The concept is simplicity itself. Picture the file directory "tree" on your Macintosh or Windows machine. If you're a DOS user, picture the output of a command like dir *.* /s that gives you a directory of all your directories and subdirectories, listing the names of the files in each.

Now imagine that everyone on campus contributes a copy of his or her file directory tree to a central database. You sign on to the database and do a search for, say, DOOM.ZIP. There is a pause, and the system gives you a list of *every* computer that has a copy of that file (a popular shareware game). It tells you who owns the computer and just where on each system DOOM.ZIP can be found.

That's how Archie works. It periodically polls hundreds of systems on the Internet, collects all their file directories into one large database,

and stores it at a given location called an *Archie server*. When you sign onto an Archie server, the Archie software will search its database for the directory names or filenames you specify. It will then tell you where all copies of that file can be found.

 # How to use Archie

There are two key points to remember about Archie in general. First, to use Archie, you've got to Telnet to an Archie server. You can do that by keying in a command like telnet archie.internic.net to get to the Archie server at that address and log on by keying in archie when prompted to do so. Or you may find that doing an Archie search is an option on a Gopher menu. (Remember that Gopher menus can give you access to just about any feature on the Net.)

Second, once you do your Archie search, you must then go get the file using FTP, the Internet File Transfer Protocol. This isn't as complicated as it sounds. But it's worth emphasizing that Archie delivers nothing but *location* information. It does not have the file, nor can it go get the file for you.

NET TIP

The current Archie server list

Here is a list of the Archie servers available at this writing. To get the most recent list, Telnet to any Archie server, log in as archie, *and key in* servers *at the Archie prompt. You will get a list of servers. Key in* bye *to log off the system and then call the server nearest you. Remember, it is good "netiquette" to use the Archie server that is nearest you since this helps cut down on network traffic:*

archie.unl.edu	*USA (NE)*
archie.internic.net	*USA (NJ)*
archie.rutgers.edu	*USA (NJ)*
archie.ans.net	*USA (NY)*
archie.sura.net	*USA (MD)*
archie.au	*Australia*
archie.edvz.uni-linz.ac.at	*Austria*
archie.univie.ac.at	*Austria*
archie.cs.mcgill.ca	*Canada*
archie.uqam.ca	*Canada*

archie.funet.fi	*Finland*
archie.univ-rennes1.fr	*France*
archie.th-darmstadt.de	*Germany*
archie.ac.il	*Israel*
archie.unipi.it	*Italy*
archie.wide.ad.jp	*Japan*
archie.hana.nm.kr	*Korea*
archie.sogang.ac.kr	*Korea*
archie.uninett.no	*Norway*
archie.rediris.es	*Spain*
archie.luth.se	*Sweden*
archie.switch.ch	*Switzerland*
archie.nctuccca.edu.tw	*Taiwan*
archie.ncu.edu.tw	*Taiwan*
archie.doc.ic.ac.uk	*United Kingdom*
archie.hensa.ac.uk	*United Kingdom*

✻ The steps to follow

There are different versions of Archie running on different systems. But here's the fastest, most efficient way for most people to use Archie:

❶ Telnet to an Archie server and log in as archie.

❷ When the Archie prompt appears, key in set search sub. That tells Archie to look for the string of characters you are about to specify *wherever* they may occur in a given directory or filename.

❸ Key in set sortby time so that Archie gives you filenames from newest to oldest. If you don't use the SORTBY command, you will have to comb through the list of files Archie gives you, identifying the newest versions on your own.

❹ Key in set maxhits 10. Most Archie servers default to giving you every matching filename or 100 hits, whichever comes first. But you only need one hit to locate a file. Limiting Archie to 10 hits makes more efficient use of this feature and gets you off and on your way faster.

❺ Key in find search-string, where *search-string* is the name of the file you're looking for or the string of characters you would expect to be part of the directory or filename. Unfortunately, Archie does not allow wildcards. It looks for exact strings of characters. (Some older versions of the software require you to use prog instead of find.)

❻ Key in q to quit Archie.

NET TIP

An Archie quick reference

Here is the sequence of commands to enter when using any Archie server:

- *Login as* archie.
- *Key in* set search sub.
- *Key in* set sortby time.
- *Key in* set maxhits 10.
- *Key in* find search-string *(where* search-string *is the file you want).*
- *Key in* q *to quit Archie when you're finished.*

Remember, too, that you can key in servers *at an Archie prompt to get the most recent list of Archie servers. You can get help by keying in* help *at the Archie prompt. But you will be better off keying in* manpage *to get the 18-page Archie manual.*

Finally, if Archie output stops after one screenful of information, hit your Spacebar or G (capital letter G).

⇨ An Archie example

Clearly, Archie works best when you already know the name of a file and want merely to turn up several locations you can tap to get it. As the Net becomes more crowded, this power will become more and more important. That's because most FTP sites—the places where you can download files—severely limit the number of users they will serve at any one time. A top limit of 50 to 100 FTP users at a site is not uncommon. (And the Internet reportedly has 20 to 30 million users!)

If you don't know the name of a file, you're not out of luck, however. Like the Macintosh, the UNIX operating system that runs most of the big computers connected to the Net permits much longer filenames than do DOS and Windows 3.x. So, while searching on the basis of a file's name is like trying to throw a baseball through a one-foot opening at a distance of 50 yards, your chances aren't as bad as they may seem.

For example, we've all heard that copies of U.S. Supreme Court decisions are available on the Net. But where? Ask Archie. If you Telnet to an Archie server, follow the steps outlined earlier, and specify *supreme* as your search string, you will get output like this. Notice that the first two items are directories and the last one is a file:

```
Host ftp.uu.net (192.48.96.9)
Last updated 06:39 18 Aug 1995

Location: /opinions
DIRECTORY     drwxrwxr-x      512 bytes   00:00   30 Jul 1993   supreme-court

Location: /doc/literary/obi
DIRECTORY     drwxrwxr-x      512 bytes   22:32   15 Aug 1994   Supreme.Court

Host nic.stolaf.edu     (130.71.128.8)
Last updated 17:09  4 Mar 1995

Location: /gopher/Internet Resources/FTP Sites
FILE     -rw-r-r—     5761 bytes   00:00 13 Dec 1991 Supreme Court Decisions
```

You will understand what all these seemingly strange items mean after you've read the next chapter. For now, notice that the host name is given. That's the site you will FTP to to get the file. The directory path location is given, as is the name of the file.

What I haven't shown you here are the half dozen *false drops* I got by searching on the word *supreme*. A false drop is a hit that matches your search but has nothing to do with the subject you're interested in. False drops are unavoidable in any search situation. Among the gems turned up this time was something called **fortress.supreme**, apparently associated with some kind of game; a file of Pennsylvania Supreme Court decisions; and a graphic file called **WH.SupremeP1.gif**.

 # Working with your friendly Gopher

Gopher, Veronica, and Jughead are the other three standard "finding" tools on the Internet. There is not a great deal to say about how to use them. After all, they are designed to be as intuitive as any feature on the Net can be. It's far more important to make sure you have a firm grasp on the concept.

If you've read Chapter 1 and tried some of the 10 Cool Things in Chapter 2, you've already had some experience with Gopher menus. If not, try keying in gopher at your campus computer's prompt. Maybe there's a Gopher on your system and you don't even know it.

Chapter 1 contains a list of publicly available Gopher servers you can Telnet to if there's no other Gopher you can use. I won't repeat that list here. The one point that bears repeating over and over again, however, is that each and every Gopher is unique!

All Archie servers, in contrast, let you search what is essentially the identical database. But the items you will find on any given Gopher menu reflect the personalities of the system administrators and staff who created the menu, as well as the resources of the institution, and the perceived needs of the Gopher's users.

That's basically a long way of saying that a Gopher at a medical school is probably going to have lots of menu items dealing with scientific and medical issues, while one at a liberal arts school might have lots of menu items devoted to full-text electronic copies of great works of literature. But either Gopher might also have a particularly extensive selection of items devoted to, say, ancient Chinese pottery or music of the Middle Ages—solely because one of the creators of the Gopher menu was especially interested in such topics.

NET TIP

Gopher commands

Some Gopher menus show a pointer (–>) that you can move up and down the left margin of the menu. But there is little reason to do so when you're exploring a Gopher, because you can select any item by keying in its number and hitting your Enter key.

The pointer can be important for the more advanced Gopher commands, however. It signifies what's called the current item *. There are lots of ways to move the pointer and go from one menu page to the next. Here are just the basics using lowercase letters. Gopher responds as soon as you hit the key—instead of waiting for you to hit Enter.*

- *To move the pointer down one item, hit* j.
- *To move it up one item, hit* k.

• *To move to the next page of a menu, hit your Spacebar.*

• *To move back a page (to back up) hit* u.

You can get a list of Gopher commands by hitting your question mark key (?) at a Gopher prompt.

You may or may not wish to invest the time needed to completely master all Gopher commands. (Gopher is supposed to simplify things after all.) But two commands not to be missed are the Information and Bookmark commands.

Information Command. *With the pointer at, say, "12. CIA World Factbook," you can hit your equals key (=) and Gopher will reveal the Internet commands that are "attached" to that entry. (With a Web browser like Netscape Navigator, you can get that information by simply moving your cursor to the item. On the Delphi Gopher, the command to use to find out about item 12 is* info 12.*)*

In this case, you'd learn that the host that Gopher Telnets to is **info.umd.edu**, *entry port* **901**. *And that the path it then follows is 1/info/Government/Factbook. This is the information you need to go do this yourself, should a Gopher be unavailable.*

Bookmark Command. *This command lets you create your own customized Gopher menu. (On Delphi, these are called your "Personal Favorites.") Simply move the pointer to an item and hit* a *to add the item to your list. Hitting a capital* A *adds the current menu to your list. With a Web browser, look for the Bookmark command on one of the pull-down menus.*

To start Gopher using your personal Bookmark list, key in gopher -b *at your system's prompt. To jump to your Bookmark list after you've started Gopher by just keying in* gopher, *key in* v *for "view Bookmark list."*

A Gopher example

In case you have not yet had the opportunity to use a Gopher, here's the kind of thing you can expect. I really think you'll love it. Here, I've Gophered to **gopher.std.com** and gotten a menu that looks like this:

```
1    OBI The Online Book Initiative            Menu
2    Internet and USENET Phone Books           Menu
3    Shops on The World                        Menu
4    Commercial Services via the Internet      Menu
5    Book Sellers                              Menu
6    Bulletin Boards via the Internet          Menu
7    Business Opportunities                    Menu
8    Consultants                               Menu
9    Government Information                     Menu
10   Non-Profit Organizations                  Menu
11   Other Gopher and Information Servers       Menu
12   Periodicals, Magazines, and Journals      Menu
```

I picked the first item, "OBI The Online Book Initiative," and was shown the following menu, from which I selected item 4, "The Online Books":

```
OBI The Online Book Initiative

Page 1 of 1

1    About The Online Book Initiative    Text
2    The OBI FAQ                         Text
3    About The OBI Mailing Lists         Text
4    The Online Books                    Menu


Enter Item Number, SAVE, ?, or BACK: 4


The Online Books
Page 1 of 12
1    Welcome to OBI              Text
2    A. Hofmann                  Menu
3    A.E.Housman                 Menu
4    ACN                         Menu
5    ATI                         Menu
6    Access                      Menu
7    Aesop                       Menu
8    Algernon.Charles.Swinburne  Menu
9    Ambrose.Bierce              Menu
10   Amoeba                      Menu
11   Anarchist                   Menu
12   Andrew.Marvell              Menu
13   Anglo-Saxon                 Menu
14   Anonymous                   Menu
15   Ansax                       Menu
16   Antarctica                  Menu
17   ArtCom                      Menu
18   Arthur.Conan.Doyle          Menu
19   Athene                      Menu
```

Notice that this is only one of 12 pages of menu items for "The Online Books." As a long-time fan of "Bitter Bierce" (Ambrose.Bierce), I picked item 9, and the following menu appeared:

```
Ambrose.Bierce
Page 1 of 1

1    Can.Such.Things.Be        Text
2    The.Devils.Dictionary     Text
3    devdict.txt               Text
4    devdict.zip               PC-DOS

Enter Item Number, SAVE, ?, or BACK:
```

Now, this will make no sense at all to those who know nothing of Bierce and his writings. But, as someone who years ago memorized numerous entries in *The Devil's Dictionary,* I about fell out of my chair to find the thing online.

NET TIP

A few devilish definitions

Fans of the original black and white Twilight Zone *know Bierce from the episode "Occurrence at Owl Creek Bridge." But they and anyone else who has yet to encounter Bierce's* The Devil's Dictionary *have a real treat in store (easily available on the Net, as we have seen). Started in 1881 and first published as a book in 1911, here are just a few choice definitions:*

Aborigines, n. *Persons of little worth found cumbering the soil of a newly discovered country. They soon cease to cumber; they fertilize.*

Absurdity, n. *A statement or belief manifestly inconsistent with one's own opinion.*

Academe, n. *An ancient school where morality and philosophy were taught.*

Academy, n. *[from Academe] A modern school where football is taught.*

Accident, n. *An inevitable occurrence due to the action of immutable natural laws.*

Accomplice, n. *One associated with another in a crime, having guilty knowledge and complicity, as an attorney who defends a criminal, knowing him guilty. This view of the attorney's position in the matter has not hitherto commanded the assent of attorneys, no one having offered them a fee for assenting.*

Tapping into Veronica & Jughead

One of the really cool things about any Gopher menu system is that it almost always includes an option to access *other* Gophers. Technically, it does this by Telnetting you to some other site. But who cares? All that matters is that you get there.

And, as you can see from the Gopher example nearby, you can have one heck of a time exploring. But after you've taken the Gopher trip several times, you will begin to wonder how Gopher can be managed and turned into a really useful tool. A useful tool that you can employ to get *specific* information instead of merely zipping around the Net looking at any interesting item that chances to cross your screen.

The answer is Veronica. Veronica is a program that uses an approach similar to that used by Archie. Except, while Archie keeps a database of filenames and their various directories, Veronica keeps a database of the menu items from Gopher sites around the world.

 ## The Veronica difference

But Veronica goes Archie one better. As I said earlier, Archie can tell you where a file is, but you've still got to FTP to a site and get it. Veronica, however, will not only present you with a list of Gopher menu items, it will also act like a Gopher. The Veronica database of all Gopher menu items is called *Gopherspace*.

Thus, if you were to use Veronica to search Gopherspace for the word *supreme*, you would almost certainly come up with a Gopher-style menu listing the places to get U.S. Supreme Court decisions. But you could then simply choose an item, and Veronica would automatically take you there.

Pretty neat. Only trouble is that Veronica doesn't always work as planned. Sometimes it hangs. Sometimes it fails to make the necessary connection when you select an item from the menu it creates for you. But when Veronica is good, it's very, very good.

 # Key points about Veronica

The only way to get to Veronica is via a Gopher client. Your local Gopher will probably include a menu item like "Search all of Gopherspace using Veronica." If it doesn't offer an item like this, you can Gopher to **veronica.scs.unr.edu** and use Veronica there.

Alternatively, you can Gopher to the Mother Gopher at **gopher.tc.umn.edu** and choose "Other Gopher and Information Servers" and then "Veronica" from the menus that will appear.

If you don't have a Gopher client, you can Telnet to one of the Gopher addresses given at the end of Chapter 1 of this book.

That's Point 1. Point B is that Veronica has a more powerful search engine than Archie. Archie can look only for specific strings of characters, and no wildcards are allowed. But Veronica can use the Boolean AND, OR, and NOT operators, nested searches, and the like.

To learn more about this facility, get the Veronica FAQ. Look for it on your Gopher menu, or Gopher to **veronica.scs.unr.edu** and select the menu item "Search All of Gopherspace using Veronica." (The FAQ is also available on the Glossbrenner's Choice disk Internet 7, Just the FAQs.)

 # A Veronica example

Here's an example of a Veronica search done at NYSERNET. I responded to the "Search for:" prompt by keying in student and loans. The system found three pages of Gopher items! Notice that the two search words appear in each menu item. Here's just the first page:

```
Search for: student and loans

Search gopherspace using veronica at NYSERNET
Page 1 of 3

1    Guide to Payment Plans and Federal Student Loans          Text
2    Guide to Private Student Loans                            Text
3    Student Loans                                             Text
4    Administration of Scholarships, Grants-in-Aid, Loans, & Stud  Text
5    Replace Guaranteed Student Loans with Direct Loans        Text
```

```
 6    Stafford Student Loans                                    Text
 7    Facts About Student Loans                                 Menu
 8    Student Loans and Debt Mgmt.                              Text
 9    Student Loans                                             Menu
10    Research paper urges change to student loans              Text
11    Government Student Loans and Bursaries                    Menu
12    Student Loans                                             Text
13    Bank-less Student Loans to be the Rule at...              Text
14    Bank of Montreal offers student loans                    Text
15    Canada and B.C. Student Loans                             Text
16    Canada Student Loans Program Interest Relief Plan         Text
17    Alberta and Canada Student Loans (Coming Soon)            Menu
18    Student Loans                                             Text
19    Scholarships, Awards, and Student Loans                   Menu

Enter Item Number, MORE, SAVE, ?, or BACK:
```

✳ And what about Jughead?

Jughead, for its part, is currently available on just a few systems. But the program is such a good idea that it is sure to spread. Basically, Jughead addresses the problem of the multiple nested menus you'll find on most Gophers. Instead of having to wend your way down many different menu paths to see if a Gopher has what you want, you can use Jughead to search all the menu items on a single Gopher all at once. As long as the search word you're looking for is on some menu item somewhere within a given Gopher's menu system, Jughead will find it.

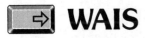

WAIS

WAIS (Wide Area Information Servers) is yet another attempt to help you find what you want on the Net. Where Archie searches a database of filenames, and Veronica searches a database of Gopher menu items, WAIS lets you search the actual text of a document or group of documents. But it does so in a way that eliminates the complex AND/OR/NOT Boolean logic and nested expressions used by people who search databases for a living.

WAIS relies on a technique called *relevance feedback* that assumes several iterations will be needed before you find exactly what you want. You can make your request using anything from "natural language" English to Boolean operators to dBASE-style data fields.

The system makes a first cut and shows you what it found. You look at the actual text and when you see a paragraph or article that's close, you, in effect, say, "Yes, you're getting there, bring me more stuff like this paragraph right here." Usually you don't have to do this more than two or three times before you find what you're looking for—assuming it is part of the WAIS database.

To use WAIS, Telnet to one of these locations and respond to the site's login prompt as shown here:

Location	Login as
quake.think.com	swais
wais.com	swais
swais.cwis.uci.edu	swais
sunsite.unc.edu	swais
info.funet.fi	info
wais.nis.garr.it	wais

 # The World Wide Web

Finally, there's the World Wide Web. The essence of the Web is *images* and *hypertext*. The hypertext features of the Web are far more important than images, however. In fact, it is here that the Web really shines. (After all, you can turn the graphics off if you want to.)

Remember how the Gopher menu system lets you use an Internet feature by merely selecting an item on the menu? Remember how I've said that on the Internet the physical location of an item and the geographical distance that separates you from it do not matter? Well, the Web takes this to its highest level. There is no menu system, there is just text filled with "hot-button" words.

 ## Hypertext Markup Language

The HTML (Hypertext Markup Language) used to create World Wide Web home pages is not difficult to learn (as you'll see in Chapter 9), so almost anyone can create an impressive-looking Web page—just as anyone can make the worst piece of writing look good by bringing the text into a desktop publishing program.

But in both cases, the good looks are often superficial. The problem with creating a really good Web page is the same faced when writing any computer program: anticipating user needs and actions and thinking long and hard about how people will actually work with and use the product.

Those are precisely the steps so many of today's Web home page programmers have neglected to take. Consequently, you will find many a Web page that is so full of large graphic images or photos that three to five minutes are required to send it to you and display it on your screen.

Similarly, many Web pages don't give you the option of speeding things up by turning off the graphics. You have to know enough to be able to do this yourself with your own local Web browser software.

NET TIP

The good, the bad, & the useless

So many Web sites, so little time. But how do you find the really good ones? Start with these "Best of" collections, plus the "Cool Site of the Day" I told you about in Chapter 2.

- *Best of the Web*

  http://wings.buffalo.edu/contest
- *Best of GNN*

  http://nearnet.gnn.com/gnn/meta/internet/feat/best.html
- *Best of PC Week*

  http://www.ziff.com/~pcweek/pcwbests.html
- *Cool Site of the Day*

  http://www.infi.net/cool.html

At the other end of the scale, you'll find the nominees for "Worst of the Web" and "Useless WWW Pages" (a.k.a. "America's Funniest Home Hypermedia") at these locations:

- *Worst of the Web*

  http://turnpike.net/metro/mirsky/Worst.html
- *Useless WWW Pages*

  http://www.primus.com/staff/paulp/useless.html

 # Tips for using a Web browser

Figure 5-1 offers a good example of one of the more elaborate World Wide Web pages you are likely to find. This is the home page for CareerMosaic, a site that offers career information and job listings on the Net.

Figure 5-1

The CareerMosaic home page on the World Wide Web.

✳ Keying in URLs

Notice the URL in the Location box at the top of the screen. If you want to go to the CareerMosaic site yourself, you must tell your Web browser program to take you to the URL **http://www .careermosaic.com/**.

Be sure to key in the URL *exactly* as you see it in print. If you make a mistake in spelling or punctuation or even spacing, it will not work. Instead, you'll get a message like "Unable to locate host" or some such.

✳ Gophers have URLs, too!

Don't forget that you can also use your Web browser to reach Gopher, FTP, and Telnet sites, as well as newsgroups. All it takes is the right URL prefix in front of the address:

To reach a Gopher site:	**gopher://**
To reach an FTP site:	**ftp://**
To reach a Telnet site:	**telnet://**
To reach a newsgroup:	**news:**

✳ Using Bookmarks & Hotlists

If you come across a Web site you like and expect to visit again, add it to your list of favorite sites. With Netscape Navigator, you can do this by clicking on the pull-down Bookmark menu and then on Add Bookmark. With NCSA Mosaic, click on Navigator and then on Hotlist. Whatever browser you use, it's sure to have a similar feature. Once you've added a site to your list of favorites, all you have to do is click on it the next time you want to go there. This is a real time saver with long and complicated Web addresses.

✳ Printing & saving files

You will want to play with your Web browser package, of course. But at some point early on, take the time to figure out how to print a Web page, and how to save it as a file.

Printing a file will probably be as simple as clicking on File and then on Print. To save a file, click on File and then on "Save as . . ." or "Save." (Use "Save as . . ." if you want to be given the opportunity to name the file yourself.) Your browser will then save the file as CAREER.HTM or some such.

✳ Working with HTML files

There are two important things you can do with .HTM files. First, you can use your browser program to view them later. Click on File and then on Open and specify the file's name. The file will be displayed, just as if you were online and logged onto that site, except that the graphics will be represented by generic icons.

Second, you can strip out all the special HTML instructions and treat an .HTM file as a text file. One easy way to do this is with a simple utility program called DE-HTML.EXE. This program will quickly eliminate all HTML codes and commands. Bring the resulting file into your word processor and adjust the paragraphs to your desired margins, and you'll be all set.

You can use Archie to look for DE-HTML.EXE on the Net. Or you can get it from Glossbrenner's Choice on the disk called Internet 8, World Wide Web Essentials.

The best search tool of all: InfoSeek

I've saved the best for last. If you're trying to find a particular site or document on the World Wide Web, one of the easiest and fastest ways to do it is with a free service called InfoSeek.

InfoSeek is one of several *search engines* that are available on the Internet. (Others include Lycos, WebCrawler, and W3.) But InfoSeek is by far the easiest to use. You can type your search request in plain English—as a complete sentence or as key words and phrases. (See Fig. 5-2 for an example.)

Within seconds, you'll receive the results—up to 10 hits that include document titles, URLs, and short summaries of the contents of each document. (See Fig. 5-3 for an example of that.)

To try InfoSeek yourself, point your Web browser at the URL **http://home.mcom.com/home/internet-search.html**. (With Netscape Navigator, just click on Directory and then on Internet Search.) That will take you to a screen like the one shown in Fig. 5-2. Search for your college, a favorite musical group, a TV show, whatever. Then prepare to be amazed!

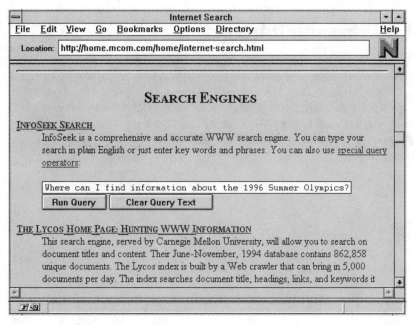

Figure 5-2

Here's the InfoSeek World Wide Web search screen.

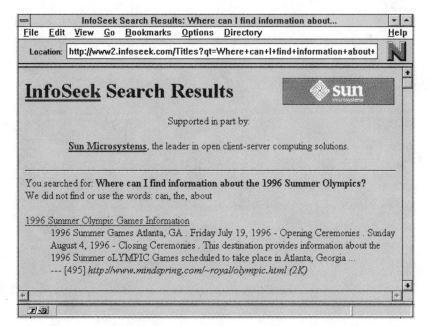

Figure 5-3

My "plain English" request for information about the 1996 Summer Olympic Games resulted in several hits, including this one.

NET TIP

Full-strength InfoSeek

If you want to generate more hits with your InfoSeek search—up to 200—you'll need to use the commercial version of InfoSeek. In addition to Web sites, the commercial version searches Internet newsgroups, several wire services, and other databases. For more information and to sign up for a 30-day free trial, visit the InfoSeek home page at **http://www.infoseek.com**.

6

How to *get* things on the Net

T HE easiest way to get things on the Internet is to let Gopher (or your Web browser if you have one) go get them for you. That's why, if you're a new user, I strongly urge you to use these methods first.

But, of course, all the Gophers in Gopherspace can't cover all the files available to you via the Internet. So you've got to learn to go get a file yourself. And you've got to learn how to process it after you get it, should it be compressed or supplied in some other non-text format.

In this chapter, we'll concentrate on the getting part. And you'll learn about some especially helpful files to get. Then I'll introduce you to the Internet Hunt, a regular just-for-fun competition that tests your Net "finding" and "getting" skills. In the next chapter, we'll zero in on the processing aspect, as you learn how to deal with files that end in .Z, .z, .tar, and other strange extensions.

 ## Anonymous FTP: A quick review

If you've read Chapter 1 of this book, you already know the steps to follow to get a file from an Internet location. The process is called *anonymous FTP*. It's anonymous because the FTP site offering the file collection does not require users to set up an account to get in

and obtain a file. It's FTP because that is the abbreviation of the File Transfer Protocol almost all Internet sites use.

You already know the basic drill. You sign on to an FTP site, move to the directory that holds the desired file, and then key in a command to get it transferred into your home directory on your campus computer. If you are using the Net by dialing up your campus computer from your own personal computer, you must then download the file from that location into your own machine.

Conceptually, FTPing a file really is a very simple procedure. But this time, the Devil and all the fiends of Hell really are in the details. So many things can trip you up. Things like the fact that UNIX is *case-sensitive*.

If, for example, you want to change to a directory called Supreme_Court and you key in cd supreme_court, the FTP system will tell you "No such file or directory." If you forget to change the FTP mode to binary transfer from its default of ASCII transfer, you may end up with garbage in your home directory instead of the file you wanted.

For these and many other reasons, you might want to make yourself a cheat sheet containing reminders and the steps you must follow to FTP a file. But let's start at the beginning.

Address, directory, & filename

You can FTP to a site and just poke around, of course. But that's likely to be a waste of time, since even UNIX's verbose filenames can be difficult to puzzle out. The best way to use FTP is to go after a file you already know about, either through a book like this or as the result of an Archie search. To FTP a file, you will need three pieces of information:

> ➤ The Internet address of the FTP site.

> ➤ The directory on that system that holds the file.

> ➤ And, of course, the name of the file itself.

Then follow the nine steps for FTPing a file presented in Chapter 1. I won't repeat them here. Instead, let's see if we can clear up some of the confusing characters that will fill your screen when you land at an FTP site. Then we'll touch on a few of the more advanced FTP commands.

NET TIP

The crowding of the Net

The number of new Internet users has grown at a fantastic rate in recent years. But the capacity of FTP sites to handle all these new folks has not grown apace. It doesn't hurt to remember that FTP site computers have other work to do. System administrators make a limited number of anonymous FTP connections available when they can. But that may or may not be during the day.

In general, unless you are specifically invited to do so, it is considered bad form to connect to most FTP sites during normal business hours as measured locally at the site. That usually means that you should avoid FTPing between the hours of 6 AM and 6 PM, their local time.

If you visit an FTP site and are told the system is "too busy to accept any more anonymous FTP connections," try again at a different time of day. Or check to see if the file you are looking for is offered at another location. Often the busy site will actually tell you about alternate sites as part of its "too busy" message.

An FTP example

Here's the kind of thing you can expect to find when you FTP to a site. In this case, I went to **rtfm.mit.edu**, logged on, and keyed in dir to get a directory. Then I changed down to the pub directory with the command cd "pub" and entered dir again. I have shortened the actual directory listings to conserve space, but this is very much like what you will see when you log onto any FTP site:

```
220 rtfm ftpd (wu-2.4(21) with built-in ls)
230 Guest login ok, access restrictions apply.
FTP> dir
200 PORT command successful.
150 Opening ASCII mode data connection for /bin/ls.
total 3807
-rw-rw-r--    1 root     system          0 Apr 14  1993 .notar
-rw-r--r--    1 root     system    1511468 Jul 15 05:55 Index-byname
```

```
-rw-r--r--    1 root      system     228722 Jul 15 05:55 Index-byname.gz
-rw-r--r--    1 root      system    1511468 Jul 15 05:55 Index-bytime
-rw-r--r--    1 root      system     144402 Jul 15 05:56 Index-bytime.gz
-rw-r--r--    1 root      system        249 Nov 10  1993 Index.README
drwxr -x--x   3 root      system        512 Apr 10 13:41 bin
drwxr-x--x    2 root      system        512 Apr 14  1993 dev
drwxr-x--x    4 root      system        512 Nov 17  1993 etc
-rw-r--r--    1 root      system     435957 Jul 15 06:02 ls-lR.Z
drwxrwxr-x   27 root      system       1536 May 25 15:38 pub

226 Transfer complete.
250 CWD command successful.
FTP> cd "pub"
250 CWD command successful.
FTP> dir
200 PORT command successful.
150 Opening ASCII mode data connection for /bin/ls.
total 3055
-rw-r--r--    1 3382      395        99943 May 23  1993 MAP.PS
drwxr-xr-x    2 3382      395          512 May 30  1995 MulticsMap
-rw-r--r--    1 3382      15010      37807 May  4  1991 chess.ps
drwxrwxr-x    2 root      3            512 Jul  8 17:54 faq-maintainers
-rw-rw--r--   1 root      system      2566 Nov 30  1995 index
drwx------    2 1         system       512 Aug  5  1995 new-usenet-addresses
drwxrwxr-x    2 3009      system       512 Apr 15  1995 popmail
drwxrwxr-x    2 3009      system       512 Feb 23 16:30 post_faq
drwxrwxr-x    2 11104     system       512 May 27 11:26 pthreads
lrwxrwxr-x    1 root      system        15 May 18  1995 usenet -> usenet-by group
drwxrwxr-x    6 3009      system       512 Aug  9  1995 usenet-addresses
drwxrwxr-x  950 3009      3          28160 Jul 15 00:25 usenet-by-group
drwxrwxr-x   37 root      3           1024 Jul 13 02:39 usenet-by-hierarchy
drwxr-xr-x    2 7783      15010        512 Jun 24 02:24 whois

226 Transfer complete.
FTP>
```

✳ Letters, dashes, & symbolic links

The style of directory listing shown here tells you that this is a UNIX system. The most important thing to look at first is the very first character in each line. If it is a *d*, you know that the line refers to a directory. (If you're a DOS user, that *d* is thus like the <DIR> that appears when you use the DIR command on your system.) If the first character is a dash (-), you know that the line refers to a file.

If the first character is a lowercase *l*, the line refers to a *symbolic link*. This is one of the more exotic features of the UNIX filing system. It makes it possible to have, on the directory of one system, an item that actually points to a file or directory on some other system (or even on the same system).

The name of the link and the name of the actual file or directory are given in the far right column, connected by an arrow, like this: usenet -> usenet-by-group. In the example above, if you were to enter the command cd "usenet", you would actually change to the directory called "usenet-by-group." System administrators have other reasons for creating symbolic links. But for us, they mainly mean a little less typing.

✳ The permissions characters

The next letters found at the beginning of each line in a UNIX directory stand for *read*, *write*, and *execute*. In UNIX-speak, these are called *permissions*. The reason there are three groups of permissions characters is due to the fact that UNIX is a multi-user operating system. Thus, the first character of a directory entry is usually either a *d* or a dash. The next three slots are the permissions for the owner of the file or directory. Followed by three slots specifying the permissions for an assigned group of people. Followed by the permissions for everyone on the system. That's us. And it's why the last three slots at most FTP sites read *r—*, allowing us only to read or copy a file.

NET TIP

Encountering non-UNIX systems

The Internet does connect non-UNIX systems as well. So the directory you see in response to the DIR command may look quite different. If each entry begins with a filename, for example, you are probably on a Digital Equipment Corporation (DEC) computer running the popular VMS operating system. On VMS systems, directory names appear like this: GRAPHIX.DIR;1. And filenames appear like this: README.TEX;1. You may even encounter systems that do not use a nested directory structure but put every file in one gigantic directory.

As always, when in doubt, key in a question mark or help. *The little details may be different, but the concepts are the same when using FTP on every kind of system.*

The main FTP commands

In all, there are nearly 60 main FTP commands and command topics, ranging from ACCOUNT through HASH and Wildcards. You can get

a list of them all by keying in help at the FTP prompt. The list ends with the "Topic?" prompt. At that point, key in any command on the list to get more information on what it means and how to use it. If you are on a UNIX system, try keying in man ftp or help ftp at your normal system prompt.

Fortunately you only need a few commands to use FTP:

dir   Shows you what's in your current location, be they files, or other directories, or both.

pwd   Stands for "print working directory." Equivalent to the DOS command CD for "check directory." Use this to find out where you are on a directory tree.

cd "directory-name"   This is the UNIX "change directory" command. That's how you move around. If you want to travel down a path all at once, use the forward slash—not the DOS backslash—to specify the path, like this: cd "/pub/faq-maintainers/". (The quotes aren't always necessary, but they never hurt.) To get to the same destination one step at a time, key in cd "pub", then cd "faq-maintainers". (If you tend to make a lot of typing mistakes, the one-step-at-a-time approach may be faster in the long run!)

cdup   Moves you up to the directory immediately above your current location.

get "filename" ¦more   Used for viewing reasonably short text files. The MORE program may or may not work on your target FTP system. Notice that there is *no* space between the pipe symbol (¦) and more.

binary   Make it a habit to enter this command before you enter the GET command. The system will respond by telling you that "type is set to I." (The *I* stands for "image" mode.)

get "filename" filename   Getting files is what it's all about. The quotes around the filename may or may not be required, but they do no harm. Make sure you enter the name of the file *exactly* as it appears in the directory listing. Case counts! The second *filename* is optional. Using it lets you give the file a different name when it arrives in your home directory on the campus system.

mget "*.Z"   The MGET ("multiple-file get") command lets you tell the FTP host to send you all files matching the criteria you specify. Here I've used *.Z to GET all files ending in .Z, but it could just as easily have been GOOD-?.DOC to get the files GOOD-1.DOC, GOOD-2.DOC, and so on.

ldir   The "local directory" command. If you are on a UNIX host, it's a good idea to issue this command after you have gotten a file with GET. That way you can make sure that the target file or files really are in your personal home directory.

exit   Gets you off the FTP site system and returns you to your own computer.

Great files: Where the getting is good

Internet FTP sites offer a stunning variety of files. Fiction, poetry, statistical reports, shareware software, music files—everything you can imagine and more. But among the most important files to get are those that help you use the Net more effectively, alert you to Net resources, and help you find other files to get.

So, now that you know how to FTP, let's get going!

Opinions are sure to differ, but in *my* opinion, there are several files no one, least of all no student, should be without. I'm not going to take the space to go into great detail. But that's okay since it's not likely to cost you anything to FTP the files, and if you don't like them, you can just delete them. (As a convenience, the most recent editions of each of these files are available on a single disk from Glossbrenner's Choice.)

The Beginner's Guide to the Internet Tutorial

FTP to **oak.oakland.edu**, Path: /SimTel/msdos/info/bgi20.zip

This DOS-based program by Patrick J. Suarez does a wonderful job of distilling the essence of the Internet into an interactive tutorial. The current version at this writing is **bgi20.zip** (Beginner's Guide to the Internet, Version 2.0). There may be a newer version, and therefore a slightly different filename, when you visit the site.

If you've got a Macintosh (II, LC, or Quadra series) and you'd like to try an interactive tutorial of your own, consider taking Merit Network's *Cruise of the Internet*. FTP to **nic.merit.edu**, Path: /internet/resources/cruise.mac/.

Special Internet Connections by Scott Yanoff

FTP to **ftp.csd.uwm.edu**, Path: /pub/inet.services.txt

This the famous Yanoff List. Mr. Yanoff basically tells you about what he feels are the best resources available on the Net for specific topics. Those topics range from "Agriculture" to "Weather, Atmospheric, and Oceanic information." The Yanoff List calls on you to use all your fundamental Internet skills to get the information or goodies you want. (For even more options and information on the current Yanoff List, try Fingering **yanoff@alpha2.csd.uwm.edu**.)

The List of Subject-Oriented Internet Resource Guides

FTP to **una.hh.lib.umich.edu**, Path: /inetdirsstacks/.README-FOR-FTP

For a student, this may well be the most important Internet resource of all. The Clearinghouse for Subject-Oriented Internet Resource Guides offers scores of text files, each of which has been prepared by someone who really knows the Net. The text files pull together in one place the newsgroup names, the Telnet and Gopher locations, the mailing lists and list servers, the electronic newsletters and journals, the World Wide Web resources, and the key e-mail addresses and FTP sites that are relevant to a *single* subject.

Here's just a sampling of the many subjects included:

➤ Alternative Medicine

➤ Art and Architecture

➤ Black/African Studies

➤ Buddhism

➤ Dance

➤ Employment Opportunities and Job Resources

➤ Environment

➤ Film and Video

➤ Journalism

➤ Latin American Studies

➤ Philosophy and Ethics

➤ Sociology and Demography

➤ Theater, Film, and Television

➤ Women's Studies and Feminism

⇨ John December's _Internet-CMC List_

FTP to **ftp.rpi.edu,** Path: /pub/communications/

The files called **internet-cmc.txt** and **internet-cmc.col** are plain text versions. (Of the two, I prefer **internet-cmc.col.**) The file called **internet-cmc.ps.Z** is the compressed PostScript version. Chapter 7 of this book shows you how to handle .Z files.

The full title of this incredible resource is _Information Sources: The Internet and Computer-Mediated Communication_ by John December. This list is essentially a wonderfully detailed table. It organizes and categorizes resources by topic and gives you the Internet feature to use (FTP, Gopher, etc.), the address to target, and the path to follow once you get there.

It's available both as plain ASCII text and as a PostScript file. Assuming you have a way to print a PostScript file, get them both. The .PS file makes a very impressive 100-page printout, while the ASCII text version can be searched on your computer using your word processor.

 # John December's *Internet Tools Summary*

FTP to **ftp.rpi.edu**, Path: /pub/communications/

Get the files called **internet-tools.col** or **internet-tools.txt** (again, I prefer the former). If you have a PostScript printer, get **internet-tools.ps.Z** as well.

Mr. December's *Internet Tools Summary* is a comprehensive guide to the tools available on the Internet for searching out files and information. Whereas the CMC List presents Internet resources organized by topic, the Tools List is organized by the name of the tool. Like the CMC List, it's updated frequently with new information about the Net.

NET TIP

The Rovers List of FTP Sites

Internaut Perry Rovers produces an impressive list of anonymous FTP sites and updates it on a regular basis. For each site, the list tells you what kinds of files and subjects are covered. Put the Rovers List into your word processor and you can search for topics of interest.

*Here are the FTP sites where Mr. Rovers posts his list. You may also want to pick up his Frequently Asked Questions (FAQ) about the site list. (Look for a file called simply **faq** in the directory with the site list.)*

USA	*FTP Address:* **oak.oakland.edu** *Path: /SimTel/msdos/info/ftp-list.zip*
USA	*FTP Address:* **rtfm.mit.edu** *Path: /pub/usenet/news.answers/ftp-list/sitelist/*
Europe	*FTP Address:* **garbo.uwasa.fi** *Path: /pc/doc-net/ftp-list.zip*
Asia	*FTP Address:* **ftp.edu.tw** *Path: /documents/networking/guides/ftp-list/*

The Internet Hunt

Some time ago, Rick Gates came up with a truly cool idea: Create a contest designed to test the skills of fellow Internauts by posing a series of questions that must be answered using Net resources. Knowing the answer to a question is not enough. You've also got to report how and where you found it on the Net. (All Trekkies, for example, know that Majel Barrett is the voice of the computer on STNG—but how can you discover that on the Internet?)

Thus was born the great Internet Hunt, with questions like these:

➤ What airline flies between Chicago, Atlanta, Newark, and Florida for one-way prices ranging from $69 to $149? The toll-free number would also be helpful.

➤ Miles Davis once recorded an album that contained the song "Surrey With the Fringe on Top." How many stars did Down Beat magazine give that album?

➤ What is ToasterNet?

➤ According to the Quilter's Ten Commandments, how many days a week ought a quilter to cook and clean?

➤ My grandfather told me that he served in the U.S. Navy Submarine Service during WWI. He was stationed aboard the USS BASS. He told me that it was sunk during WWII in U.S. coastal waters. How could this have happened?

➤ In 1991, the United States Postal Service issued a set of postal stamps with fishing flies on them. What five fishing flies appeared on the stamps?

➤ In what Gilbert & Sullivan operetta was "Sir Speak" mentioned?

➤ What are *Wired* magazine's Seven Wonders of the World?

➤ Which novels were nominated for the Hugo Award in 1985? Which author/novel won that year?

➤ According to Mark Twain's character, Pudd'nhead Wilson, what is a cauliflower?

To an information and Internet junkie, the challenge is irresistible! To tap into the Hunt, FTP to **ftp.cic.net**, Path: /pub/hunt/about/. Get the file called **intro.txt** for instructions on what to do next. (You can also find the Hunt at the Gopher site **gopher.cic.net**). Have fun!

NET TIP

Finding sports information

After a hard day of FTPing, why not relax and Finger some sports scores and team standings? Here are some sample Finger commands to help you check up on your favorite teams:

- *Baseball Scores/Standings*
  finger jtchern@headcrash.berkeley.edu

- *Baseball and Football Scores/Standings*
  finger robc@xmission.com

- *International Hockey League Newsletter*
  finger 074345@xavier.xu.edu

7
How to
process files

YOU have heard, perhaps, about waiting for the second shoe to drop? No? Well, never mind. This chapter is the "third shoe." You know how to *find* files with Archie and friends. You know how to *get* files with anonymous FTP. Here you'll learn what to do with files after you get them.

Sadly, this is not a trivial point. It would be wonderful if you only had to worry about text files and compressed archives created with, say, the PKZIP program. (Or the StuffIt program, if you're a Macintosh user.) It would be wonderful if there were only one flavor of graphic image file—say, .GIF—and one flavor of sound file—say, .WAV—but that is far, far from the case.

In the computer field, everyone thinks he or she has a better idea. So, "let a thousand formats bloom." Unfortunately, for most people it is irrelevant whether, say, the ZOO method of file compression saves a kilobyte here and a kilobyte there by being a "better" compressor than PKZIP, or my favorite, LHA. Nor do most people care whether .GIF or .PCX or JPEG is the best graphic format.

If only things could be *simple*! But they're not. And that's reality, so let's deal with it.

Compression, archiving, & all that

All anyone really needs to know about file compression and file archives can be summarized very quickly. First, almost any file can be compressed by replacing multiple characters—like *the*—with a single character. Indeed, that's exactly what file compression programs do. They run through a file making those replacements and then prepare a translation table indicating what they have done.

Such a table might have a line reading something like this: @ = the. Since the table is included with the compressed file, it's easy for a decompression program to read it. In this case, the decompression program would run through the file replacing every @ with the letters *the*. This makes it easy for the decompression program to create a perfect copy of the original file on your disk.

But why go to all this trouble? To save storage space and transmission time, that's why. After all, it's much more economical to "compress" orange juice into frozen concentrate and ship it north from Florida than it is to freeze regular orange juice and ship it that way. The difference is that reconstituted frozen orange juice bears little resemblance to the real thing, while a reconstituted file is a perfect copy of the original.

In the personal computer world, at least, individual compressed files came first. Then someone hit on the great idea of not only compressing files but also packing related files into a compressed *archive*. No longer would users have to download a program file *and* a documentation file. By downloading an archive, you could get everything at once.

And that, ladies and gentlemen, is just about all any normal person needs to know about the theory of file compression and archiving. The only piece that's missing is this: IBM, Macintosh, and Internet/UNIX users have all developed their own file compression and archiving programs. The techniques used by each range from similar to identical. But that does not change the fact that you need a special program to process each type of compressed or archived file.

 # How do I know which tool to use?

The best way to deal with this problem is to take the "if/then" approach. "If the file ends in .SIT, then I need UNSTUFF.EXE if I'm a DOS user (or StuffIt or StuffIt Lite if I use a Mac) to decompress and unarchive it." Or "If the file ends in .ps or .PS, then I need to be able to print it as a PostScript file." In short, the file extension will tell you which software tool you need. Then all you have to do is obtain and apply the right tool.

 # The master list of file extensions

Here's a master list of the file extensions you are likely to encounter at FTP sites on the Internet and how to handle each one. See the NetTips that follow the master list for a summary of the most common file extensions for DOS users and for Macintosh users, along with the names of the programs for dealing with them.

.ARC	Compressed archive. Requires ARC from SEAware, PKARC, or Vernon Buerg's tiny, free ARCE or ARC-E programs to extract. Macintosh program ArcMac and UNIX program arc5521 will also work.
.ARJ	A compressed archive requiring the ARJ program to uncompress.
.btoa	Binary to ASCII. A binary file in text format that must be converted back to binary with the UNIX program BTOA or the DOS program ATOB. (The file extension .atob is, of course, ASCII to Binary.)
.com	A DOS program file. Type the filename at the DOS command line to make it run.
.cp or .cpio	Archives created by UNIX CPIO (copy-in/copy-out) tape archiving program. An early competitor

to TAR. UNIX users may use the PAX program to deal with such files or with .TAR files, for that matter. For DOS users, the program to get is PAX2EXE. PAX stands for *portable archive exchange*.

.cpt   Macintosh file created by Compactor.

.doc or .DOC   A text file (*document* or *documentation*). View on screen or with your word processor when offline.

.exe   A DOS program file that is usually larger than a .com file. To run it, key in the filename at the DOS command line. Note: Self-extracting archive files created by PKZIP and LHA may have this extension as well. Just key in the filename at the command line. No need to use—or even own—PKZIP or LHA.

.gif   A Graphics Interchange Format file. CompuServe created this format to make it possible to exchange graphic images among different computer systems. Look at the file with a *viewer* program that can handle .GIF (pronounced "jiff") files.

.gz   Compressed archive requiring a UNIX interpretation of PKZIP, specifically the GZIP (GNU Zip) program from the GNU Project. See also .z.

.Hqx or .hqx   Macintosh compression format. Requires the Mac program BinHex, the DOS program XBIN, or the UNIX program MCVERT to convert.

.jpg   A file in the Joint Photographic Experts Group (JPEG) format. Can be viewed on any system with a JPEG-compatible viewer program.

.lha or .lzh   DOS compressed archive requiring the use of the public domain program LHA, which can handle archives created by its predecessor if you specify the /O (for "old version") switch.

.mpg   A video file that can be viewed on any system with the right software.

.pict   A Macintosh-format picture file.

.pak   A DOS compressed archive created by the PAK program. Rarely seen these days.

.pit   A file created by the Macintosh program PackIt.

.ps or .PS   A PostScript document (in Adobe's page description language). Make ready your PostScript printer and simply "copy" such a file to the printer. The results are often desktop publishing quality.

.sdn   Rarely seen these days. A compressed archive file created by the Shareware Distribution Network. Try running the ARJ or PAK programs against it, taking care to specify the full filename, including the .sdn extension.

.sea   A Macintosh self-extracting archive.

.shar, .sh, or .Shar   A *shell archive* created by the UNIX SHAR program. Use UNSHAR to uncompress.

.sit or .Sit   A compressed archive created with the Macintosh StuffIt or Stuffit Deluxe program.

.?q?   A squeezed DOS file. This technique is so ancient that you really must question how current any such file can be.

.sqz   A squeezed DOS file of similar vintage to the kind cited above.

.taz or .tgz   Shorthand for *.tar.z*. Use the GZIP program first on such files, and then TAR.

.tar or -tar	Short for *tape archive*. TAR files are archives packed into a single file by the UNIX TAR program. Use TAR to unpack.
.tif	A graphic Tagged Image Format File (TIFF). TIFFs come in many flavors, and not all viewer programs can display all types.
.txt or .TXT	Short for *text*. Should be nothing but plain, standard ASCII text that you can display or print out easily.
.uu or .uue	A binary file in ASCII format requiring the UUDECODE program or a clone to convert back into binary form.
.wp	A WordPerfect file.
.xtoa	X to ASCII. Data transformation standard to convert binary files to 7-bit ASCII.
.xxe	An ASCII file created from a binary file by a program like UUENCODE. The newer versions of UUENCODE and its clones should be able to handle such files the same way they handle .ue and .uue files.
.Z	A compressed file requiring the UNIX UNCOMPRESS program or a clone, like the DOS program U16 or the Mac program MacCompress.
.z	Case counts! A lowercase *z* usually indicates an archive requiring the free GZIP program from GNU Project. To reduce confusion, newer versions of the GZIP program create files ending in .gz instead.
.zip or .ZIP	Compressed archive created by the DOS program PKZIP.
.zoo or .ZOO	Compressed archive created by the ZOO program, which is required to uncompress it. Versions of ZOO exist for most platforms.

DOS compression programs

Listed below are the filename extensions you are most likely to encounter on the Internet, followed by the name of the DOS program you'll need to deal with it.

*All of these programs are available on the Net by FTP. Look for them at PC archive sites like **oak.oakland.edu** or **archive.umich.edu**. They are also available from Glossbrenner's Choice on a single disk.*

File extension	Name of required program
.arc	ARCE
.arj	ARJ
.btoa	ATOB
.cpio	PAX2EXE
.gz or .z	GZIP
.hqx	XBIN
.pak	PAK
.pit	UNPACKIT
.shar	TOADSHR
.sit	UNSTUFF or UNSIT
.tar	TAR or EXTAR
.uue	UUEXE (Richard Marks) or NCDC
.Z	U16 or COMP
.zip	PKZIP
.zoo	ZOO

Macintosh compression programs

These are the compression programs that Macintosh users will need in order to deal with the most common types of compressed files. Notice that for .ARJ, .gz or .z, and .cpio files there is no Mac program to use. At least not at this writing. Fortunately, you will usually find a .Sit (StuffIt) version of a compressed file in the same directory that holds the .z, .gz. or .ARJ version.

File extension	Name of required program
.ARC	ArcMac
.ARJ	no equivalent
.Hqx	BinHex

.bndl	Bundle
.cpt	Compactor
.cpt	Compact Pro
.Z	MacCompress
.gz or .z	no equivalent
.cpio	no equivalent
.dd	DiskDoubler
.ish	ISHMAC
.LZH	MacLHarc
.lzss	LZSS
.pit	PackIt
.ZIP	ZipIt or UnZip
.shar	UNSHAR
.stf	STF
.Sit	StuffItLite
.tar	UNTAR
.UUE	UUTOOL
.ZOO	MacBooz

New FTP sites offering Macintosh software are constantly appearing. For starters, FTP to one of these sites to look for the compression/ conversion utilities you need: **mac.archive.umich.edu**, **oak.oakland .edu**, *or* **sumex-aim.stanford.edu**.

How to actually process a file

Since you are likely to be FTPing lots of files, it's a good idea to develop good habits for dealing with them. If you take just a moment to set things up correctly, dealing with files will soon become second nature. In general, the concept is to move the file to its own area and then perform the extraction, and, after that, any conversion that may be required. Follow these steps:

❶ If it's a program file you're dealing with, it's a good idea to test it for viruses before running it. DOS comes with a virus detection program. If you do not have such, ask around.

❷ If the file is clean, run the program.

❸ Look at the program documentation with your word processor or text editor. Check especially for any special installation or startup instructions.

❹ Then remove the original compressed archive from your disk, either by deleting it or by copying it to a floppy.

⇨ Sounds & images

Once you get a program or text file unarchived and uncompressed, it is pretty obvious what to do next. You run the program and you look at or print out the text file. But files that contain images, sounds, and animation require still more processing. Or at least, they each require a special program of some sort.

In the next chapter you will learn how to view images—after first capturing them as text messages on a newsgroup and then converting them to a binary file. As you will see, all that's required is a *viewer program* capable of displaying the graphic file, be it .PCX, .GIF, .TIF, or whatever.

Same thing applies to image files you get via FTP. The only difference between getting an image file via FTP and taking the newsgroup route is the extra step the newsgroup route entails as you convert from text to binary format. (There is also the fact that no image you will ever get via FTP will ever be as, uh, "interesting," as one you'll find in a newsgroup like **alt.sex.binaries**.)

⇨ Sound sites by FTP

But what about sound? What about animation? As it happens, there are lots and lots of Internet sites with tons of sound and animation files for you. If you're interested in sound files, start with one of the many sound archive sites available by FTP:

➢ FTP address: **ee.lbl.gov**
Path: /sounds/

➢ FTP address: **f.ms.uky.edu**
Path: /pub3/sounds/

> FTP address: **plan9.njit.edu**
> Path: /pub/sounds/

> FTP address: **sol.ctr.columbia.edu**
> Path: /pub/DA/sounds/

> FTP address: **valhalla.ee.rochester.edu**
> Path: /pub/sound/

> FTP address: **vela.acs.oakland.edu**
> Path: /pub/sound/

⇨ Sound sites on the World Wide Web

If you have a Web browser, you might also visit some of the World
Wide Web sites that are devoted to sound files. The Rutgers
University Sound Home Page shown in Fig. 7-1 is just one of many
Web sites that offer pointers to vast collections of sound files from
all around the world. Here are just a few:

> Computers:Multimedia:Sound (extensive collection of sounds
> from TV, movies, and elsewhere)
> **http://www.yahoo.com/Computers/Multimedia/Sound/**

> Rutgers University Sound Home Page (animals, Barney,
> cartoons, Chinese, classical, modern music, Monty Python, Star
> Trek)
> **http://www-caip.rutgers.edu/Rutgers_Sounds/**

> Sound Archive (pointers to lots of sound files and information)
> **http://www.comlab.ox.ac.uk/archive/sound.html**

> Sunsite Sound Archive
> **http://sunsite.sut.ac.jp/multimed/sounds/**

> UnderWorld Links Sound (birds, cartoons, comedy,
> commercials, and more)
> **http://www.nd.edu/StudentLinks/jkeating/links/sound.
> html**

> World Wide Web Virtual Library: Audio (pointers to information
> on audio sounds available around the world)
> **http://www.comlab.ox.ac.uk/archive/audio.html**

Figure 7-1

The Rutgers University Sound Home Page makes it easy to get animal
sounds, Barney, cartoons, classical music, and more.

NET TIP

Playing sound on a PC

*Macintosh computers have long had sound built in, but users of
DOS/Windows machines must do one of two things to play sound
files. You've either got to add a SoundBlaster sound board (or
compatible) and a pair of speakers. Or you've got to load the
Microsoft PC Speaker driver, SPEAKER.DRV. (Add a line like this to
your CONFIG.SYS file:* device=c:\dos\speaker.drv.)

*SPEAKER.DRV is widely available online and from Glossbrenner's
Choice. It's limited to playing .WAV sound files in Windows. But with
SOX, a program discussed later, you can convert most other sound
formats into .WAV files.*

Sounds via newsgroup

As you'll see in the next chapter, converting binary images into text files and posting them to various newsgroups is a favorite pastime on the Net. But graphics files aren't the only binary files you'll find in newsgroups. You'll also find sound files people have sampled, digitized, and converted into one or more text messages for posting with the UUCODE program discussed in the next chapter.

If sounds are what you're after, use your newsreader to access one or more of these groups:

alt.binaries.sounds.cartoons	Sounds from copyrighted animated shows.
alt.binaries.sounds.d	Sounding off.
alt.binaries.sounds.erotica	Erotic noises.
alt.binaries.sounds.midi	MIDI binaries.
alt.binaries.sounds.misc	Digitized audio adventures.
alt.binaries.sounds.mods	MODs and related sound formats.
alt.binaries.sounds.movies	Sounds from copyrighted movies.
alt.binaries.sounds.music	Music samples in MOD/669 format.
alt.binaries.sounds.tv	Sounds from copyrighted television shows.
alt.binaries.sounds.utilities	Sound utilities.

Because messages do scroll off newsgroup boards, there is no guarantee that you will find any given sound file at any given time. But you can post requests for sound clips, and whatever you do find is sure to be interesting. Recent postings to the group **alt.binaries.sounds.tv** included:

➤ Anyone know where I can find the O.J. Simpson CNN theme?

➤ REQUEST: Addams Family "Whoop Whoop—Mail's in" sound

➤ Gilligan's Island theme

➤ Beavis & Butt-head: Here's more Mr. Buzzcut!

And recent postings to the group **alt.binaries.sounds.movies** included:

➢ Monty Python (4 msgs)

➢ Lion King

➢ Forrest Gump anyone?

➢ HIGHLANDER: Better to burn out . . .

➢ Was 20th Century Fox Theme .WAV reposted? (2 msgs)

➢ FlintStones Theme!!

➢ REQUEST: Caddyshack

NET TIP

SOX: the sound converter

You almost certainly received a program for playing sound files with your SoundBlaster or other sound board. But, since there seem to be nearly as many sound file formats as there are formats for graphics files, you'll also want a good sound conversion program. Perhaps the best is the SOX (SOund eXchange) program you will find available for most machines.

SOX supports the following file types:

Raw (no header)	Sndtool
IRCAM Sound Files	Sounder
SoundBlaster	NeXT .SND
Sun SPARC .AU (w/header)	Windows 3.1 RIFF/WAV
Mac HCOM	Turtle Beach .SMP
PC/DOS .SOU	Apple/SGI AIFF and 8SVX

SOX is available for DOS users on the Sound Tools disk from Glossbrenner's Choice, but you can also find it in DOS and other formats at various locations on the Net. Look for it in one of the FTP archives devoted to sound files or PC/Macintosh software collections. Or try an Archie search for SOX.EXE or SOX.ZIP. Or post a request on the newsgroup **alt.binaries.sounds.utilities***.*

 # Animation considerations

At this writing, animation is very much "the undiscovered country" in the world of computing. It is used in CD-ROM-based encyclopedias to illustrate things like the functioning of a four-stroke internal

combustion engine. But most of the time, animation files are just enjoyable novelties. Still, they're a lot of fun.

Naturally, there are many conflicting, incompatible file formats and relatively few software tools and utilities. Fortunately, a standard does appear to be emerging. It is the .FLI ("flick") file format popularized by the Autodesk Animator program. The key program to get to play .FLI files in DOS is AAPLAY. This is the AutoDesk Automated Animator Player. It's quite serviceable and does a nice job.

If you're a Windows user, you can play .FLI files with the built-in Windows Media Player. Two things are necessary to do this. First, you must have a copy of the proper driver file for the animation files you want to play. At this writing, look for MCIAAP.DRV, a 17K file that is available in the ASOFT forum on CompuServe and in many other places.

Second, you must have the animation files themselves. Like AAPLAY and MCIAAP.DRV, both are readily available from public domain and shareware sources, including Glossbrenner's Choice. You might also try an Archie search to see where these files might be on the Net.

NET TIP

Animation online!

If you are interested in animation, the Internet has lots of invaluable information to offer. Here, for example, are the names of the main newsgroups that focus on the subject.:

alt.binaries.multimedia	*Sound, text, and graphics rolled in one.*
comp.graphics.animation	*Technical aspects of computer animation.*
comp.sys.ibm.pc.soundcard	*Hardware/software aspects of PC sound cards,*
rec.arts.animation	*Discussion of various kinds of animation.*
comp.graphics	*Computer graphics, art, animation, image processing.*
rec.arts.anime	*Japanese animation discussion.*

You'll also want to check out the VT/ANSI Animation mailing list. Its sole purpose is to provide a distribution channel for VT/ANSI ANIMATION files and a forum for discussion of how these files can be created easily. (Regis Graphics and Regis Animation files are also discussed.)

To subscribe, prepare a letter with something like "Please add me to the VT/ANSI Animation List" in the message area and send it via e-mail to **ANIM-L@rmcs.cranfield.ac.uk**.

GhostScript instead of PostScript

Files that end in .PS are PostScript files, and those that end in .EPS are Encapsulated PostScript files. Neither type of file will do you any good if you do not have a PostScript printer or a way to print PostScript files.

If you *do* have a PostScript printer or a PostScript emulator cartridge, the printed results of .PS or .EPS files can be absolutely stunning! You will think you are reading pages from a commercially printed book. All you have to do is get the .PS or .EPS version of the file on your disk, make sure your PostScript printer is enabled, and key in copy filename.ps prn or type filename.ps > prn (where *filename.ps* is the name of your file). In a couple of minutes, printing will begin. If you're a Mac user, drag the file and drop it on the printer.

Fortunately, if you do *not* have PostScript capabilities, all is not lost, thanks to an intriguing option called GhostScript. The GhostScript package lets you view and print PostScript files—even if you do not have a PostScript-compatible program or printer.

But, although it is free software, you will "pay" in disk space. The main program file, compressed, is over 1.2 megabytes in size. GSMENU.EXE, an add-on utility I like a lot, adds another 200K. And the font files you will need to really use GhostScript take up a couple of megabytes more. Still, if you've got the space on your hard drive and you don't have PostScript, GhostScript is a very credible option.

All necessary files are available on the Net and via Glossbrenner's Choice.

 # Text-treating programs

Over the years, untold hours have been spent using word processing programs to laboriously "process" files downloaded from some computer. And nowhere is the problem more manifest than on the Internet.

For example, some creator of a file on the Net may have indented every line five spaces because he or she thought it looked better that way. Or you may find that something funny has been done at the end of each line. Many files have tab characters (ASCII 9) embedded in them to save space. Others may simply have a lot of non-displayable junk characters.

In any event, the key to solving such problems quickly and easily lies in a collection of the right utility programs:

LIST   Every PC user should have a copy of Vernon Buerg's famous shareware LIST program. LIST can quickly clean up a file, filtering out junk characters and who-knows-what. It also lets you search for text strings and clip out sections to be dumped to disk under a different name. I use LIST dozens of times a day and simply could not work without it.

TEXT   Walter Kennamer's TEXT program is also invaluable, for it lets you remove all leading white space on each line of a file. Or remove all trailing blanks. Or convert all white space into the number of spaces you specify. And so on.

CHOP   The CHOP program, also by Walter Kennamer, will cut a file into as many pieces as you specify. You might use it for dealing with the 64K limit on Internet newsgroup and e-mail messages.

CRLF   This program by Rahul Dhesi, the creator of the ZOO method of file packing, makes sure that every line in a text file ends with a carriage return and a linefeed so it can be displayed and edited

properly. If the file was created on an old Apple computer, for example, there's a good chance that each line will end in a carriage return but be missing the linefeed character. If the text was created on a mainframe, each line may end in two carriage returns or two linefeeds. Whatever the case, CRLF is smart enough to fix things up.

These are just a few of the *text treater* tools I use every day when dealing with text files downloaded from the Net. Archie may be able to help you find these files (or equivalent utilities) on the Net itself, but looking up every one of them could take lots of time. If you find it more convenient, you can order all these tools through Glossbrenner's Choice.

8
How to view "interesting" pictures

THE Internet has so many goodies to offer that at times it seems like a treasure house of old. There are *wonderful* things: pictures, graphics, animation, sound, plain text files, and files you can simply copy to your printer to produce a professional typeset look.

Trouble is, as with the treasure houses of myth and legend, you often have to go through an ordeal before you can lay your hands on the prize. In this case, it is an ordeal by software. You already know about unzipping, unarcing, unstuffing, or otherwise unpacking the file that lands on your disk after an Internet session. But you probably don't know about the *uudecoding* of text gotten from Usenet newsgroups.

And there are so many different graphics formats that you may not know what to do with a decoded or unpacked file that ends in .GIF, .PCX, .JPG, and so on. This chapter will straighten things out and get you going right away.

In keeping with the ancient treasure house theme, ordeals may have been necessary to obtain the prize. But magic spells and incantations could also save you a lot of time and bother. In this world, the equivalent of a magic spell is the right piece of software. All it takes is the right program to turn some dumb file into a spectacular (and possibly sexy) graphic.

In short, all will be revealed in the pages that follow. We'll start off with the whole UUDECODE thing. Then we'll take a look at graphics viewers, converters, and paint programs. Finally, we'll clue you in to the best sources for graphics software and image files.

 # Pictures, graphics, & binary files via newsgroups

The simplest, easiest way to get and view photographs, clip art, and other graphic images is to find what you want as a binary file. FTP it or otherwise download it using Zmodem or some other error-checking protocol, load a graphics viewing program, and voilà, you're in business.

Getting such a file in zipped or stuffed or some other compressed format is okay, too. After all, once you've got an unarchiving program, you can quickly produce a copy of the runnable, viewable, or usable full-sized file. Remember to delete the file containing the archived version from your disk to conserve space, and you're all set.

A lot of binary files are available via e-mail and on newsgroups, however, and these types of files require a bit more processing.

You wouldn't think that newsgroups would have files. After all, the reason newsgroups exist is to make it possible for Internauts to exchange ideas, opinions, and information with people all over the world by typing at their keyboards. You could argue that images are information, but why not simply direct someone to an FTP site and a specific file you want to share?

As it happens, there are two very good reasons why this is not possible and, therefore, why a number of newsgroups carry binary files:

➤ For reasons of security, most FTP sites do not permit uploads. There is thus no easy way for a user to place a binary file on the Net for others to obtain via FTP.

➤ The information available at FTP sites is controlled by the people who run the site. Newsgroups, on the other hand, are typically not controlled or *moderated*. That means no one reviews the material that is posted or controls what messages will or will not appear.

The catch is that, if it's going to appear on a newsgroup, it's got to be in 7-bit ASCII text. There is also the fact that no newsgroup message can be longer than 64K. The same restrictions apply to Internet e-mail.

NET TIP

QuickShot: Getting & viewing graphics

Here's a quick summary of the steps to follow for getting and viewing graphics files:

1   *Get a copy of the UUENCODE/UUDECODE program for your machine. If you're using a UNIX workstation at the computer center, this program is probably already available to you.*

2   *Access a newsgroup with the word* binaries *in its title.*

3   *Most images will consist of several parts, each one a separate message labelled 1 of 4, 2 of 4, and so on. Open your comm program's capture buffer and get them all.*

4   *When the last message in the series is safely in your capture buffer file on disk, sign off the Net.*

5   *Run the UUDECODE program against the capture buffer file to reconstitute the binary file. If your version of the decoding software is not smart enough to handle this, you will have to use a text editor to cut the capture file into a file for each message in the series. Then run the decoder against the entire group.*

6   *Load your favorite viewer program and look at the file. Most viewer programs will also let you make a printout.*

NET TIP

Hows & whys:
The lowest common denominator

Internet newsgroups and e-mail are used by millions of people equipped with all sorts of computers. Consequently, these features are designed around what we can think of as the lowest common denominator in computer communications: 7-bit ASCII text. Here's what it all means:

- *Computers operate on the binary numbering system that consists of only two digits: 1 and 0. Each digit is symbolized by a bit, actually a particular voltage level on a wire.*

- *The binary numbering system can symbolize any number using just 1's and 0's. But for technical reasons, computers tend to use eight-bit chunks called bytes. (Since each bit is symbolized by a*

voltage level on a wire, eight wires are required to transport one eight-bit byte around inside your system.)

- *Text is symbolized in a computer by assigning a number to each upper- and lowercase character of the alphabet. Numbers are also assigned to the digits from 0 through 9 and to punctuation marks and a bunch of other things.*

- *The kicker is this: In the binary numbering system, seven bits are all that are required to represent the decimal numbers 0 through 127, and those numbers offer all the slots needed to assign one number to each letter of the alphabet, and so on. In fact, there are even some slots left over.*

- *It is this code chart from 0 through 127 (called Standard ASCII) that everyone in the world agrees on.*

- *The only reason the 7-bit in 7-bit ASCII is significant is that computers have an eighth bit to work with. The binary numbering system being what it is, adding an eighth bit lets computers symbolize an additional 128 characters (128 through 255). But no one agrees on what characters should be assigned to these high ASCII codes.*

Now here's the payoff: If you can get whatever it is you want to communicate into 7-bit ASCII format, anyone, anywhere can use it. That's what the UUDECODE/UUENCODE programs are all about.

Converting to text with UUENCODE

The question is this: I've got this wonderful scanned image file of, oh, let's say, the Mona Lisa. And I want to share it with the world on the Internet. How can I do it?

Believe it or not, it's really simple. Assume you have obtained a copy of the UUENCODE/UUDECODE program for your computer and that your image file is called MONA.GIF. (The .GIF stands for *graphics interchange format*, a topic we'll look at in a moment.) The filesize is approximately 144K. Here's what you do:

Key in uuencode mona.gif.

That's it. There really is only one step. The program will automatically create the files MONA1.UUE through MONA4.UUE.

None of them will be larger than about 60K, and when you add up the sizes of each of these four files, you will see that they total over 200K. Converting binary files to 7-bit ASCII text always increases the amount of data that must be sent by 30 to 40 percent.

And speaking of 7-bit ASCII text, please see Fig. 8-1 for a sample of what the first few lines of MONA1.UUE look like.

Figure 8-1

```
Running a UUENCODE program against a binary file of any sort
usually results in the creation of several text files. The
program will number each in order and use the extension .UUE in
naming the files. Here are what the first few lines of MONA1.GIF
look like. Hard as it is to believe, La Gioconda's enigmatic
smile is in there somewhere:

section 1 of uuencode 5.25 of file mona.gif      by R.E.M.

begin 644 mona.gif
M1TE&&.#EA@`+@`==`==.`=`=.`=.`=.`=.`J@"J`.`"Jj@"j``jjjh``*h`jji5`*jjje555555_u7_
M557___J55?J5___5?___Ql$"q4$"0<' "`x)"a4*!!4*"a4*#a4*%1l*!!l*
M"al*#Ql*%2$*#r8*$!4/!!40"a40$!40%1l0!!40&ql0"al0$!l0%2$0!!l0
M&r$0"b$0$"$0%2$0&r80$b80&rx0$0\/#s46%a45"145$!86&!l5!!l6"al7
M$!l7%r$7!!l7&r$7"al7(b$7$"$7%r$7&r87"2$7(b87"87%r87&r87(bx7
```

The Mona Lisa as 7-bit ASCII text.

Now all you have to do is transmit these four files to the appropriate newsgroup, each one as a separate message labelled Part 1 of 4, Part 2 of 4, and so on as appropriate. (In the case of a scanned file of the Mona Lisa, the newsgroup **alt.binaries.pictures.fine-art .digitized** would probably be the right place.)

A day passes, and some other art lover sees your posting. That person opens the capture buffer of the comm program being used and records each of your messages on disk. Let's assume that there are four of them. When the last line of the last message has arrived, the art lover closes the capture buffer and signs off.

 # Reversing the process with UUDECODE

Let's now assume that *you* are the art lover and that you sign on to a newsgroup and see that there is a group of messages that are the parts of an image of the Mona Lisa. You want it.

So open your comm program's capture buffer to make sure that everything gets written to a disk file. (If you are using a newsreader on a hard-wired system, see if you can save the file by pressing s and entering a filename. If you are asked if you want to save it in mailbox format, opt for n for no.)

Call your capture file MONA.TXT (or anything you like). Then begin "reading" each of the four Mona Lisa messages in turn. The subject line of the message should indicate the part number and the total number of parts. If the word *part* is not used, look for something like *[03/04]* in the subject line.

The first time you try this, you will be amazed at how long it takes. Getting all four parts of the Mona Lisa file means capturing over 200,000 characters of text, or the equivalent of about 120 typed, double-spaced pages. At 9,600 bps, this is going to take close to four minutes. For technical reasons, characters per second is always one tenth of the bit-per-second speed.

NET TIP

Calculating the cost

If you're using the Internet on campus, you're probably not concerned about how long it takes to get a given file or set of messages. But what would it cost to get, say, 350K worth of data if you were using a commercial system like Delphi? Assume that you're online at 9,600 bps, you're downloading in the evening, and Delphi's rate is $4 per hour. Assume also a perfect connection and no overhead imposed by Zmodem or any other error-checking protocol.

When the last message has been transmitted to your computer, close your capture buffer and get off the Net. Now it's time to reverse the UUENCODE process. We'll assume that your capture buffer file is

called MONA.TXT and that it contains only one set of image file
messages. Now, to convert those text messages into the original
binary file, key in UUDECODE mona.txt.

That's pretty much it. You will see something like this on your screen:

```
C>uudecode mona.txt
UU-DECODE 5.25 FOR PC. by Richard Marks
Destination is MONA.GIF
Decoding MONA.TXT, Section 1
input section passed sum -r and size tests
Decoding MONA.TXT, Section 2
input section passed sum -r and size tests
Decoding MONA.TXT, Section 3
input section passed sum -r and size tests
Decoding MONA.TXT, Section 4
input section passed sum -r and size tests
output file passed sum -r and size tests
Completed decode of file MONA.GIF
```

Now you've got MONA.GIF on your disk. You can view it on your
screen in full color, or produce a printout like the one in Fig. 8-2.
The next step is to delete MONA.TXT to conserve disk space. (I keep
harping on this because I know that if I don't delete a file the moment
it is no longer needed, files will accumulate on my disk like coat
hangers multiplying in a darkened closet. Eventually, I will run out of
disk space.)

Figure 8-2

*And heeeee—re's Mona!
For more GIF files like this,
check the FTP site at*
ftp.wustl.edu, Path:
/multimedia/images/gif/.

NET TIP

A copyright lawyer's nightmare!

Of course, any image file can be altered and modified with the right paint program. The modified file can then be uploaded to a CompuServe forum library, America Online, or someplace else. Or it can be converted to 7-bit ASCII text again and transmitted to a newsgroup on the Net or to anyone with an Internet mail address.

This is the kind of thing that can give a copyright lawyer nightmares. The technology to make a digital copy of nearly any image is as cheap as a $200 hand-scanner. And that image can be altered, adapted, changed, and transmitted anywhere. I'm all for the free flow of information, but I'm also a writer whose living depends on royalties paid for intellectual property, so I have mixed feelings.

If you think about it, though, there may be a lot less here than meets the eye. So an art lover obtains a copyrighted image as a disk file. What can the person do with it? The moment he or she tries to make a profit from it, the lawyers can pounce. Until then, it seems to me, no harm has been done.

Certainly not as much "harm" as a library does to authors' royalty statements by making it possible for people to read a book without paying for it. And what about all those used textbooks you see for sale on campus? What about the photocopied magazine articles your professor hands out? As you can see, the copyright issues are anything but simple. The Net simply adds fuel to the fire.

 # Caveats & considerations

The reason it was so easy to convert MONA.GIF to four UUENCODED text files and then back again to its original form is the superb programming of Richard Marks's UUENCODE/UUDECODE package for DOS users. Mr. Marks's program is an example of a "smart" UUCODER.

That means it can usually read an entire capture file and automatically detect where each MONA?.UUE message begins and ends. Most of the time it will not be distracted by any non-relevant text the file may contain. Other UUCODER programs are not that smart and thus require special preparation.

The first UUENCODED file will contain the word *begin* followed by the name of the original binary file. The last file will contain the word *end* at its end. Files in between start and conclude with lines used for error checking. Should you find both words in the same message, it's a sure sign that this is a single-part file.

It may be that your decoder program is smart enough not to be distracted by extraneous text appearing before the word *begin*. But you will find that many UUENCODED messages on the Net include a line reading "Cut Here" to tell you to delete that line and all the text above it before running your decoding program.

NET TIP

Caution: use a text editor or non-document mode

If you decide to edit out extraneous information, it is very, very important that you either use a text editor or make sure you save the edited file in non-document mode *from your word processor. Text editor programs produce pure ASCII text, but word processing software typically adds special non-standard ASCII codes to a file for its own convenience—unless you specifically tell it to save the file in non-document, unformatted mode.*

NET TIP

Automatic decoding

Some Usenet newsreading programs have a built-in extract *capability that will automatically decode messages for you. You will need a direct connection of the sort available at your university or college computing center to take advantage of this. Ask the administrator about newer versions of the* **rn***,* **nn***, and* **trn** *newsreaders, which might have this capability. Or check the UNIX* man *(short for* manual*) page.*

 # Getting the facts

Okay, okay, sorry for the pun. But there really is a super three-part series of FAQs (Frequently Asked Questions) files covering decoding and encoding newsgroup messages, compression, and graphic-viewing software. It's the FAQ for **alt.binaries.pictures**, and it's

uploaded to that group and to **news.answers** every other Monday. It is also available by anonymous FTP:

➢ FTP to **pit-manager.mit.edu**
Path: /pub/usenet/news.answers/pictures-faq/
Files: part1, part2, part3

➢ FTP to **ftp.cs.ruu.nl**
Path: /pub/NEWS.ANSWERS/pictures-faq/
Files: part1, part2, part3

➢ FTP to **ftp.uu.net**
Path: /usenet/news.answers/pictures-faq/
Files: part1, part2, part3

If you have time to get only one part, make it Part 3, because that's the one with the lists of FTP sites; the decoding, decompressing, and other software to get for your particular computer system; and where to get it.

If you have a bit more time, and especially if you are interested in this aspect of the Net, be sure to get and read all three parts. This is one of the best and best-written FAQ files you will find. Its author and maintainer is Jim Howard of Cadence Design System, Inc. Remember as you read Mr. Howard's FAQ that the tilde (~) character in UNIX-speak is simply shorthand for *the top directory*. Thus ~ftp/pub/pc/ means the same as /ftp/pub/pc/.

 # Where to get UUENCODERS/ DECODERS

As you can see, turning text file messages on newsgroups back into binary files is simply a matter of having the right software. There is no need to even think about what's going on. (It's kind of boring in any case.) All you've got to do is get the decoder needed for your system, retrieve all the parts of the image file, sign off, and "turn the crank."

If you are a DOS or Windows user, the program to get is Richard Marks's UUEXE. You will find it on the Net and on most commercial online systems under a name like UUEXE*.EXE or UUEXE*.ZIP, where the asterisk (*) is a three-digit number representing the current

version. (Version 5.32 is current at this writing, but if you want to run it down using Archie, I suggest specifying just UUEXE as your search phrase.) There are other smart programs; this just happens to be the one I like. For instructions on obtaining alternative smart programs, see Part 3 of Jim Howard's FAQ file for **alt.binaries.pictures**, as discussed in a nearby NetTip.

Richard Marks's UUEXE program is available via Glossbrenner's Choice. But if you'd like to FTP a copy, try the PC software archives at **oak.oakland.edu** or **archive.umich.edu** or **wuarchive.wustl.edu**. Or look for it at one of these locations, which I turned up with an Archie search:

> ➢ FTP to **beethoven.cs.colostate.edu**
>   Path: /pub/olender/uuexe*.zip

> ➢ FTP to **ftp.halcyon.com**
>   Path: /disk2/waffle/miscnets/uuexe*.zip

> ➢ FTP to **ftp.isi.edu**
>   Path: /pub/incoming/uuexe*.zip

If you're a Macintosh user, the program of choice is UUTOOL. This is available on most commercial systems (CompuServe, Delphi, etc.) that have Internet special interest groups or forums. But you can also FTP it from **sumex-aim.stanford.edu**, Path: /info-mac/util/uutool-*.hqx.

 # Graphics viewers, converters, & paint programs

There are many different graphics file formats, including .TIF, .PCX, JPEG, Windows BMP, and Macintosh PICT. But there are basically just three types of programs associated with graphics files: *viewers*, *viewer/converters*, and *paint programs*.

Fortunately, excellent shareware packages exist in all categories, and all types of graphics programs are widely available. However, the type I recommend is the viewer/converter.

A plain viewer program will show you the image and possibly let you print a copy. A paint program has those powers as well, but paint programs bring more firepower to the party than you really need. Paint programs let you modify the image and add all manner of special effects. But those extra features mean that a paint program tends to take longer to load.

That's why I like viewer/converters for routine image viewing. These programs typically handle a large number of graphics file formats and let you convert, say, a .GIF file into a .PCX file. Conversion can be important when you're dealing with a paint program or a desktop publishing program that can only deal with one or two formats. Viewer/converters may also let you crop or resize an image.

Where to get the software

If you're a DOS user, the program to get is Steve Rimmer's Graphic Workshop. Fast, fun to use, and powerful, I simply cannot say enough for this program. See Fig. 8-3 for a sample screen. If you're a Windows user, I recommend Mr. Rimmer's Graphic Workshop for Windows.

```
┌─[ Page 1 of 1 ]──────────────────────────────────┐  ┌─[ ? for help ]─┐
│                          ┌─[ Write to ]───────────┐           │
│                          │ ART (PFS:1st Publisher) │           │
│    ..            GWS.EX  │ BMP (Windows 3)         │           │
│ 3CLOWNS.PCX      GWSINS  │ CUT (Halo)              │           │
│ 3WITCHES.PCX     HURRIC  │ EPS (PostScript)        │           │
│ A_S_MONA.TIF     IBD138  │ EXE (Self displaying)   │           │
│ BETH.TIF         IBD171  │ GEM/IMG (Ventura)       │           │
│ BRUCE.GIF        KIMMC.  │ GIF (CompuServe)        │           │
│ BRUCE.PCX        LILVAM  │ HRZ (SSTV)              │           │
│ BRUCE2.PCX       MERMLE  │▓JPG (JFIF JPEG)▓▓▓▓▓▓▓▓▓ │           │
│ CATLOGO.GIF      MONA.G  │ IFF/LBM (Amiga)         │           │
│ CEMETERY.PCX     MONA.P  │ MAC (MacPaint♦)         │           │
│ CINDY.PCX        MSI1.P  │ MSP (Microsoft Paint)   │           │
│ EXAMPLE1.IMG     MSI1.T  │ PIC (PC Paint/Pictor)   │           │
│ EXAMPLE2.GIF     PHAN04  │ PCX (PC Paintbrush)     │           │
│ EXAMPLE3.GIF     PHAN04  │ RAS (Sun Raster)        │           │
│ GHOST.PCX        PIC1.G  │ RLE (Windows 3)         │           │
│ GIF.TIF          PONDER  │ TGA (Truevision Targa)  │           │
│                          │ TIFF                    │           │
│                          │ TXT (Text files)        │           │
└─[ Graphic Workshop 7.0   │ WPG (WordPerfect)       │chemy Mindworks Inc. ]─┘
                           └─────────────────────────┘
```

Figure 8-3

Graphic Workshop for DOS.

Look for both programs at the FTP site **uunorth.north.net**, Path: /pub/alchemy/. The files to get are GRAFWK*.EXE (Graphic Workshop) and GWSWIN*.EXE (Graphic Workshop for Windows). Or visit Mr. Rimmer's Web site at **http://uunorth.north.net:8000/ alchemy/html/alchemy.html**. Both packages are also available from Glossbrenner's Choice.

If you're a Macintosh user, you might want to get either GIFConverter or Imagery, available at the following FTP sites:

➤ FTP to **sumex-aim.stanford.edu**
Path: /info-mac/art/gif/gif-converter-*.hqx

➤ FTP to **sumex-aim.stanford.edu**
Path: /info-mac/app/imagery-*.hqx

➤ FTP to **mac.archive.umich.edu**
Path: /mac/graphics/graphics.utilities/imagery*.hqx

NET TIP

Graphics resources on the Net

If you have trouble finding any of the programs I've told you about in this chapter, you might want to visit the Johns Hopkins Gopher at **gopher.gdb.org** *and choose "Search and Retrieve Software" from the main menu. Then choose the menu item for "Search and Retrieve Graphics Software and Data." What you'll find is a huge collection of graphics resources—software, FAQs, image collections, the works.*

On the World Wide Web, visit the Graphic Utilities Site at **http://www.public.iastate.edu/~stark/gutil_sv.html#DOS** *for another great collection of resources.*

 # Where to get graphic images

As I said earlier, the simplest, easiest way to get pictures and graphic images from the Net is to get them from an FTP site (like **ftp.wustl.edu**, Path: /multimedia/images/gif/). Or you can visit a World Wide Web site like the WebMuseum (**http://sunsite.unc.edu/louvre**), where you'll find stunning images of Paris as well as famous paintings from the Louvre and other museums. (See Fig. 8-4 for just one example.)

Figure 8-4

The May Jaunt, a pageant celebrating the "joli mois de Mai," from Les Très Riches Heures du Duc de Berry. See it in full color at the WebMuseum home page on the World Wide Web.

However, that's not nearly as much fun, and the images you will find won't be nearly as, er, varied, as you will find in the following Internet newsgroups:

alt.binaries.multimedia	Sound, text and graphics data rolled in one.
alt.binaries.pictures	Huge image files.
alt.binaries.pictures.12hr	Pictures of clocks.
alt.binaries.pictures.animals	Pictures of all types of animals.
alt.binaries.pictures.anime	Images from Japanese animation.
alt.binaries.pictures.ascii	Pictures composed of ASCII characters.
alt.binaries.pictures.astro	Very black pictures.
alt.binaries.pictures.cartoons	Images from animated cartoons.
alt.binaries.pictures.celebrities	Unrated pictures of famous people.
alt.binaries.pictures.d	Discussions about picture postings.
alt.binaries.pictures.erotica	Gigabytes of copyright violations.
alt.binaries.pictures.erotica.amateur.d	Amateur subjects/photographers.
alt.binaries.pictures.erotica.amateur.female	Amateur subjects/ photographers.
alt.binaries.pictures.erotica.amateur.male	Amateur subjects/ photographers.
alt.binaries.pictures.erotica.anime	Anime erotica
alt.binaries.pictures.erotica.blondes	Copyright violations featuring blondes.
alt.binaries.pictures.erotica.cartoons	Copyright violations featuring toons.
alt.binaries.pictures.erotica.d	Discussing erotic copyright violations.
alt.binaries.pictures.erotica.female	Copyright violations featuring females.
alt.binaries.pictures.erotica.furry	Erotic furry images.

alt.binaries.pictures.erotica.male	Copyright violations featuring males.
alt.binaries.pictures.erotica.orientals	Copyright violations featuring Asians.
alt.binaries.pictures.fine-art.d	Discussion of the fine-art binaries.
alt.binaries.pictures.fine-art.digitized	Art from conventional media.
alt.binaries.pictures.fine-art.graphics	Art created on computers.
alt.binaries.pictures.fractals	Cheaper just to send the program parameters.
alt.binaries.pictures.furry	Funny animal art.
alt.binaries.pictures.girlfriend	Pictures of girlfriends.
alt.binaries.pictures.girlfriends	Commercially controversial group.
alt.binaries.pictures.misc	Have we saturated the network yet?
alt.binaries.pictures.nudism	Images featuring nudists.
alt.binaries.pictures.supermodels	Yet more copyright violations.
alt.binaries.pictures.tasteless	That last one was sick.
alt.binaries.pictures.utilities	Posting of pictures-related utilities.

9

How to create your own Web home page

IF you spend much time on the World Wide Web, you'll soon discover that some of the most imaginative and entertaining sites you'll visit are the creations of students at colleges and universities around the world. Some of them are quite basic. But others are so professional-looking—with graphics and icons and navigation buttons and hypertext links—that you're likely to find yourself asking, "How in the world was a college student able to do that?"

The answer in most cases is that they took advantage of free tools— tools that are widely available on college campuses and on the Net itself—for creating personal Web home pages. I'll leave it to you find the people and resources at your particular school. (Hint: You might start by checking one of the lists of college and university home pages you'll read about in Chapter 21 to see if your school has a Web site. Then use your Web browser to visit the site and see what kinds of things are offered.)

What we'll concentrate on in this chapter is where you can look on the Internet for some of the best home-page creation tools and resources. Armed with that and a little imagination, you too could soon be "publishing on the Web."

Home Page Construction Kit

One of the best places to start is at the site of the Home Page Construction Kit created by Ellie Cutler and John Labovitz. The site is one of O'Reilly & Associates' Global Network Navigator offerings, and you'll find it at this address:

http://nearnet.gnn.com/gnn/netizens/construction.html

As you can see from the opening screen, shown in Fig. 9-1, the kit simplifies home page creation by organizing it into four major topics:

➤ Creating a Home Page
➤ Publishing a Home Page
➤ Home Page Template
➤ Sample Home Pages

Figure 9-1

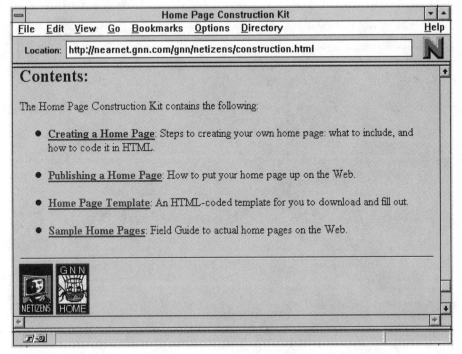

The Home Page Construction Kit makes creating your first home page a breeze.

Start with some examples

My suggestion is that you first click on "Sample Home Pages." That will take you to a delightful set of examples representing what the creators call "some of the more interesting and popular manifestations of *genus* home page." The examples are classified according to their place in the evolution of the home page—from Elementary (actually created by elementary school students and described as "charming testaments to the virtue of simplicity") to Home Pageant ("densely loaded with imagery, links, lists, documents, recipes, and writings").

Each of the examples is quite different, and quite original. Among them you'll find the "cozy Home on the Net" created by Phoebe Sengers, a graduate student at Carnegie Mellon University (see Fig. 9-2), and the very business-like home page of Jim Croft, director of the botany section of the Australian National Botanic Gardens (shown in Fig. 9-3).

Figure 9-2

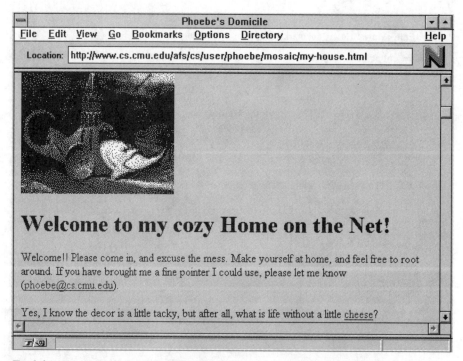

Feel free to root around in "Phoebe's Domicile" to find ideas for your own home page.

Figure 9-3

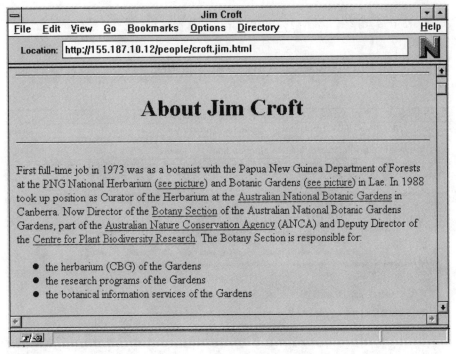

Jim Croft's home office page is neat and to the point, but it contains a few surprises as well.

NET TIP

From Yahoo to Who's Who

For still more examples of home pages, many of them created by students, check the Yahoo collection at Stanford. You'll find it at this address:

http://www.yahoo.com/Entertainment/People/

*Once you've created your own Web page and made arrangements to put it on the Web server at your school, you can send an e-mail message to the folks at Yahoo (**admin@yahoo.com**) and they'll add your page to the collection.*

You might also want to consider getting listed in Who's Who on the Internet, billed as the "Complete Directory of Internet Personalities." From the opening screen, shown in Fig. 9-4, all you have to do is click on "How to add your own..." and then fill out the online registration

115

form. *(No references or recommendations required!)* You'll find Who's
Who at this address:

http://web.city.ac.uk/citylive/pages.html

Figure 9-4

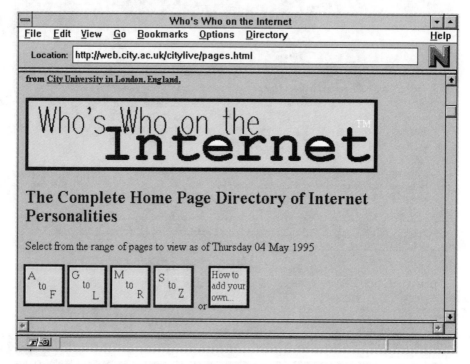

You can become an "Internet personality" by listing your Web page with
Who's Who on the Internet.

⇨ Home page template and other tools

After studying some of the sample home pages, you'll be ready to
explore the other parts of the Construction Kit. Be sure to download
the sample Home Page Template and play around with it. (You'll be
amazed at how easy it is to modify the template to create your own
page, and to give it a totally different look and feel by making
relatively simple changes to the template file.) Then use the
"Creating" option to learn more about HTML coding. Finally, click on

"Publishing" for some pointers on actually putting your completed home page on the Web.

There's no question about it—the Home Page Construction Kit beats crayons and construction paper all hollow!

HomePage Publisher

Anyone with a Web browser can use the Home Page Construction Kit to create a personal Web home page. But what if your school doesn't have a Web server for you to put it on once you create it? What if they do have a Web server but don't allow students to use it for their personal home pages?

The solution might just be the HomePage Publisher (HPP) at Ohio State University. By all means check first with your local system administrator to see if you can put your home page on the system at your school. If the answer is no, then visit the HomePage Publisher at this address:

http://www-bprc.mps.ohio-state.edu/HomePage/

Be sure to read and abide by the "Rules for Creating Home Pages on this Server" (five-page maximum, no advertisements allowed, no pornographic material, etc.) This is a free service, after all. If people abuse it, it could go away. You must also be sure to modify your home page at least once a month or it will be considered inactive and removed from the system.

Like the Home Page Construction Kit, HomePage Publisher offers guidelines for writing HTML documents and includes hypertext links to other excellent home-page creation resources on the Web.

Still more Web page resources

You'll probably find just about everything you need for creating your first Web page at the Home Page Construction Kit and HomePage Publisher sites. But if you decide to get serious about Web pages (or perhaps even become the "home page expert" on campus), you should know about these resources as well:

- *HTML Editors*
  A large collection of software for creating HTML documents, maintained by Gabriel White.
  http://werple.mira.net.au/~gabriel/

- *Web Developer's Virtual Library*
  http://www.charm.net/~web/

And you'll want to read one or more of these HTML guides and tutorials:

- *A Beginner's Guide to HTML*
  From NCSA, the creators of Mosaic software.
  http://www.ncsa.uiuc.edu/demowab/html-primer.html

- *Crash Course on writing documents for the Web*
  Written by Eamonn Sullivan, a technical editor with PC Week Labs. Provides a good overview of HTML, and includes topics like "The Absolute Essentials" and "HTML Philosophy."
  http://www.ziff.com/~eamonn/crash_course.html

- *Whatsupdoc HTML Tutorial*
  Includes practice exercises to test your HTML skills. Also covers how to handle foreign language accent marks and special characters.
  http://fire.clarkson.edu/doc/html/htut.html

- *Composing Good HTML*
  Offers suggestions on how to make your home page attractive and usable.
  http://www.willamette.edu/html-composition/strict-html.html

 # Adding icons & graphics

Once you've mastered the basics with your Web page, the next step is to add icons and graphics. No, they're not necessary, and large graphics can slow things down considerably even under the best of circumstances. But, hey, they're fun! Here are some sites that house collections of images you can use. Check your local Web server as well for logos and artwork specific to your college or university.

➤ Images, Icons, and Flags
From the Webmaster of the Planet Earth Home Page in San Diego, a huge collection of images classified by subject.
http://white.nosc.mil/images.html

➤ Rutgers University Network Services WWW Icons and Logos
A collection of icons and button graphics in GIF format. See Fig. 9-5 for some samples of what's available.
http://www-ns.rutgers.edu/doc-images/

➤ Tony's Icons
http://www.bsdi.com/icons/tonys.html

➤ Anthony's Icon Library
http://server.berkeley.edu:80/pub/AIcons/appl/

Figure 9-5

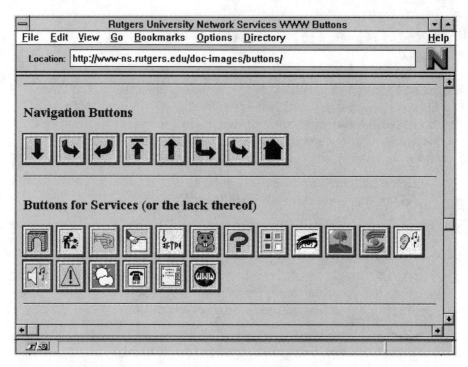

Give your home page a professional look with navigation buttons and special icons from this collection at Rutgers University. The "Under Construction" button (the second one in the second row) is one of the most popular for student home pages that are "in progress."

10
Making the most of mail!

ELECTRONIC mail or e-mail is one of the most popular—and powerful—of all Internet features. Among other things, it gives everyone who participates in it both greater range and greater control. You can contact people via e-mail whom you would never dream of calling on the telephone. And, as long as you are both on the Internet, the communication will probably not cost either of you anything. What's more, the sender can send when convenient, and the receiver can read the message when convenient. E-mail thus puts an end to telephone tag.

There's also the fact that you can send things to people via e-mail that you would never read over the phone or into the person's telephone answering machine. For example, if you wanted advice from someone on a distant campus concerning a paper you're writing, sending a copy to the person via e-mail is the ideal solution. You'd certainly never read the thing over the phone or into someone's answering machine. And it is much easier for someone to make comments on an electronic copy than on a fax.

In this chapter, we'll touch on a few e-mail fundamentals. But the bulk of the chapter is devoted to the *sine qua non* of e-mail. Namely, e-mail addresses. If you don't know the right e-mail address, you obviously can't send mail. Fortunately, the Net is stuffed with features to help you ferret out the addresses you want.

 # E-mail essentials

If you want to learn the best way to prepare and send mail on your campus system—ask! Ask a friend or someone in the system administrator's office. You may discover that there are several mail preparation programs available for you to use. Try them all, find one you like, and stick with it.

The one thing to be wary of, however, is learning too many commands. Oh, go ahead, if you feel so moved. But e-mail is simple, and you should resist every attempt to make it complicated. Forget about the precise commands at this point and concentrate on the concept. The main steps to be followed in preparing any e-mail message are:

❶ Run the system's mail program, often by simply keying in mail at the system prompt. From within your mail program, you can read, delete, file, and forward messages received.

❷ You can also prepare and send mail, often by keying in send.

❸ The mail program will prompt you for an address (To:) and a subject line (Subj:). You will then be able to enter the text of your message.

❹ When you've finished typing your message, enter whatever command your mail program wants to see to tell it that you're through. It may be a Ctrl-Z or a Ctrl-D or something else.

❺ That's really all there is too it. To read new messages, you typically run the mail program again and key in dir to get a numbered list of messages in your mailbox. You can then key in read 2 to read message number 2. When finished, you can key in a command like delete 2 to delete that message.

 ## The best way to prepare a message

The specific commands required for preparing e-mail messages vary from program to program, of course. To learn more, try keying in mail and then help. The one thing to stay away from, in my opinion, is any set of commands designed to let you edit your messages online. Why force yourself to learn how to use the text editor offered by your

campus mainframe when the Mac- or PC-based word processor you know and love will do just as well?

Any time you're preparing a brief note, either as an answer to some piece of mail or as new mail, you'll find it convenient to use the text editor available in the mail program on the campus computer. If you make a major mistake, enter a Ctrl-C—or whatever command is needed to exit without sending—and start over.

Longer messages and messages requiring careful consideration are best prepared using your favorite personal computer word processing program. The only twist is to make sure you save the resulting file to disk as *plain ASCII text*. If you need to indicate italics or bold, frame the target word with asterisks, like *this*. Don't use a font.

Next, sign on to your campus computer from your dorm room or wherever; run the mail program; and when it gets to the point where you are supposed to enter text, use your computer's comm program to transmit the ASCII text file to the mail program. The mail program will not know that you are not sitting there typing the message. When the file has been sent, just tap in the "all done" command to tell the mail program to send your message.

Finally, to give yourself even more options. Find out whether it's possible to *insert* a file from your home directory on the campus system into a mail message. This can be very helpful if you want to send the same text to several people—like to your parents' e-mail address as well as the e-mail addresses of friends or brothers and sisters at other schools.

How to encrypt e-mail messages

Electronic mail is not private. Of course, it is not likely that anyone will want to read your mail. But some people can, if they want to—people other than your correspondent.

That's why I strongly urge you to encrypt any sensitive message. It's easy to do, and the programs needed to do it are either free or shareware. In the Glossbrenner's Choice collection you'll find a disk with everything a DOS or Windows user needs to keep the National Security Agency guessing, including Philip Zimmermann's Pretty

Good Privacy (PGP) encryption program. Versions for the Mac are available on the Internet and elsewhere.

Basically, you prepare your file. Then you run an encryption program against it. The encryption program will ask you to supply a key that it can use to control just how it scrambles the file. The key might be whale or xyzzy or anything else. As long as your recipient has the same program and as long as you give the person the key (either by voice phone or by a separate e-mail message), he or she will be able to transform the gibberish back into readable text in an instant.

⇨ All about Internet e-mail addresses

Internet e-mail addresses consist of two parts: the stuff to the left of the at sign (@) and the stuff to its right. As an example, consider the address **bilbo@shire.midearth.edu**. Note that, just this once when dealing with UNIX, the case of the letters does not matter. Thus, **bilbo@shire.midearth.edu** and **Bilbo@Shire.midearth.edu** are equivalent.

If Bilbo were giving you his address, he would say, "I'm Bilbo at Shire dot Midearth dot Edu." But Internet computers read this kind of address from right to left. So the address tells them (and us) that the address is at an educational institution called Midearth, on a computer called Shire that's part of that system. And Bilbo is the logon name of the individual person.

The information to the right of the at sign is called the *domain*. Indeed, Internet addresses all follow the *Domain Name System* of addressing. Under this system, all Internet addresses end in one of the following *zone* name extensions:

.com U.S. commercial businesses
.edu U.S. college and university sites
.gov Governmental bodies
.int International bodies, like NATO
.mil Military organizations
.net Companies or organizations that run large networks
.org Nonprofit organizations and others that don't fit anywhere else

Following the zone is the organization's name, in this case, Midearth. If the organization is a large one, it may have several computers or network servers, each with its own name. In this case, the computer at the Midearth organization where Bilbo hangs out is called Shire.

The Internet mail system effectively reads these addresses from right to left. The computers that route and transport the mail know that it is their responsibility to deliver a message to the "highest" subdomain in the full domain name, in this case, the Midearth system. After that, it is the responsibility of the subdomain name system to take over routing and transport within its own network.

NET TIP

Internet Protocol addresses

The Domain Name System is designed to hide each system's numeric Internet Protocol (IP) address. Somewhere along the way to our friend Bilbo, one or more Internet **name-server** *computers will convert the Domain Name System address* **bilbo@shire.midearth.edu** *into something like* **bilbo@123.45.67.89**. *This might translate as "network number 123.45, and computer 67.89 on that network."*

Most of the time, you will have no problem using the domain name version of an e-mail address. But if a letter gets bounced back to you, it may be necessary to use the IP address. Before you do that, however, check the address you used to make sure that you did indeed type it correctly.

NET TIP

Getting a list of country codes

I should add here that e-mail addresses for users outside the U.S. typically end in a country code. For example, .AU is Australia, .KH is Cambodia, and .NP is Nepal. Internaut Larry Landweber maintains a complete list of such codes. To get a copy, FTP to **ftp.cs.wisc.edu**; *Path: /connectivity_table/. Look for a file called* **Connectivity_Table.text**.

There's also an International E-Mail FAQ, which is posted regularly on the newsgroups **comp.mail.misc** *and* **news.newusers.questions**. *Or you can request a copy by sending e-mail to* **mail-server@rtfm.mit.edu**. *Leave the subject line blank, and in the message area key in the one-line message* send usenet/news.answers/mail/country-codes.

How to send mail to a Bitnet address

Bitnet, the network that is associated with a nonprofit consortium of educational institutions known as Educom, does not follow the Internet style of addressing. Instead, a native Bitnet address consists of a user name, an at sign (@), and a computer name. No .edu or .com or any other dot extensions.

Thus, if you ever see an address like **listerv@thumbovm**, you will know that it is a Bitnet address. To convert it to an Internet address, all you have to do is add **.bitnet** to the end of the address: **listserv@thumbovm.bitnet**. This will work most of the time.

The .bitnet extension is needed to smooth out the incompatibility of the Internet and Bitnet. That extension tells your mail system to forward your message to a computer that serves as a gateway between the Internet and Bitnet. If your particular site does not recognize .bitnet, however, the message will be bounced back to you. Should that happen, you might consider sending your message to a known gateway site using a *bang path* address. (The name comes from the traditional computerese term for an exclamation point—a *bang*.)

Thus, if sending a message to **listserv@thumbovm.bitnet** does not work on your system, you might try an address like this:

cunyvm.cuny.edu!thumbovm.bitnet!listserv

Notice that the format starts with the name of the gateway system (**cunyvm.cuny.edu**), followed by a bang, followed by the name of the computer in the original Bitnet address (**thumbovm**), followed by **bitnet** and a bang and the user name, in this case, **listserv**. The general template is thus:

gateway!computer.bitnet!userid

If you are using a UNIX computer running the C-Shell, you must precede the exclamation point with a backslash (\!).

If you gotta do it, you gotta do it. But bang path addresses should be avoided whenever possible. It is difficult to imagine a more bytehead,

computeristic chore than having to specify the computer-to-computer path your message should take.

Still, here are several of the main Internet-to-Bitnet gateway systems you might consider using if your local system chokes on the .bitnet pseudo domain:

**cornell.cit.cornell.edu
cunyvm.cuny.edu
mitvma.mit.edu
pucc.princeton.edu
vm1.nodak.edu**

✳ What does the percent sign signify?

Sometimes you will encounter an e-mail address that contains a percent sign (%). Like this: **bilbo%ndsuvm1.bitnet@vm1.nodak.edu**

In addresses of this sort, the percent sign is always to the left of the at sign (@). In most cases, it's used to separate the name of a user from the name of a local computer.

Thus a message sent via the Internet to the above address would go first to the Bitnet/Internet gateway computer **vm1.nodak.edu**. Then it would go to Bitnet, and Bitnet would deliver it to the computer called **ndsuvm1**. That computer would in turn deliver it to the user ID **bilbo**.

You can use the format **userid%computer.bitnet@gateway** to send a message to a Bitnet computer, instead of the format described earlier. But the percent-sign format is not officially supported, even though it usually works.

NET TIP

Size limits & binary files

The Internet always goes for the lowest common denominator. That's why all e-mail messages—and articles posted to newsgroups—must be in plain, 7-bit ASCII text (no special foreign-language, box-drawing, or other characters with ASCII codes above decimal 127). And they can be no longer than 64,000 characters (64K). A message of 64K is the

> equivalent of about 35 pages of double-spaced text, assuming 65
> characters per line and 28 text lines per page.
>
> Leaving aside the actual limits, that's far too long for an e-mail
> message in any case. If your message is longer than a page or two (one
> page is just under 2K), send it as a file on disk through snail mail
> (a.k.a. the postal system).
>
> These limitations also make it inconvenient to send binary files on the
> Net. That's why, if you have an archive, a graphic image, or other
> binary file, you'll be better off sending it from your personal computer
> to a bulletin board system you and your correspondent can both use,
> or sending it via CompuServe, America Online (AOL), or GEnie.

 # How to find e-mail addresses

The absolute, foolproof, quickest way to get someone's Internet e-mail
address is to pick up the telephone and call the individual. But suppose
you met someone at a party, and all you know is the person's name
and school. You could probably track the person down by calling the
college or the appropriate directory assistance operator. But wouldn't
it be neat if the person you are trying to reach just signed on to the
campus system one day and found an e-mail message from you?

It's a nice, emotionally safe way to start a relationship. Much, much
better than trying to pick the person up at a party and a heck of a lot
more risk-free than calling on the phone! A little note. A poem (your
own or someone else's). A funny character graphic (like Bill the Cat or
some such).

I'll leave you to use your imagination. All that matters on the
technical front is that the person has an Internet account and checks
for mail regularly. Otherwise, it's back to the phone and paper mail.

College/university address tools

The Net has so many wild and wonderful things, that it probably will not surprise you to learn that there is a FAQ (Frequently Asked Questions) file called the College E-mail FAQ. Prepared by David Lamb, this FAQ pulls together all the information any college student needs to find e-mail addresses, especially e-mail addresses of other students, on the Net.

There are several ways to get the College E-Mail FAQ:

> ➢ E-mail: Send a message to **archive-server@qucis .queensu.ca**. In the subject line, key in send dalamb/college-email. Leave the message area blank.

> ➢ FTP to **ftp.qucis.queensu.ca**
> Path: /pub/dalamb/college-email/faq*.text

> ➢ FTP to **rtfm.mit.edu**
> Path: /pub/usenet/mail/college-email/part*

> ➢ Newsgroups: The FAQ is posted periodically to **soc.college**, **soc.net-people**, and **news.answers**.

> ➢ World Wide Web
> **http://www.qucis.queensu.ca:1999/FAQs/college-email/college.html**

What are your options?

The Internet supposedly has 20 to 30 million users worldwide. You will undoubtedly hear about schemes to create a single, master address book for everyone, but, for the time being, take it all with a cup of salt. In reality, the Internet White Pages and similar attempts in this area include only about one or two percent of Internet users. Hardly worth your time or mine.

That's why you'll like David Lamb's College E-mail FAQ. The techniques he presents for running down the address of someone at a college or university are far from foolproof. But then, no techniques

are. There are any number of reasons why the person you want to contact might not show up. Starting with the fact that he or she may not have taken the steps necessary to open an account on a college system. And then there's the main Achilles heel of e-mail: If the person doesn't check for mail regularly, many of the advantages of e-mail are lost.

David Lamb's College E-mail FAQ

But let's not look on the negative side. David Lamb has done an absolutely splendid job of pulling together and summarizing the tools that are at your disposal for locating someone's e-mail address on the Net.

In the first place, he takes each major college or university and gives you a write-up like this:

```
Arizona State University:

Academic Machines: Grad, Undergrad.

The phonebook for ASU's Faculty/Students is available online by
Telnetting to asuvm.inre.asu.edu and logging on as HELLOASU. The
phonebook has both e-mail addresses for academic machines as well
as the phone numbers.

Engineering machines: Grad, Undergrad
enuxha.eas.asu.edu--Unix--can FINGER first/last names or userids
enuxva.eas.asu.edu--Unix--same as above
envmsa.eas.asu.edu--VMS--Only userid FINGER-ing works.

Usually CSC and EEE undergrads who use comps get accts on ENUXHA,
and almost all grads have accts on ENUXHA which is the most
popular machine due to USENET.
```

Additional options

David Lamb's FAQ is positively bursting with possibilities. But three of the techniques you will find most useful are Finger, Gopher, and the Usenet Address Server. Be sure to get the David Lamb FAQ. But here is just a quick sample of these three other techniques.

✳ Using Finger to find people

The Finger program is a wonderful idea. But it only works if the person you want to Finger has previously prepared a *plan file*. That's the file that is displayed when you Finger someone, and if it does not exist, you'll get nothing.

Still, let's assume that you're at a party and you meet someone really cool. His last name is Bromley, and you sure as heck don't want him to know how you feel—at least not right now. All you know is that he is a student at Arizona State University. But the band was playing, so you didn't catch his first name.

On Sunday, back at your own campus, you sign on to the system and key in finger bromley@asu.edu. Who knows, maybe you'll get lucky. Electronically, at least. And lo and behold, here is what you see:

```
      >>>> Welcome to the ASU Electronic Post Office <<<<
-------------------------------------------------------------------------
--
Note: There are no accounts on this machine. Results are E-mail aliases.
--
-------------------------------------------------------------------------
Exact alias match for <BROMLEY> does not exist. Searching for
partial matches...

FRED.R.BROMLEY
REBECCA.BROMLEY
KARRIE.BROMLEY
STEPHANIE.BROMLEY
RUTH.BROMLEY
MATTHEW.BROMLEY
ELIZABETH.BROMLEY
DAVID.BROMLEY
APRIL.BROMLEY
CRAIG.BROMLEY
```

Let's assume that the guy you're interested in is Matthew Bromley. (Actual names have been changed to protect ... whomever.) Now you've got his address: **matthew.bromley@asu.edu**.

The only other thing you need to know is that different sites return different information in response to the Finger command. If you were to Finger someone named Bromley at Princeton, for example, you might see something like this:

```
finger bromley@cs.princeton.edu

Karen Bromley (Kar-Kar) is not presently logged in.
Last seen at elan on Wed Jul  6 13:42:29 1994
```

✳ Using a Gopher

As you know, because I have repeated it so frequently, *every* Gopher menu is unique. But one thing that most Gophers at colleges and universities have in common is a menu item for a "College Phonebook." The other thing many Gophers offer is an item that will let you search for the Gopher you want to use. Thus, if you know that the person you want to reach goes to the University of Virginia, you may be able to log onto *your* Gopher and search for that Gopher. Finding it, you can connect and see something like this:

```
Univ of Virginia (CWIS) [gopher.virginia.edu]
Page 1 of 1

1    About this Service                                   Menu
2    News and Announcements                               Menu
3    Library Services                                     Menu
4    Arts and Sciences                                    Menu
5    Schools of the University                            Menu
6    Health Sciences                                      Menu
7    Academic Information                                 Menu
8    Administrative Information                           Menu
9    Search for UVa Faculty, Staff, or Students         Search
10   Organizations and Publications                       Menu
11   Computing and Communications                         Menu
12   Worldwide Internet Services (i.e., non-UVa services) Menu

Enter Item Number, SAVE, ?, or BACK: 9
```

Notice that item 9 lets you "Search for UVa Faculty, Staff, or Students." Choose it and respond to the "Search for:" prompt by keying in Bromley. Again, I've made up the names, but here is the kind of thing you will *see*:

```
Search for UVa Faculty, Staff, or Students
Page 1 of 1

1    Bromley, E. W.       (ewb7y)    Staff       Graduate   Text
2    Bromley, Carl E.     (ceb3m)    Grad        Hospital   Text
3    Bromley, David E.    (deb8k)    Grad        Hospital   Text
5    Bromley, Hal L.      (hlb5h)    Undergrad   Admission  Text
6    Bromley, Schlomo     (sbb4w)    Grad        Hospital   Text
7    Bromley, Peter S.    (psb9g)    Undergrad   College    Text
8    Bromley, Lemkie      (lkb2e)    Undergrad   Hospital   Text
9    Bromley, Olivia      (ob8a)     Staff       School O   Text

Enter Item Number, SAVE, ?, or BACK:
```

✳ The Usenet Address Server

Most posters to Usenet newsgroups are not aware of it, but there is a database to keep track of who has posted what to which group. To query the database, send an e-mail message to the Usenet Address Server at the following address: **mail-server@rtfm.mit.edu**. In the body of the message, key in send usenet-addresses/name.

The "name" should be one or more space-separated words for which you want to search. Thus, to discover the address of Internaut and boffo FAQ author Kevin Savetz, you would key in a line like this in your message: send usenet-address/savetz. Be aware, however, that the mail server will stop after it's got 40 matches. So if you are searching for a relatively common name, it probably won't do you much good.

 # Conclusion

As you've seen, the tools do indeed exist to find the e-mail addresses of people on the Net. There are just two points to bear in mind. First, as I said at the very beginning of this chapter, the best way to find an address is to pick up the phone, call the person, and ask. Second, not everyone can be found. I've got accounts on lots of commercial systems, for example. And I can send and receive Internet mail from any of them. But you probably won't find those addresses using conventional Internet techniques. (If you do need to reach me, use the address **alfred@delphi.com**.)

There are two reasons for this. Systems like CompuServe, America Online, Prodigy, Delphi, and GEnie do not require subscribers to be listed in their system-wide directories. Indeed, if you want to be listed, you must take specific steps to add your name to the directory on these systems. Second, these systems do not support incoming Finger requests, and their directories do not appear on any Gopher menus.

All of this could change in the future, of course. But, for now, your best bet for getting an e-mail address is still to call and ask for it.

11
What to tell your parents

HAT to tell your parents?" Are you kidding?

Every student since the dawn of time has known the answer to that one. And that answer is this: It doesn't matter what you say, as long as you punctuate *every other* sentence with one or more of the following:

"No, really, I'm fine. It's just a head cold."

"Of course I'm eating three meals a day. The dining hall food is great! Just last night we had creamed chipped beef on toast. Mmmmm."

"Well, maybe I am a little tired. I've pulled an all-nighter or two trying to get ready for mid-terms."

"Well, yes, now that you mention it, I am running a little short. What with all the books I've had to buy and . . ."

The point of this chapter, though, is: How would you like to be able to do all of this through *e-mail*?

I'm serious. Get your folks hooked up to a system that lets them receive and send Internet e-mail, and you can send them a message anytime you want. (And read and respond to their messages at your convenience!) Not to mention the fact that exchanging e-mail is much cheaper than phoning every Sunday night. It won't replace voice calls, but it may help you get them down to one or two calls a month, instead of one each weekend.

How to get your parents connected

I'm going to take the gloves off here. I don't care whether your parents are married, separated, or divorced. I don't care whether you've got one living grandparent, four, or none. And the *number* of brothers and sisters you've got is of no concern. What I want to burn into your brain is that you *all* can communicate, regularly, conveniently, and cheaply via the Net. And it almost doesn't matter which systems everybody's on.

If you've got friends or brothers or sisters at other schools, insist that they get an account on their campus systems and pursue the Internet e-mail option. If your parents or grandparents don't already have a computer . . . well, I'm not sure I'd suggest they get one merely to exchange mail with you, as beloved as you may be. But computers are available in a huge and growing percentage of homes these days—and you'd be amazed at how many seniors are online. It is thus well worth looking into getting the family connected.

Bottom-line time

Each computer will, of course, need a modem and a communications program. But, while you need an account on your campus system, what your relatives need is an account on some commercial system that lets them access the Net.

The main difference is that they will have to pay a monthly fee for their account—and they may have to pay for the Internet messages you send them on their chosen system—while your Internet access is most likely free.

If we start from the point where the parent or grandparent or other relative you want to be able to exchange e-mail with already owns a computer, then the next step is to get them equipped to communicate, and to get them an account on a commercial system.

It's entirely possible that the person you want to communicate with already has a modem but is not aware of it. One sure sign is if there are two sockets, one above the other, at the back of the computer that will accept a phone plug. (One socket is to connect the internal modem to the phone line; the other is to make it possible to plug in a regular phone.) Don't try to do this over the telephone. Ask for the airfare, or whatever, to make a quick trip home!

 # Which system to choose?

College students have been known to go through withdrawal when facing the prospect of graduating and losing their free Internet accounts. But such is life.

So, yes, your parents and relatives will actually have to *pay* for the Internet access you currently get for free. Fortunately, the fees are low: probably no more than about $9 a month. And for that $9, they not only get to correspond with you via e-mail, they get access to many other features as well.

If you plan to advise your friends and relatives, at this writing, here is what you need to know.

 # Ways to connect

There are at least five ways for non-students to connect to the Internet:

❶ Use an employer's Internet connection. Many large companies and institutions have been on the Net for years. But don't be surprised to find that Internet connections are not automatically made available to all employees. It may be necessary to ask someone like the network administrator how to gain access.

❷ Use a commercial online system. Any Internet user can exchange mail with users of America Online (AOL), CompuServe, Delphi, GEnie, MCI Mail, Prodigy, and nearly any other general-interest system you can name. Policies and charges vary, but almost all systems have an Internet mail connection of some sort, as well as other Internet services. Call these numbers for a free information packet:

America Online   800-827-6364
CompuServe   800-848-8199
Delphi   800-695-4005
GEnie   800-638-9636
MCI Mail   800-779-0949
Prodigy   800-776-3449

❸ A Bulletin Board System (BBS). Some BBSs, especially FIDO systems, exchange mail with the Internet. Such boards are fun, whether or not there is a membership fee involved, but they are not the place for a new user to start. There is a lot of FIDOnet activity on the Net. Start with the newsgroup **comp.org.fidonet** to get more information.

❹ Local freenets. Some *freenets* offer access as well. Freenets are systems that focus on some particular community or region. Corporations and institutions donate money, time, and computer facilities to make it possible for others in the community to use the system free of charge. Check the newsgroup **alt.online-service.freenet** for tips and information.

Be aware, however, that the quality of service you get from freenets can vary widely. If your relatives already use one, fine. But this is probably not the kind of place you want some new online communicator to start.

❺ SLIP and PPP connections. A Serial Line Internet Protocol (SLIP) or Point-to-Point Protocol (PPP) connection gives you full access to the Internet. It's just like having a student account. The difference is that it costs $20 or more a month, and the user has to dial up the account the way you dial into your campus computer from your room. Companies that provide SLIP/PPP accounts are called Internet Access (or Service) Providers. Two of the best known and most widely available are Netcom (800-501-8649) and PSINet (800-827-7482).

➡️ And the winner is . . .

If your parents, friends, or relatives are not currently online with some system or another, and if you want them to be able to easily exchange mail with you, then America Online is the choice to make. It's quick, it's intuitive, and it's pretty. One look at the screen shots in Fig. 11-1 and Fig. 11-2 and you'll see exactly what I mean.

I recommend America Online for parents and grandparents alike. In fact, AOL is the home of SeniorNet, a really nifty set of features aimed at people 55 and older.

Figure 11-1

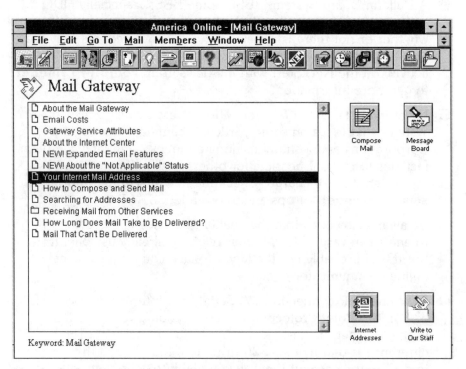

Here's the Internet mail gateway screen on America Online. Is it pretty and pretty intuitive, or what?

Figure 11-2

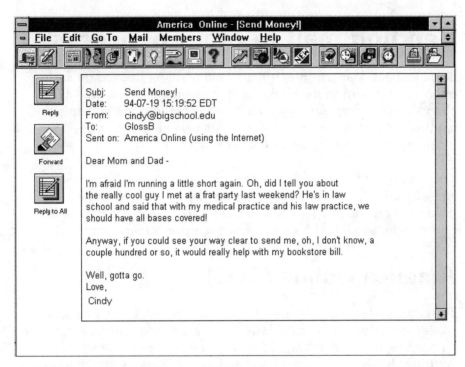

And here's the kind of thing your folks can expect to see when receiving Internet mail from you via the Internet. Again, AOL makes it easy

NET TIP

Getting it on with America Online

To access AOL, you load the special AOL software (Windows, DOS, Mac, etc.) and just start clicking. The software is free and often comes with a credit good for 10 free hours online.

The idea is to give you a taste of the service to see if you like it. If you wish to continue, subscriptions are $9.95 per month. That includes five hours of connect time. After that, the connect time cost is $2.95 per hour. The price is the same whether you go online at 2,400 bps or 9,600 bps.

For more information, call 800-827-6364.

 # Sending mail to other networks

Once you get your parents, friends, and relatives hooked up and online with one or more of the leading commercial systems, it's almost clear sailing. All they have to do is get into the system's mail feature and key in the text of a letter they want to send you—or enter a command to read the letter you've sent them.

The only thing that might trip them up is the proper form of e-mail address to use when messaging you on the Net. For your part, you'll need to know the proper address format for their system as well. Fortunately, you'll find both sides of each coin summarized here.

 ## America Online (AOL)

To send mail from the Internet to someone on AOL, remove any spaces from the person's AOL user name and add **@aol.com** to get an address like **jsmith@aol.com**. If you don't know the user name, your best bet is to call the person and ask. AOL does not charge users for mail sent or received via the Internet.

To send mail from AOL to an address on the Internet, just put the person's Internet address in the "To:" field before composing your message. Thus, **bjones@bigschool.edu**.

 ## CompuServe

Although you may soon see English language "aliases" introduced as CompuServe addresses (**CSI:EMILYG**, for example), CompuServe users have traditionally had numerical addresses, in the form **789102,678**.

To send mail from the Internet to a CompuServe user, change the comma to a period and add **@compuserve.com**. That gives you an address like **789102.678@compuserve.com**. CompuServe users must pay a minimum of 15 cents for each message received from the Internet.

To send mail from CompuServe to someone on the Internet, use an address in the form **INTERNET:bjones@bigschool.edu**. The colon (:) is required.

Delphi Internet Services

To send mail from the Internet to a Delphi subscriber, use an address consisting of the person's Delphi user name plus **@delphi.com** to get an address like **jsmith@delphi.com**. Delphi charges $3 a month for full, unlimited Internet access. Delphi users can have megabytes of messages and files transferred to their personal workspace on the system, without charge, as long as they download or delete the material within 48 hours.

To send mail from Delphi to someone on the Internet, the form is **internet"jsmith@company.org"**. (The quotation marks are required.)

GEnie

To send mail from the Internet to GEnie, add **@genie.geis.com** to the end of the GEnie user name. For example: **jsmith@genie.geis.com**.

To send mail from the regular GEnie Mail system (Menu Page 200) to someone on the Internet, use the person's Internet address plus the constant **@INET#**. The address will look like this: **jsmith@company.org@INET#**.

To send mail to an Internet address from GEnie's Internet Mail Service (Menu Page 207), just key in the person's Internet address when you are prompted to "Enter Destination Internet Address." (No need to include the **@INET#** constant in this case.)

 # MCI Mail

To send mail to someone with an MCI Mail account, add
@mcimail.com to the end of the person's name or numerical
address. For example: **555-1234@mcimail.com** or
jsmith@mcimail.com. (You're better off using the numerical address
if the person has a relatively common name, since there can be no
doubt about the John Smith at 555-1234, but considerable doubt
about JSMITH.)

To send mail from MCI Mail to an Internet address, at the "To:"
prompt, key in the person's name and (EMS). At the resulting
"EMS:" prompt, key in internet. At the resulting "MBX:" prompt, key
in the recipient's Internet address.

Prodigy

To send mail from the Internet to a Prodigy user, add **@prodigy.com**
to the person's Prodigy user ID. For example: **jsmith@prodigy
.com**. As with CompuServe, Prodigy users must pay extra for
Internet e-mail.

To send mail from Prodigy to an Internet address, you'll need
Prodigy's Mail Manager software, which is available for download
from the system. After composing your message offline using Mail
Manager, send it to the person's normal Internet address, like
jsmith@company.org. No special punctuation is required.

12

How to use Internet Relay Chat (IRC) & TALK

INTERNET Relay Chat or IRC (pronounced "irk") is, in effect, a real-time conferencing system with elements of citizens band (CB) radio tossed in. One difference: There may be 1,000 or more "channels" active at once. And you can join almost any one of them. (The same IRC technology is used for Internet MUDs and MUSEs and other text-based, multiplayer games.)

IRC was developed in Finland in 1988 by Jarkko Oikarinen. It's designed to let you hold live keyboard conversations with people all over the world. When you key in something on your computer, it is instantly "broadcast" to whomever happens to be on the same channel. At this writing, IRC links systems in more than 60 different countries, but your system may or may not have IRC access. Here's an easy way to find out. If you are on a UNIX system, just key in irc followed by the nickname you want to use. For example: irc dr-crusher.

Deciphering what you'll see

All conversation on IRC takes place on channels. Thus, you can either join a channel when you sign on, or you can create one of your own. Notice how many people have done just that in the sample IRC session shown here. Each of the channels with only one user listed is an instant creation.

```
/list
***          Channel: Users  Topic
***          #aussie:    1
***          #IceDog:    1
***          #wetsex2:   1    Horny girls welcome here
***          #gcl:       1    GNU Common Lisp
***        #gaychicag*   2    Gay Chicago
***        #LondonLNO:   1    LOOT Night Out
***        #DeltaSig:    1    Delta Sigma Pi - Co-Ed Professional Business
                              Fraternity
***        #randland:    1    Let the Dragon ride again on the winds of Time
***            #BAD:     3    [BAD] Bitchin' ANSi Design [BAD]
***           #void:     1
***         #echoes:     1    Pink Floyd!
***         #jasmin:     1
***        #Highway:     1
***            #sun:     1    Hier scheint immer die Sonne
***            #dv8:     2
***       #femuscle:     1    Women muscle and wimps
***           #genx:     1
***        #niceguy:     1    I'm a nice guy ... come talk to me
***           #pars:     2
***         #tacoma:     2
***        #nicecafe:    7    Nice people, nice conversation...a great place
                              to be!
***             #cc:     1
***        #Forum-V:     1
***         #kanada:     2    Kean LOVES Linda with all his heart :)
***           #psyc:     1
***        #gblf.de:     4    hier sind alle lieb und artig
***        #Private:     3
***           #KMKI:     4    Keluarga Mahasiswa Katolik Indonesia
***       #amigascne:   10    Alles Was Ein Piss Braucht - Saku
***       #Antwerpen:    1    AANTWAARPS IS EEN WEIRELDTOAL
***       #Socialism:    1
***        #francais:   12
***           #india:   30    TU CHEZ BADI HEY MAST MAST
***           #happy:   13    We don't need no stinkin topic
***         #camelot:    5
***          #wetsex:   24    Welcome to WETSEX .......SirJeStErs Casino
           #hottub:    11    Billy Joel/Elton John - what a show!!!/join
                              #hottub
```

To participate in any discussion, all you have to do is enter the /JOIN command, followed by the channel name. Thus, /join #hottub will get you into that channel. The #HOTTUB channel is one of the longest running channels on IRC. I'm not sure it ever shuts down, because, as the earth revolves, a cadre of sysops in each time zone takes the reins.

 # The crucial IRC commands

Typically, IRC has more commands than you will ever use. And, naturally, there are at least two versions of the IRC software, so some commands work or don't work, depending on the version your IRC server happens to be running. Fortunately, regardless of your server, you can get a complete list of commands by keying in /help once you are in IRC.

As you will notice, all IRC commands begin with a slash (/). That's to tell the system not to display to other users the text that follows, but to expect the text to be a command. The most important IRC commands are these:

> /list -min *n*

Try keying in just /list to get a complete listing of all channels of every sort. That will help you appreciate what happens when you use the command with the "-min *n*" modifier. This command lets you list channels with a minimum of *n* users. Replace "-min *n*" with "-max *n*" and you can get a list of channels that have no more than *n* people.

> /join *channel*

Probably the most important command. Connects you to the channel you specify. Most channel names begin with a pound sign (#). You can also use this command to create a channel of your own. Key in /join #goodstuff and the system will first search for such a channel. If #GOODSTUFF does not exist, the system will create it, making you its *Channel Operator*.

As Channel Operator, you can use the /MOD command to make a channel secret, private, anonymous, invite-only, moderated, or otherwise control it. You can also give other users Channel Operator status. Those with Channel Operator status have an at sign (@) in front of their names (@Bobbsy, @PumpkinFace, etc.).

> /leave *channel*

Leave the target channel. When you enter IRC, you are on the Null Channel (Channel 0). You can enter commands, but you

can't chat. When you leave a channel that you have joined, you return to the Null Channel.

➤ /quit or /signoff

Lets you quit IRC completely. You can enter this command wherever you happen to be.

➤ /help or /help *command*

If you key in /help, you will get a list of all IRC commands. If you key in /help join you will get information on how to use the /JOIN command, and so on.

NET TIP

IRC-oriented newsgroups

It's worth noting that IRC is the focal point of a number of Usenet newsgroups. If you really want to get into things, here are the groups to check out:

alt.irc   *Internet Relay Chat material*

alt.irc.announce   *Announcements about IRC*

alt.irc.hottub   *Discussion of the #HOTTUB channel*

alt.irc.ircii   *The IRC II client program*

alt.irc.questions   *How-to questions for IRC*

alt.irc.recovery   *Recovery from too much IRC*

 Learning more

If you want to learn about IRC, start by going online and experiencing it first-hand. That way you'll have a better idea of what people are talking about in the files that tell you how to use IRC—files like the IRC Primer, the IRC Tutorial, and the IRC FAQ.

The IRC Primer is the one to start with. It's available in both plain ASCII and PostScript format. You can find all three IRC documents on the Internet, or you can get them from Glossbrenner's Choice on the disk called Internet 7, Just the FAQs.

To get the files via FTP, look for filenames like **IRCprimer**, **tutorial**, and **alt-irc-faq** in these locations:

➤ FTP to **cs-ftp.bu.edu**, Path: /irc/support/

➤ FTP to **coombs.anu.edu.au**, Path: /pub/irc/docs/

➤ FTP to **nic.funet.fi**, Path: /pub/unix/irc/docs/

Or visit the IRC Web site at
http://www.ugcs.caltech.edu/~kluster/ircwww.html.

➡ An IRC lexicon

As you will discover throughout the Net, different groups have developed different cultures. IRC is no exception, and it naturally has its own "language." The following list of words, while far from comprehensive, will help you get a leg up in understanding the phrases and abbreviations you will encounter.

MOTD   Message Of The Day. The greeting screen that is created by the IRC Operator at the IRC site you are using.

#Twilight_Zone   The channel most IRC Operators monitor. They'll usually answer technical questions, but this is not the place to go for chat.

BOTS   Short for *robots*—scripts run by someone using IRC client software. The scripts or *software robots* can be turned loose on IRC. For this reason, most IRC Operators now ban any form of BOTS on their systems.

^G   If the person creating a channel has added a description and included one or more Ctrl-G characters, they may show up on your screen as ^G. A Ctrl-G is an ASCII 7, and it has always been used to ring a "bell" at the receiving site. These days, some systems respond to a Ctrl-G with a beep, and some simply ignore it.

Lurking   Joining a channel and simply watching the conversations without contributing or participating yourself. Nothing wrong with it. But those who *are* participating don't like to feel they're putting on a show.

TALK on the Internet

In addition to world-wide IRC conversations, there is also TALK. TALK is the Internet equivalent of a telephone conversation. It requires that both you and the person you want to talk to have access to this function, and that both of you are online at the same time.

To use it from a UNIX system, follow these steps:

❶ Key in talk user@site.name, where *user@site.name* is the e-mail address of the other person. That person will see something like this on the screen:

```
talk: connection requested by yourname@site.name
talk: respond with:   talk yourname@site.name
```

❷ To start the conversation, your correspondent should then type at the host's command line talk yourname@site.name, using *your* e-mail address in the TALK command. This is the equivalent of picking up the phone, and if your correspondent does not do this, no connection can be made. That's all there is to it.

Conclusion

Both IRC and TALK are fun to play with. But neither is what one could call an outstanding feature. If you're bored and want to play some evening—and if your connect time is not costing you anything—then it can be enjoyable to dip into IRC. Just be aware that most of the people you will encounter are bored, too, and the conversations are usually less than scintillating. Same thing's true of the chat services on CompuServe, America Online, and similar systems.

Still, your Internet experience will never be complete until you've at least tried IRC. And—who knows?—you just might luck into a wonderful conversation or debate with wonderful people.

13
Library card catalogues

IT'S just possible that this could be the most important chapter in this book. We've had a lot of fun on the Net already, and we're going to have tons more. But if college is about anything, it's about learning—or more to the point, learning *how* to learn. Your paper on Jane Austen or Einstein's approach to a unified field theory isn't likely to set the world on fire. But the *process* you go through to research and prepare such papers will serve you well the rest of your life.

As will your familiarity with libraries, librarians, and information resources. Probably the biggest mistake I made when I was at school was ignoring the library. It was only after I graduated—and some years later returned to my college town as a writer—that I realized what I had missed. Only then did I really learn how to use this resource. I had to. My profession demanded it.

I hope you won't make the same mistake. I hope you will realize that *information* is the steel, plastics, and automotive industry of today and of the future. And discovering how to find and manipulate it may well be the single most important skill you learn at college.

I am absolutely serious about this. After all, to a large degree, the same information is available to everyone. But it's the person who knows how to search for and find the fact, figure, quote, book, article, or government report that is relevant to the question at hand who will win the game.

Okay. Let me rephrase that. In some cases, it's the person who knows enough about information and what's available to hire a professional searcher to go get the desired item who will win. You don't have to be the information expert yourself. But, you truly must know something about what can be and is being done.

 # Start with your friendly librarian

The absolute best place to begin is with the librarians at your campus library. Make friends with these people and bind them to your soul with hoops of steel.

Libraries and librarians don't get even one tenth of the respect and veneration they deserve. In a just society, they would rank with doctors, lawyers, and certified public accountants in respect, pay, and position. After all, they are the guides and gatekeepers to 10,000 years of human culture and knowledge!

You may rail at their classification systems, but if it weren't for librarians and the systems they implement and enforce, no one would ever be able find anything. If the librarians you have known in the past have seemed a bit possessive of the library's materials, give them a break. Everyone with library training I have ever known has been totally *dedicated* to making the most knowledge available to the most people possible.

Yes, some may be a bit retentive about it. But believe me, this is their one true passion. Once you realize that, it's easy to see why a librarian would be concerned about how you treat a book or a magazine, and why he or she would be concerned that things are put back in their proper place. If a patron mutilates a book or other item, it will not be available to or usable by anyone else. And if everyone returned books to the shelves willy-nilly, it would not take long before the shelves were a complete jumble and no patron could find anything.

 # Get them on your side

Basically, the men and women who work at your college or university library can be some of the most important people you'll meet in your

entire college career. They are all professionals and will appreciate it if you treat them as such. If you come to them saying "Geeze, I've got a paper due on Middle Kingdom Egyptian art on Tuesday. What do I do?" they will try to help.

But you will be much better off if you first do your part. For example, in this chapter, you'll learn how to search the Library of Congress on the Internet. Once you know how to do that, you can go to your campus library and say, "I did a search of the Library of Congress and found this long-out-of-print book on my topic. How can I borrow a copy?" You're sure to get an enthusiastic reception.

 # Getting the book: Interlibrary Loan requests

Other authors rave about the fact that you can use the Internet to search the Library of Congress and many other libraries around the country and around the world. But no one tells you what good this does you.

For example, what good does it do you in California to be able to search, say, the holdings of the Kenyon College Library in Gambier, Ohio? The answer is that, thanks to the Interlibrary Loan program, you *can* borrow books from distant libraries.

You fill out a request—using the bibliographic information about the book you have obtained via the Internet—and hand it in at your campus library. Two or three weeks later, the book will have arrived at your library for you to borrow for a specified time. You may or may not be charged for the cost of mailing the book back and forth.

 ## Not quite a largess universal

Of course, you can't borrow absolutely everything. Books that are heavily used at the library, audio/visual materials which tend to be fragile, rare manuscripts, and so on usually aren't made available through Interlibrary Loan. Nor are you likely to be able to borrow

from the Library of Congress, because it holds the "copyright copy" of the work.

But you can borrow from nearly everywhere else. Indeed, it is an unwritten code among the world's librarians that all reasonable Interlibrary Loan requests are honored. This makes a lot of sense, because there is no telling when one of the librarian's patrons will want to borrow something from a distant location.

 # Making the most of online card catalogues

There are just a few things you need to know to turn the searching of library card catalogues via the Internet into a truly powerful tool. First, the best way to locate and access a card catalogue is to use the Gopher system on your campus computer. Every Gopher menu is different, but most do contain menu items to let you find and connect to library card catalogues. (Technically, when you select a library, your Gopher Telnets you to the location and automatically logs you on.)

Second, many such locations require you to emulate a VT-100 terminal. That may not be an issue if you go in via your campus computer center terminal. But if you are dialing into the campus system from your dorm room, you may have to set your computer software to emulate a VT-100.

Third, don't be surprised to discover that each library's system has its own requirements for how you enter a search or view results. These procedures may or may not be intuitive. But help is always available, so be sure to take advantage of it.

It is also worth noting that online searching of any sort is a skill. You simply cannot plunk yourself in front of a terminal, key in a phrase, and expect to get a list of all the publications that are relevant to your area of inquiry. You'll probably get a lot of them, but the list won't be comprehensive. (Which may or may not matter, depending on your research needs.)

 # Books past & present

Finally, the best reason for searching any library catalogue is to develop a list of items that have been published about your topic in the *past*. Printed directories of out-of-print books do exist, but they are far from comprehensive. None contains the literally millions of titles in the Library of Congress.

On the other hand, for *current* books, you are probably better off searching the print or electronic version of the publication *Books in Print*. The electronic version is available on many commercial systems and may even be available at your library on CD-ROM. If not, you are sure to find a copy of this multivolume publication at your campus bookstore. (You can search by author, title, or subject.)

 # How to search the Library of Congress

Founded on April 24, 1800, the Library of Congress is surely, by any measure, one of the great libraries of the world. And, while you probably will not be able to borrow books from its collection, you can search its card catalogue via the Internet. The main reason to do this is to develop a reasonably comprehensive list of the works that have been published on your topic. And I do mean comprehensive—some Library of Congress volumes were published in the 1400s and before!

Probably the best way to gain access is to run your local system's Gopher and opt to connect to a specific Gopher site. The site you want is **marvel.loc.gov**. MARVEL stands for Machine-Assisted Realization of the Virtual Electronic Library. And LOC is short for LOCIS, the Library of Congress Information System.

If you have a Web browser, you can start your search at the Library of Congress home page on the World Wide Web. Point your browser at **http://lcweb.loc.gov** to reach the opening screen, shown in Fig. 13-1. (This Web site is worth a visit even if you're not looking for a book. You'll find information on special exhibits, historical collections, recently discovered manuscripts, and more.)

Figure 13-1

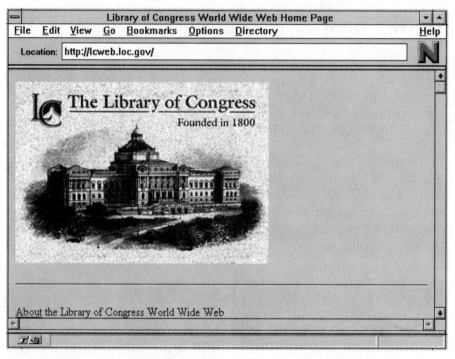

The Library of Congress home page on the World Wide Web.

Once you're connected to the Library of Congress, you will see menus like this:

```
Page 1 of 1

1    About LC MARVEL                                      Menu
2    Events, Facilities, Programs, and Services           Menu
3    Research and Reference (Public Services)             Menu
4    Libraries and Publishers (Technical Services)        Menu
5    Copyright                                            Menu
6    Library of Congress Online Systems                   Menu
7    Employee Information                                 Menu
8    U.S. Congress                                        Menu
9    Government Information                               Menu
10   Global Electronic Library (by Subject)               Menu
11   Internet Resources                                   Menu
12   What's New on LC MARVEL                              Menu
13   Search LC MARVEL Menus                               Menu

Enter Item Number, SAVE, ?, or BACK: 6

Library of Congress Online Systems
```

```
Page 1 of 1

1    Overview--Library of Congress Information System (LOCIS)   Text
2    How to Connect to LOCIS                                    Text
3    Hours and Availability                                     Text
4    Quick Search Guides for LOCIS                              Menu
5    Connect to LOCIS (Public Users - No Password Needed)       Telnet
6    Connect to LOCIS (LC and Congress - Requires Password)     Telnet
7    Other LC Online Systems                                    Menu

Enter Item Number, SAVE, ?, or BACK: 5
```

Notice that I opted for item 6 on the first menu to get to the Library of Congress and then chose item 5, "Connect to LOCIS (Public Users - No Password Needed)." That leads to a display like the one shown in Fig. 13-2. Select item 1, "Library of Congress Catalog," from that menu, and you will see Fig. 13-3. Here, you should probably pick item 3, "Combination of files 1 and 2 above (LOCI and PREM)," to make sure you search everything.

Figure 13-2

```
       L O C I S :  LIBRARY OF CONGRESS INFORMATION SYSTEM

          To make a choice: type a number, then press ENTER


     1   Library of Congress Catalog        4   Braille and Audio

     2   Federal Legislation                5   Organizations

     3   Copyright Information              6   Foreign Law

   *    *    *    *    *    *    *    *    *    *    *    *

     7   Searching Hours and Basics
     8   Documentation and Classes
     9   Library of Congress General Information
    10   Library of Congress Fast Facts
    11   * * Announcements * *      New Interface for Some Files!



    12   Comments and Logoff
         Choice: 1
```

The main menu for the Library of Congress Information System (LOCIS).

Figure 13-3

```
                    LIBRARY OF CONGRESS CATALOG
CHOICE                                                        FILE

  1    BOOKS: English language books 1968-, French 1973-, German,    LOCI
       Portuguese, Spanish 1975-, other European languages 1976-77,
       non-European languages 1978-79.  Some microforms 1984-.

  2    BOOKS earlier than the dates above.  Some serials, maps,      PREM
       music, audiovisual items.

  3    Combination of files 1 and 2 above  (LOCI and PREM).

  4    SERIALS cataloged at LC & some other libraries since 1973.    LOCS

  5    MAPS and other cartographic items (except atlases) cataloged  LOCM
       at LC 1968- and some other research libraries 1985-.

  6    SUBJECT TERMS and cross references form LC Subject Headings.   LCXR
       NOTE:   Choices 1,4, and 5, depending on commands used, also
               include ALL catalog files.  See HELP screens.
 12    Return to LOCIS MENU screen.

       Choice:
                                                        LC CATALOG
```

Pick item 3 to be sure of getting everything.

⇨ Entering your search terms

The LC MARVEL system represents a nice compromise between power and ease of use. And the price is right. Searching the identical database on DIALOG costs $57 an hour (95 cents a minute, plus charges for each record you view). As you can see from Fig. 13-4, you will be prompted with "READY FOR NEW COMMAND." At that point, I keyed in browse york, pa. It seemed reasonable to assume that this Pennsylvania town that once served as the capital of the country might be the subject of an American History research paper.

✳ Searching for York, Pennsylvania

Of course, there was also the fact that I knew that a relative, one Adam J. Glossbrenner (1810–1889), had published a history of York County in 1834. The search produced over 40 items, including:

➤ Hartley, Thomas (1748–1800). Observations on the propriety of fixing upon a central and inland situation for the permanent residence of Congress. Humbly offered to the consideration of the honorable members of the Senate and House of

Representatives of the United States. {New York} Printed in the year MDCCLXXXIX.

➤ Polk's York, Pennsylvania, city directory (1898).

➤ York, Pennsylvania: A Dynamic Community Forges Ahead. Published by the York Chamber of Commerce in 1957.

➤ Spotlight on York. Published by the League of Women Voters in 1952.

➤ The First Printers of York, Pennsylvania (1940).

➤ The economic geography of York, Pennsylvania (1935).

➤ "Some important reading abilities and types of procedure to give training in these abilities." York, Pa. Board of education (1927).

➤ York, Pa. City engineer's office. Report on the sanitary sewerage system and disposal works (1917).

➤ It's illegal; quaint laws in York, Pennsylvania's past. York, Pa., Strine Pub. Co., (1973).

But no Adam. No *History of York County, from its erection to the present time*, 1834. No A. J. Glossbrenner. I found it, of course, by searching on the author's name. But why it didn't turn up when I looked for publications about York, PA, is a puzzle. I also discovered

Figure 13-4

```
PREM- THE LIBRARY OF CONGRESS COMPUTERIZED CATALOG
      is now available for your search.
      The Term Index, updated on 07/19/94, contains 8,403,670 terms.

CONTENTS: PREM contains records for older materials: books and serials
cataloged at the Library from 1898 to 1979 (with records from 1968 forward
containing mostly non-English materials); and maps, musical scores, sound
recordings and audiovisual materials cataloged through 1984. Most records
contain incomplete, unreviewed information derived from the LC card catalog.
Names and subject headings are the terms originally assigned, reflecting
over 80 years of cataloging practice. Errors are gradually being corrected.

TO SEARCH, USE FIRST WORDS OF:              EXAMPLES:
        subject ------------------->     browse aeroplanes
        author  ------------------->     b faulkner, william
        title   ------------------->     browse gone with the wind
        partial LC call #-------->       b call QA76.9
        LC record # ------------->       prem 44-27203

UPDATE:    Index terms are added and updated each night.
FOR HELP:  Enter HELP for PREM info, or HELP COMMANDS for command list.
   READY FOR NEW COMMAND: browse york, pa
```

"Browsing" with the keywords "York, PA."

that in at least one reference, old Adam's name was spelled "Clossbrenner." Many of my own books were listed as well, but at least one listing showed my first name as "Alred." Kind of makes you wonder what other data-entry errors have been made, doesn't it?

 # Now what?

There are a number of comments to make about the search of the Library of Congress catalogue I did. First and foremost, you will be stunned by how far back the documents go and at the minutiae they cover. I mean, a "Report on the sanitary sewerage system and disposal works" as they existed in a small Pennsylvania town in 1917? A report from the local board of education from 1927?

This kind of detail is an historian's dream! And if it exists for this one town in Pennsylvania, what *else* might be among the holdings of the Library of Congress! There's just one problem: How to get your hands on it.

It is not at all uncommon for graduate students and doctoral candidates to travel the world to visit key libraries and view books and documents that are crucial to their areas of study. But that's not practical for most of us. At least not for those of us who do not have some kind of government grant.

What to do? Let's suppose that I wanted to borrow Adam Glossbrenner's history of York County. I know that the Library of Congress probably will not lend it via Interlibrary Loan. So where else do I look?

I'll save you the suspense. Where I looked was at the Penn State library. I used Gopher to get to a menu of library card catalogues in Pennsylvania. Then I just picked Penn State because I figured it was the largest and most likely to have the book.

The system asked me for a password. But I simply hit my Enter key and was told that my activities would be limited to "search only." Fine with me.

Armed with the bibliographic information about Adam's book that I got from the Library of Congress, it was easy to search the Penn State library catalogue for that work. In seconds, I found four copies. I printed out the information Penn State provided. I could now take this to my local county or township library and initiate an Interlibrary Loan request.

 # Conclusion

And you and your parents and friends can do the same! Your friends and relatives can search the Library of Congress themselves via the Internet using America Online or Prodigy or some other online service. They can also search the Penn State library and many other university libraries using the same systems.

And, with the information thus provided, they and you and everyone else can go to any public library and submit an Interlibrary Loan request to actually get your hands on the publication.

It takes some skill. It takes some patience. But it costs next to nothing. It is only a slight overstatement to say that with this feature alone, the Internet lays the entire world of human knowledge at your feet. Or at your fingertips!

14
Newsgroups & mailing lists

IF library card catalogues are the button-down, sport-coat-and-tie aspect of Internet information, then newsgroups and mailing lists represent the laid back, wild and woolly, anything-goes side of things. Not that newsgroups and mailing lists don't address serious topics in serious ways. Many of them do. But a lot of them are simply off the wall.

How many? Probably a couple of thousand. After all, there are reportedly some 12,000 newsgroups in existence. And there are thousands of mailing lists as well.

A college student's perspective

So what's all this mean to you? It means two things. First, newsgroups and mailing lists can be the source of endless hours of fun and intellectual enjoyment. You've just gotta love a newsgroup devoted to Spam (**alt.spam**, of course.) And how can you resist a group called **alt.flame.roommate** that's described as "Putting the pig on a spit"?

But there are also newsgroups like **misc.writing**, **rec.arts.cinema**, **sci.mech.fluids**, **sci.med.radiology**, and **alt.culture.hawaii** (described as "Ua Mau Ke Ea O Ka 'Aina I Ka Pono"). And there are mailing lists on subjects as diverse as balloon sculpting and wind energy development.

As you learned at the Internet 5-Minute University in Chapter 1, a Usenet newsgroup is essentially a player-piano roll of messages devoted to a particular topic, and a mailing list is a list of people interested in some topic and willing to receive all articles posted to the list by any member. Now you know that both can be used for work as well as for fun.

The key questions, then, are these:

❶ How can I get a comprehensive list of all the newsgroups that are available?

❷ How can I best locate and read the groups that are of interest to me?

❸ How can I get a current list of all the mailing lists that exist?

❹ How can I best participate in any mailing list?

Believe it or not, each of these four questions has a reasonably simple answer. Let's start at the top.

Finding a comprehensive list of newsgroups

Gene Spafford created the original, comprehensive list of Usenet newsgroups. Then David C. Lawrence took it on. Maintaining such a list is an awesome task, and Mr. Lawrence has done a wonderful job.

The list is organized into two major parts: the Alternative Newsgroup Hierarchies (all the ALT groups) and the List of Active Newsgroups (everything else, i.e., all the non-ALT groups). As a convenience, all the files are available on the Newsgroup Essentials disk from Glossbrenner's Choice. Or you can get them via FTP or newsgroup postings. Just be sure to get all the files in each directory (part1, part2, etc.):

➢ FTP to **ftp.uu.net**

Path: /usenet/news.answers/active-newsgroups/part*

Path: /usenet/news.answers/alt-hierarchies/part*

> ➤ FTP to **rtfm.mit.edu**

    Path: /pub/usenet/news.answers/active-newsgroups/part*

    Path: /pub/usenet/news.answers/alt-hierarchies/part*

> ➤ Newsgroups:

    news.lists

    news.groups

    news.announce.newgroups

    news.answers

Searching offline

Once you've got the comprehensive list of newsgroups on your disk, the next step is to identify the ones you want to read. That way, you will be able to tell your newsreader program exactly which group to go to.

So, with your list of newsgroups on disk, it just makes sense to use your computer's power to search it. The program I like for this purpose is Vernon Buerg's famous shareware LIST program, but any word processing program with a search function will do. Just key in any topic that occurs to you and activate the search function. That's what I did to locate these newsgroups, all having to do with college life:

alt.flame.professor	Professor Bunsen's high enthalpy chem classes.
alt.flame.roommate	Putting the pig on a spit.
alt.folklore.college	Collegiate humor.
alt.fraternity.sorority	Discussions of fraternity/sorority life and issues.
alt.college.college-bowl	Discussions of the College Bowl competition.
alt.college.food	Mystery meat and so forth.
alt.college.fraternities	College and university fraternities.
alt.college.sororities	College and university sororities.
alt.college.tunnels	Tunnelling beneath the campuses.
alt.shenanigans	Practical jokes and other fun stuff.

clari.news.education.higher	Colleges and universities.
clari.sports.basketball.college	NCAA basketball coverage.
clari.sports.football.college	NCAA football coverage.
rec.sport.baseball.college	Baseball on the collegiate level.
rec.sport.baseball.fantasy	Rotisserie (fantasy) baseball play.
rec.sport.basketball.college	Hoops on the collegiate level.
rec.sport.baseball.college	Baseball on the collegiate level.
rec.sport.basketball.college	Hoops on the collegiate level.
rec.sport.disc	Discussion of flying disc based sports.
rec.sport.football.college	US-style college football.
soc.college	College, college activities, campus life
soc.college.grad	General issues about grad school
soc.college.gradinfo	Information about grad schools
soc.college.org.aiesec	Int'l Assoc of Business & Commerce Students
soc.college.teaching-asst	Issues affecting collegiate TAs

 # Other approaches to finding newsgroups

Of course, you don't absolutely have to have the complete list of newsgroups in order to find the ones that might be of interest to you. You can get recommendations from friends. You'll see references to specific groups in books and articles about the Internet, and in the subject-specific resources you'll read about in Chapter 15.

You can also use search tools like the commercial version of InfoSeek (described in Chapter 5) to find a group on a particular topic. Or look for a menu item on your local Gopher that allows you to search for newsgroups by keyword.

If you have a Web browser, you might want to try MaxThink's newsgroup search service at **http://maxthink.com/news**. My search for newsgroups dealing with the environment resulted in a number of hits, the first several of which are shown in Fig. 14-1.

Figure 14-1

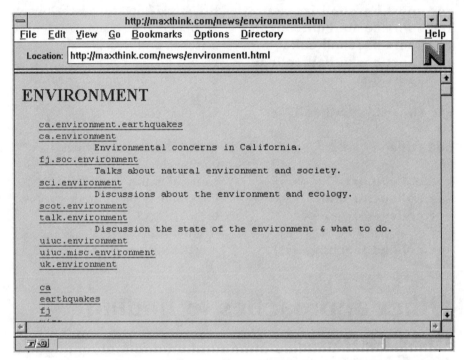

The results of a newsgroup search using MaxThink's search service on the World Wide Web.

 # Newsgroups via Gopher & e-mail

It's always possible that once you find a particular newsgroup you're interested in, you'll discover that it's not carried on the system you use. (Remember, not all Internet sites carry all groups.) You might try contacting the system administrator on campus and asking that person about the possibility of carrying the group you want. It's a longshot, perhaps, but you won't know unless you ask.

Another possibility would be to look for the newsgroup at one of these sites, all of which offer a selection of newsgroups on their Gopher menus:

➤ Gopher to **gopher.bham.ac.uk** and choose "Usenet News Reader" from the menu.

➤ Gopher to **gopher.msu.edu**. Choose "News & Weather" and then "Usenet News."

➤ Gopher to **gopher.gdb.org**. Choose "Usenet News and FAQs" and then "Read Usenet News Groups."

As a last resort, you could try reading and posting to the newsgroup via e-mail. It won't be the same as having full access to the group. But it might be better than nothing.

For more information on reading newsgroups via e-mail, send a message to **listserv@blekul11.bitnet** or **listserv@cc1. kuleuven.ac.be** with the command **/nnhelp** in the body of the message.

To post a message to a newsgroup via e-mail, you can send it to one of several locations. Again, not all locations carry all groups, so you'll have to experiment. Replace the periods in the newsgroup name with hyphens, and then add the name of the site. For example, to post a message to **alt.bbs** using the University of Texas site, you would use the address **alt-bbs@cs.utexas.edu**. Here are the sites offering a selection of newsgroups via e-mail:

newsgroup-name@cs.utexas.edu
newsgroup-name@news.demon.co.uk
newsgroup-name@undergrad.math.uwaterloo.ca
newsgroup-name@nic.funet.fi

NET TIP

Newsgroup hierarchies

To make it easier for people to find what they're looking for, Usenet newsgroups are divided into topics. Each main topic is further divided, and the result is often divided again and again, as areas are created for discussions of ever greater specificity.

For example, a group called **alt.music** might be formed to discuss music in general. But as people really get into the swing of things, some may decide that they really want to focus on baroque, jazz, and hip-hop. So **alt.music.baroque** might be formed, along with **alt.music.jazz** and **alt.music.hip-hop**. And so on.

Here are the main topic categories of Usenet newsgroups:

alt   *Alternative newsgroups. Basically, topics that don't fit neatly anywhere else. Many Usenet sites don't carry these groups.*

bionet *Biology, of course.*

bit   *Topics from Bitnet Listserv mailing lists.*

biz   *The accepted place for advertisements, marketing, and other commercial postings. Product announcements, product reviews, demo software, and so forth.*

clari *ClariNet is a commercial service. For a subscription fee paid by the site that carries its feed, ClariNet provides UPI wire news, newspaper columns, and lots of other goodies.*

comp *Topics of interest to both computer professionals and hobbyists, including computer science, software source code, and information on hardware and software systems.*

ddn   *Defense Data Network.*

gnu   *The Free Software Foundation and the GNU project.*

ieee   *Institute of Electrical and Electronic Engineers*

k12   *Topics of interest to teachers of kindergarten through grade 12, including curriculum, language exchanges with native speakers, and classroom-to-classroom projects designed by teachers.*

misc   *Groups addressing themes not easily classified under any of the other headings or which incorporate themes from multiple categories.*

news   *Groups concerned with the Usenet network and software (not current affairs, as you might think).*

rec   *Groups oriented towards the arts, hobbies, and recreational activities.*

sci   *Discussions relating to research in or application of the established sciences.*

soc   *Groups primarily addressing social issues and socializing.*

talk   *Groups largely debate-oriented and tending to feature long discussions without resolution and without appreciable amounts of generally useful information.*

How to read newsgroups

The only way to actually read the articles in a newsgroup is with a *newsreader program*. If you are accessing the Net from a UNIX site, your computer almost certainly has the **nn** newsreader available. This is the old standby, but any number of more powerful, more friendly newsreader programs exist, including **trn** and **tin**.

Your best bet is to contact your system administrator and tell that person that you want to be able to read newsgroups. Ask what options are available and what the administrator recommends.

The most important point to bear in mind about reading newsgroup articles is that the newsreader software keeps track of which messages you've read and which you have not read, either because they are new or because you chose to pass them by in the past.

Thus, the first time you start to read a newsgroup, all messages will be new to you. My advice is to scan things quickly, reading a message of interest here and there. Then use your newsreader program's command to mark all messages as read. That way, the next time you enter the group you won't have to confront 1,000 or more messages. Note that anything of lasting value—like FAQ files—will be reposted to the group on a regular basis.

NET TIP

The really key groups

These are some of the key newsgroups for new Internet users:

news.announce.newusers   *A series of articles that explain various facets of Usenet.*

news.newusers.questions   *This is where you can ask questions about how Usenet works.*

news.announce.newgroups   *Information about new or proposed newsgroups.*

news.answers   *Lists of Frequently Asked Questions (FAQs) and their answers from many different newsgroups.*

alt.internet.services   *Looking for something in particular on the Internet? Here's where to ask.*

alt.infosystems.announce   *People adding new information services to the Internet will post details here.*

 # News filtering from Stanford

The Department of Computer Science at Stanford University offers a service called the Stanford Netnews Filtering Service. Basically, you set up a profile for yourself consisting of the keywords you think are most likely to appear in articles that would be of interest to you.

The filtering software then searches all the newsgroups carried at Stanford for those keywords. (Notice that you yourself do not have to specify any newsgroup names, just the keywords.) Newsgroup articles that match your keywords are mailed to your Internet e-mail address. Automatically. For free.

For more information, visit their Web site (shown in Fig. 14-2) at **http://woodstock.stanford.edu:2000**. Or send an e-mail message to **netnews@db.stanford.edu**. In the message area, key in help. The system will automatically mail you a set of instructions for creating and activating a profile.

Figure 14-2

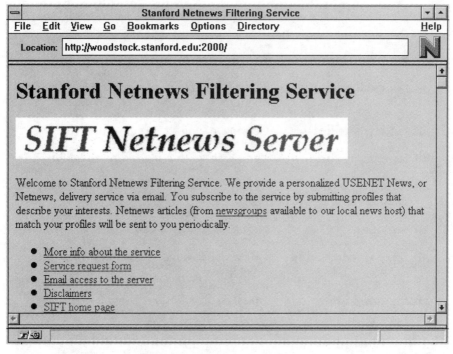

The Stanford Netnews Filtering Service on the Web.

Posting an anonymous message

Anonymity can at times be desirable. Unfortunately, with computers, everything you do on a system is registered and tagged with your name and account. Yet what computers can give, they can also take away. So, if you are interested in how one might post a message to a newsgroup *anonymously* (purely for scientific purposes, of course) contact the Anonymous Posting Service. Just send a blank e-mail message to **help@anon.penet.fi** or **acs-info@chop.ucsd.edu**. You'll soon receive complete instructions on getting and using an anonymous ID.

NET TIP

ALT-dot-FAN-dot what?

When it comes to cool stuff, clearly, the ALTs have it on the Net. Among the most popular ALT groups are **alt.sex**, **alt.beer**, **alt.bigfoot**, **alt.lies**, *and* **alt.stupidity**.

And then there's the ALT.FAN hierarchy. Here are just a few of the neat groups you'll find in it:

alt.fan.blues-brothers   Jake & Elwood ride again!

alt.fan.cecil-adams   The brother Douglas Adams never talks about.

alt.fan.chris-elliott   Get a Life, you Letterman flunky.

alt.fan.conan-obrien   Late Night with a big red pompadour.

alt.fan.dave_barry   Electronic fan club for humorist Dave Barry.

alt.fan.dune   Herbert's drinking buddies.

alt.fan.g-gordon-liddy   Crime does pay, or we wouldn't have so much of it.

alt.fan.hofstadter   Douglas Hofstadter, Godel, Escher, Bach, and others.

alt.fan.howard-stern   Fans of the abrasive radio & TV personality.

alt.fan.karla-homolka   Why are there so few hot, exhibitionist, S&M women?

alt.fan.letterman   One of the top 10 reasons to get the alt groups.

alt.fan.penn-n-teller   The magicians Penn Jillette & Teller.

alt.fan.pern   Anne McCaffery's s-f oeuvre.

alt.fan.ren-and-stimpy   For folks who couldn't find alt.tv.ren-n-stimpy.

alt.fan.shostakovich   Fans of the music of Shostakovich.

alt.fan.surak   That wild and crazy Vulcan.

alt.fandom.cons   Announcements of conventions (SciFi and others).

Moving on to mailing lists

Now for mailing lists. There are technically two types: those that originate on Bitnet and those that originate at non-Bitnet sites. The difference is one of procedure, not content, and it really does not have to concern you. All you need to know is that Bitnet is one of the largest networks linked by the Internet, and that its software does not allow the equivalent of Usenet newsgroups. So Bitnet users invented the mailing list and the *list server*—a computer that looks for special words in the subject line or the body text of the letters it receives. Upon finding them, it automatically adds the name of the letter's sender to a given mailing list.

Internet users decided that this was a good idea and took two steps. First, they created automatic list servers of their own. Second, some Internauts created Internet newsgroups to "mirror" Bitnet mailing lists. This second step should not be underestimated, for the great disadvantage of any kind of mailing list is that everyone gets everything, whether they want it all or not. With a newsgroup, in contrast, you are free to pick and choose among the messages and articles, opting to read only those that are of interest to you.

 # Getting a list of mailing lists

Subscribing to an Internet or Bitnet mailing list is easy. In most cases, you simply send a request to a *subscription address*, where a human being or a computer reads it and adds you to the list. From then on, you read and respond to messages from the list's *main address*. (Note that the subscription address and the main address are *different*.)

Naturally, though, before you can do anything, you've got to know what lists are available, what they cover, their names, and their subscription address. As you might imagine, a number of such lists are available on the Net. Two of the most comprehensive and well-respected lists are:

✳ **The SRI List of Lists**

This list covers both Internet and Bitnet. It is updated regularly, and currently weighs in at over 700K. A hardcopy, indexed version of this list is published by Prentice Hall under the title *Internet: Mailing Lists*, edited by T. L. Hardie and Vivian Neou. It sells for $29.

You can get the SRI list via FTP, e-mail, or newsgroup posting.

➤ FTP to **sri.com**

Path: /netinfo/interest-groups.

➤ Request via e-mail by sending a message to **mail-server @sri.com**. Include the line send interest-groups in the body of the message.

➤ Look for the list on the following newsgroups:

news.lists

news.answers

✳ **Publicly Accessible Mailing Lists**

This list, maintained by Stephanie da Silva, concentrates mainly on Internet lists. It is widely available via FTP, newsgroups, and the World Wide Web. You'll often see it referred to as the PAML list.

➤ FTP to **rtfm.mit.edu**

Path: /pub/usenet/news.answers/mail/mailing-lists/

➤ Look for the list on the following newsgroups:

news.lists

news.answers

➤ World Wide Web

http://www.neosoft.com/internet/paml

As a convenience, both of these lists are also available from Glossbrenner's Choice on a disk called Mailing List Essentials. This disk also includes DOS search software to make it easy to find mailing lists of interest. See the Glossbrenner's Choice section at the back of the book for details.

NET TIP

Selected Internet/Bitnet lists

Here are just three of the mailing lists you can subscribe to on the Internet and Bitnet. I've picked them by searching the SRI List of Lists on disk. I had no idea that these three lists existed, but I felt certain that if I searched for Camelot, Generation X, and Early Music I would find something.

- *Camelot*

```
CAMELOT@CASTLE.ED.AC.UK
   Subscription Address: CAMELOT-REQUEST@CASTLE.ED.AC.UK
   Owner: Chris Thornborrow <ct@castle.edinburgh.ac.uk>
   Last Update: 2/1/92
   Description:

A mailing list on the subject of Arthurian legend and Grail
Lore. The 'Matter of Britain', as it is known, in all its
guises and all related subjects, discussed in an unmoderated
mailing list. There is a related anonymous FTP repository with
FAQs, GIF pictures and interesting articles at
sapphire.epcc.ed.ac.uk (129.215.56.11). After connecting, "cd
pub/camelot" and get the README to find the contents.
```

- *Generation X*

```
GENERATION X
   Subscription Address: MMILOTAY@GALAXY.GOV.BC.CA
   Owner: Mark S. Milotay <MMILOTAY@GALAXY.GOV.BC.CA>
   Last Update: 5/2/93
   Description:

This is a forum for the twenty somethings to hang out and
interface in the manner we all love best, remotely by
computer. This is a moderated forum but is open to any remarks
relevant to our generation.

To subscribe send a request to for subscription with your name
and e-mail address to MMILOTAY@GALAXY.GOV.BC.CA. To
unsubscribe send a message to the same address asking to
unsubscribe.
```

- *Early Music*

```
EARLYM-L@AEARN.EDVZ.UNI-LINZ.AC.AT
   Subscription Address: LISTSERV@AEARN.EDVZ.UNI-LINZ.AC.AT
   Owner: Gerhard Gonter <gonter@awiwuw11.wu-wien.ac.at>
   Last Update: 10/12/91
   Description:
```

> EARLYM-L and the newsgroup rec.music.early are linked. They
> provide a forum for exchange of news and views about medieval,
> 'art' and 'folk') derived as part of European culture, its
> researchers, performers, instruments, instrument-makers,
> festivals, concerts and societies, records, song texts and
> translations, machine-readable notations of (early) music;
> authenticity in music of (these and) later periods (e.g.
> classical and romantic).

 # How to subscribe to a mailing list

To get your name added or removed from a mailing list, whether it
originates on the Internet or on Bitnet, you send an e-mail message
containing your request to a designated location. The lists of mailing
lists just discussed will give you the specifics of what to do to
subscribe or unsubscribe. But not every set of instructions is equally
complete. The points to zero in on are:

➤ Where should the subscription request be sent?

➤ What, specifically, should the message contain?

➤ Where should actual contributions to the list—as opposed to
subscription requests—be sent?

 ## On the Internet...

On the Internet, you should assume that the list is being managed by
a person. In the absence of instructions to the contrary, to subscribe
to a list managed by a human being, send a short note to the
subscription-request address. (Once again, remember that the
subscription-request address is special and should not be used to post
messages.) Something like this will do:

Please add me to the S-F Lovers list. My address is
JOHNR@bigschool.edu. Thanks!

This message would be sent to **sf-lovers-request@rutgers.edu**.
Mailing lists are supposed to have a request address in the form

listname-request@host.site.domain. But, of course, not all list owners follow this format. Still, it's worth a try, since it will work most of the time.

Once you're part of the list, you would send postings to the address of the list itself, in this case, **sf-lovers@rutgers.edu**.

On Bitnet...

Bitnet mailing lists are usually managed by a machine. The main programs or *list managers* are LISTSERV, MAJORDOMO, and LISTPROC. Thus, to subscribe to the Fiction Writers Workshop, you might be told to send a message to the address **listserv@psuvm.psu.edu**.

Or you might need to send a message to an address in the form **majordomo@host.site** or **listproc@host.site**. You will want to verify the specific requirements for each list, but in general, all you have to do is include a line in the following format in your message to the automated list server: subscribe listname your_name.

In this case, *your_name* is your first name and last name, not your network e-mail address. Leave the subject line in your message blank, because it will be ignored anyway. (Don't forget to add ".bitnet" to a Bitnet address when you send mail to it.)

NET TIP

LISTSERV commands

Written by Eric Thomas in 1986, the LISTSERV program that in most cases automates the entire Bitnet mailing list process has been updated frequently and has grown to embrace many functions beyond the basic subscribe and unsubscribe.

You don't need to know even a small fraction of these commands, but a comprehensive list is readily available. They are summarized and presented in the LISTSERV REFCARD (reference card). If you want to get the command reference card for a given list server, simply send it a message containing the line get refcard. *The reference card contains all kinds of other possibilities as well, but you probably will*

*not need them. In any case, you will find a complete refcard on the
Glossbrenner's Choice disk called Mailing List Essentials.*

*As always when talking to a list server, leave your subject line blank.
The most useful commands are these:*

- *To subscribe to a list, you send a message to a list server
  containing the line* subscribe listname your_name.

- *To unsubscribe, the command to use is* unsubscribe listname
  your_name.

- *For a list of all of the available mailing lists, use the command* list
  global.

- *Perhaps the most powerful command of all is* list global/topic,
  where topic *is something you are interested in, like Early Music,
  SCUBA, Poetry, Plasma Physics, or whatever. So your command
  might be something like* list global/SCUBA.

*This is a really neat service, and you might try it right now by
addressing your message to* **listserv@bitnic.bitnet**. *You may be
startled at how fast Bitnic gets back to you!*

 # Conclusion

Newsgroups and mailing lists represent one of the fundamental
strengths of the Internet, and that's people. When you've got 30
million or more souls worldwide tapping into the Net, each with his
or her own interests and expertise, you have a resource of
unimaginable power. A resource that has never existed before in all of
human history. It's almost like a collective *consciousness*.

You won't want to miss out on newsgroups and mailing lists. But, as
I'm sure you are already aware, with literally thousands and thousands
of groups and lists to sample, you could easily end up "majoring in
the Internet" and flunking all of your courses. My advice is to set
aside some time to plunge in and just go wild! Don't just get your feet
wet—go for total immersion.

Later, you can pull back and focus on finding and using groups and lists
that can really help you with your studies. And you'll know which groups
to tap when the walls are closing in and you need a little fun. One way
or another, I'm sure you'll agree that newsgroups and mailing lists are
among the most incredible features on the entire Internet.

15
The Internet: Organized by subject

W HEN it comes to subject-specific information on the Internet, the good news and the bad news are the same: There is more of it on every subject imaginable than you will ever be able to find. Fortunately, longtime Internet users are well aware of this. That's why some of them have taken it upon themselves to produce lists and guides. It's also why, no matter where you land, you'll find many people who will voluntarily point you to other, related resources. One thing, in other words, almost always leads to another.

As you will quickly discover, you don't have to find everything on the Net related to your subject of interest. All you have to do is find what you need. What's required is a starting point. That's what you'll find in this chapter—a starting point. Lots of starting points in fact.

In this chapter, I'll introduce you to four truly excellent resources on the Internet:

➤ The Rice University Gopher (RiceInfo)

➤ The Clearinghouse for Subject-Oriented Internet Resource Guides

➤ The Gopher Jewels

➤ The Library of Congress MARVEL Gopher

The resources available through the Internet are so vast that any number of attempts have been made to get a handle on things. After all, information doesn't do anybody any good if no one can find it—or even knows it's there.

The best printed reference I have seen is *The Internet Yellow Pages* by Harley Hahn and Rick Stout (Osborne/McGraw-Hill). But for online access, the four features profiled here are hard to beat. I'll also tell you how to track down information on scholarly societies in your field of interest.

 # The RiceInfo Gopher

The folks at Houston's William Marsh Rice University have built a Gopher that is specifically designed to present Internet resources by *subject area*. They call it, naturally enough, the RiceInfo Gopher. To get to it, Gopher to **riceinfo.rice.edu** and choose "Information by Subject Area" from the menu. (The Web version can be found at **http://riceinfo.rice.edu/**.)

Selecting "Information by Subject Area" on the main RiceInfo Gopher menu leads to over 40 subject-specific submenus. The first six selections from the first menu page are shown here, but to save space, I have stripped out everything but the actual subject items for the succeeding entries. Just keep in mind that each subject item on the list will lead you to a submenu containing items and resources related to that subject.

```
Information by Subject Area (RiceInfo)

1.  About the RiceInfo collection of "Info. by Subject Area"    Text
2.  More about "Information by Subject Area"                     Menu
3.  Clearinghouse of Subject-Oriented Internet Resource Guides   Menu
4.  Search all of Gopherspace by title: Jughead (from WLU)       Search
5.  Search all of Gopherspace by title: Veronica                 Menu
6.  Search all of RiceInfo by title: Jughead                     Menu
```

Aerospace	Grants, Scholarships, & Funding
Agriculture & Forestry	History
Anthropology & Culture	Jobs & Employment
Architecture	Language & Linguistics
Arts	Library & Information Science
Astronomy & Astrophysics	Literature, Electronic Books, & Journals
Biology	Mathematics
Census	Medicine & Health

 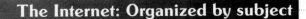

Chemistry	Military Science
Computer Networks/Internet Guides	Music
Computing	News & Journalism
Economics & Business	Oceanography
Education	Physics
Engineering	Reference
Environment & Ecology	Religion & Philosophy
Film & Television	Scholarly Societies (from U Waterloo)
Geography	Sociology & Psychology
Geology & Geophysics	Travel
Government, Political Science, & Law	Weather, Climate, & Meteorology

The Clearinghouse for Subject-Oriented Internet Resource Guides

The University of Michigan's University Library and the School of Information and Library Studies (SILS) have established a system for creating and distributing some truly incredible subject-oriented guides to Internet resources. The full title of this project is given in the headline above. Here I'll just call it the Clearinghouse.

At this writing, over 170 guides are available. More are sure to have been added by the time you read this. The guides are prepared by longtime Internauts and by SILS students working under a faculty advisor as part of the Internet Resource Discovery Project.

Although they vary in quality and comprehensiveness, most are on the order of 20 pages or more of single-spaced text. And they typically cover *everything*: Gophers, Telnet sites, World Wide Web home pages, files you can FTP, newsgroups, mailing lists, bulletin board systems—the works!

How to get to the Clearinghouse

There are lots of ways to get to the Clearinghouse at the University of Michigan. Perhaps the easiest is to simply pick the relevant item off your local Gopher. If your Gopher doesn't have such, use the RiceInfo Gopher (**riceinfo.rice.edu**). As you can see on the "Information by Subject Area (RiceInfo)" list presented earlier in this chapter, item 3

will take you to the Clearinghouse. You can also get there by FTP, Gopher, Telnet, and the World Wide Web:

➤ FTP to **una.hh.lib.umich.edu**; Path: /inetdirsstacks/. Then get the file called **.README-FOR-FTP**. Or simply use the DIR command. The filenames in this directory are self-explanatory.

➤ Gopher to **gopher.lib.umich.edu** and select "What's New and Featured Resources" and then "Clearinghouse…"

➤ Telnet to **una.hh.lib.umich.edu 70**.

➤ Use your Web browser to visit one of these sites. Note the tilde (~) before the letters *lou* in the second address:

http://www.lib.umich.edu/chhome.html

http://http2.sils.umich.edu/~lou/chhome.html

Figure 15-1 will give you an idea of what you can expect when you tap into the Clearinghouse via the Web.

Figure 15-1

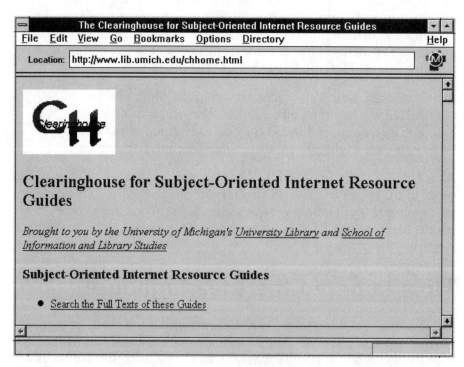

The Clearinghouse home page on the World Wide Web, where you'll find more than 170 detailed subject guides to the Internet.

 # Clearinghouse topics

In my opinion, the fastest, most satisfying way to use the
Clearinghouse is via Gopher. When you access it this way, you will get
a short opening menu that contains a selection for "Clearinghouse for
Subject-Oriented Internet Resource Guides." Choose it, and you will
see a submenu that looks like this:

```
Clearinghouse for Subject-Oriented Internet Resource Guides (UMich)


Page 1 of 1


1   About the Clearinghouse (UMich)                      Menu
2   Search full texts of these Guides                    Search
3   All Guides                                           Menu
4    Guides on the Humanities                            Menu
5    Guides on the Sciences                              Menu
6    Guides on the Social Sciences                       Menu
7   The Internet Resource Discovery Project (UMich)      Menu
8   Helpful Information on using the Internet            Menu
9   Clearinghouse Updates (last updated 01/11/95)  (UMich)  Text


Enter Item Number, SAVE, ?, or BACK: 3
```

Choose Item 3 from this menu to display a list of all the subject-
specific guides. Here's a sampling:

```
All Guides
Page 1 of 1


1    Search full texts of these guides                       Search
2    Academic Computing Training & User Support; M. Kovacs; v8; 0  Text
3    Adult/Distance Education; J. Ellsworth; 07/01/94            Text
4    Aerospace Engineering; C. Poterala, D. Dalquist; v2; 3/15/94  Text
5    Agriculture, Veterinary Science & Zoology; L. Haas; v8; 03/9  Text
6    Agriculture; W. Drew; v4.0; 08/08/94                        Text
7    Alternative Medicine; J. Makulowich; 07/29/94               Text
8    Anesthesia & Critical Care; A. Wright; v17; 12/26/94         Text
9    Animals; K. Boschert; v3.0; 06/01/94                         Text
10   Anthropology, Cross Cultural Studies, & Archaeology; G. Bell  Text
11   Aquatic Biology; B. Brown; v2; 07/04/94                      Text
12   Archaeology, Historic Preservation; P. Stott; v3.08; 01/07/9  Text
13   Architecture, Building; J. Brown; 01/95                      Text
14   Archives; D. Anthony, N. Kayne; v2; 05/27/94  (UMich)        Text
15   Art & Architecture; K. Robinson; v8; 03/94                   Text
(etc.)
```

The "All Guides" menu goes on to include a total of over 170 selections. Everything from Black/African Studies to Buddhism, Conservation, Film and Video, Journalism, Law, Medical Resources, Midwifery, Tibetan Studies, and West European History and Culture.

Remember, each of these guides consists of *lists* and *descriptions* of Internet subject-specific resources. You won't find information on, say, botany, here. But you *will* find a file that tells you were to look on the Net for information about botany and botanical subjects. Also, notice that the very first selection on the "All Guides" menu is "Search full texts of these guides." This can save you a lot of time because it helps you identify just those Clearinghouse documents that contain the keyword or phrase you specify.

A Clearinghouse example

As an experiment, I looked at quite a few of the Clearinghouse guides. One of the most impressive was Art "Rambo" McGee's guide to resources "related to Black/African people, culture, and issues." It's 24 single-spaced pages long, and among many other things, it includes:

➤ Phone numbers for over 125 BBSs specializing in Black/African issues, including suggestions on the files you should get when you log on.

➤ Voice phone numbers for nearly everyone who is anyone in African studies at colleges and universities. Classified by specialty: Diversity, Islamic Resources, International/Sustainable Development, Social/Progressive Activism, and so on.

➤ Internet e-mail addresses for same.

➤ Hundreds of Internet and Bitnet mailing lists and news services that deal with or focus on African, African-American, African-Caribbean, or African-Latin people, culture, and issues.

➤ Plus scores of newsgroups, including:

alt.current-events.somalia Discussion of the situation in Somalia

bit.tech.africana Technology in the Motherland

clari.news.group.blacks	News of interest to black people
rec.music.afro-latin	Music with Afro-latin, African influences
soc.culture.african.american	Discussions about Afro-American issues
za.ads.jobs	Looking for a job?/Offering a job?
alt.discrimination	Quotas, affirmative action, etc.
soc.couples.intercultural	Interracial Relationships
alt.activism.death-penalty	Capital Punishment & Executions
alt.motherjones	Mother Jones magazine

Not all Clearinghouse resources lists are as thorough and complete as this one. Some, I've found, don't go much further than offering a list of mailing lists. That's certainly helpful, but when you see a guide like Arthur McGee's, it makes you appreciate the kinds of things that can be done by someone who is truly dedicated to a particular topic and willing to invest the huge amount of time required to prepare a thorough resource list.

 # The Gopher Jewels!

The RiceInfo Gopher and the University of Michigan Clearinghouse are two of the most important subject-oriented services on the Net. But another one you should know about is a Gopher feature called *Gopher Jewels*. Created by the Gopher Jewels Project under the leadership of David Riggins, this feature celebrated its second birthday on June 1, 1995.

The basic concept is simple: Collect the Gopher menus from many leading Gopher sites. Then go through them all, classifying each menu item by subject. When you're done, rearrange all the items into a new, master menu in which everything is presented by *subject*.

You will find the general structure of the Gopher Jewels menu system below. But, as an example, if you were to pick the second main item, "Community, Global, and Environmental," you would be taken to a menu offering items like the "National Environmental Scorecard"; Global Warming; plus gateways to the EchoGopher and the GreenGopher at the University of Virginia, as well as the Great Lakes Information Network.

⇨ Contents of the Gopher Jewels

Like all Gophers, the Gopher Jewels menu is easy to use and incredibly seductive. If you have one tenth of an ounce of curiosity in your body, you will find yourself signing on to research one topic and end up an hour later with a stack of printouts that have nothing to do with your original quest. Which is not only just fine, it's wonderful!

Why? Because the information you collect by letting your curiosity run free may not help you finish that philosophy paper by tomorrow morning, but it will definitely expand your intellectual horizons. Everything—absolutely *everything*—you read or see is grist for the mill. It may be years before you use it, but the item you find via the Gopher Jewels today will have an effect, however tiny, on who you are and what you think. So, don't miss this one!

Here is the general layout of the Gopher Jewels menu system. Notice that everything is categorized by subject. (The slash at the end of some lines is the Gopher symbol meaning that particular item leads to another menu.)

```
                    CONTENTS OF GOPHER JEWELS
1. Gopher Jewels Information and Help/
   1. About Gopher Jewels.
   2. Gopher Help Documents/
   3. Gopher Jewels Announcement Archives/
   4. Gopher Jewels Discussion   Archives/
   5. Other Archives and Related Information/
2. Community, Global and Environmental/
   1. Country Specific Information/
   2. Environment/
   3. Free-Nets And Other Community Or State Gophers/
   4. Global or World-Wide Topics/
3. Education, Social Sciences, Arts & Humanities/
   1. Anthropology and Archaeology/
   2. Arts and Humanities/
```

```
      3. Education (Includes K-12)/
      4. Genealogy/
      5. Geography/
      6. History/
      7. Language/
      8. Religion and Philosophy/
      9. Social Science/
  4. Economics, Business and Store Fronts/
      1. Economics and Business/
      2. Products and Services - Store Fronts/
  5. Engineering and Industrial Applications/
      1. Architecture/
      2. Engineering Related/
      3. Manufacturing/
      4. Safety/
  6. Government/
      1. Federal Agency and Related Gopher Sites/
      2. Military/
      3. Political and Government/
      4. State Government/
  7. Health, Medical, and Disability/
      1. AIDS and HIV Information/
      2. Disability Information/
      3. Medical Related/
      4. Psychology/
  8. Internet and Computer Related Resources/
      1. A List Of Gophers With Subject Trees/
      2. Computer Related/
      3. Internet Cyberspace related/
      4. Internet Resources by Type (Gopher, Phone, USENET, WAIS, Other)/
      5. Internet Service Providers/
      6. List of Lists Resources/
  9. Law/
      1. Legal or Law related/
      2. Patents and Copyrights/
 10. Library, Reference, and News/
      1. Books, Journals, Magazines, Newsletters, and Publications/
      2. General Reference Resources/
      3. Journalism/
      4. Library Information and Catalogs/
      5. News Related Services/
      6. Radio and TV Broadcasting/
 11. Miscellaneous Items/
 12. Natural Sciences including Mathematics/
      1. Agriculture and Forestry/
      2. Astronomy and Astrophysics/
      3. Biological Sciences/
      4. Chemistry/
      5. Geology and Oceanography/
      6. Math Sciences/
      7. Meteorology/
      8. Physics/
```

 # How to get to the Gopher Jewels

To reach the "Mother Site" of the Gopher Jewels, Gopher to **cwis.usc.edu** and choose "Other Gophers and Information Resources" and then "Gopher Jewels."

Once you reach the Mother Site, you will be able to get information on *mirror sites*, locations that duplicate the Mother Site but may be located closer to your location. By opting to use them instead of "Mother," you will help reduce Net traffic.

On the World Wide Web, you can reach the Gopher Jewels at these locations:

➤ **http://galaxy.einet.net/gopher/gopher.html**

➤ **http://galaxy.einet.net/GJ/index.html**

➤ **gopher://cwis.usc.edu/11/Other_Gophers_and_ Information_Resources/Gophers_by_Subject/ Gopher_Jewels**

➤ **gopher://info.monash.edu.au/11/Other/sources/ Gopher_Jewels**

➤ **gopher://gopher.technion.ac.il/11/Other_gophers/ Gopher_Jewels**

NET TIP

Ask Dr. Math!

*If what you're looking for on the Internet is the answer to a vexing math question, a simple e-mail message to Dr. Math may be all it takes. Write to **dr.math@forum.swarthmore.edu**. All messages are answered by members of "The Swat Team" at Swarthmore College, who claim that "no problem is too big or too small."*

 # Library of Congress MARVEL Gopher

The United States Library of Congress has got to be one of the primary information sources in the entire world. And to its everlasting credit, in my experience over the past decade or so, it has vigorously pursued a goal of making its information and catalogues accessible by electronic means.

It thus comes as no surprise to find that the Library of Congress has a very strong and impressive presence on the Internet. But the key thing to remember is that the Library of Congress (LC) MARVEL Gopher is not limited to the books and other Library of Congress resources I told you about in Chapter 13. Far from it. The design philosophy of the LC MARVEL Gopher is to get you plugged into the Net *by subject*. So you will find that this Gopher may be but a starting point from which you will be taken to other Gophers and resources.

To get to the Library of Congress Gopher, check first for references to LC MARVEL on your local Gopher menu. If you don't find one, look for an entry like "All the Gophers in the World," or otherwise get into a position where you can specify a given Gopher address. When prompted, Gopher to **marvel.loc.gov**.

You will see a menu that looks like the one shown here. Choose "Global Electronic Library...," to display the subject-matter menu:

```
Library of Congress MARVEL Gopher
Page 1 of 1

1    About LC MARVEL                                Menu
2    Events, Facilities, Programs, and Services     Menu
3    Research and Reference (Public Services)       Menu
4    Libraries and Publishers (Technical Services)  Menu
5    Copyright                                      Menu
6    Library of Congress Online Systems             Menu
7    Employee Information                           Menu
8    U.S. Congress                                  Menu
9    Government Information                          Menu
10   Global Electronic Library (by Subject)         Menu
11   Internet Resources                             Menu
12   What's New on LC MARVEL                         Menu
13   Search LC MARVEL Menus                         Menu

Enter Item Number, SAVE, ?, or BACK: 10
```

```
Global Electronic Library (by Subject)
Page 1 of 1

 1   About this menu                        Text
 2   Reference                              Menu
 3   Library Science                        Menu
 4   Philosophy and Religion                Menu
 5   Language, Linguistics, and Literature  Menu
 6   The Arts                               Menu
 7   Social Sciences                        Menu
 8   Law                                    Menu
 9   Economics and Business                 Menu
10   History and Geography                  Menu
11   Medicine and Psychology                Menu
12   Natural Science                        Menu
13   Mathematics                            Menu
14   Applied Science and Technology         Menu
15   Sports and Recreation                  Menu

Enter Item Number, SAVE, ?, or BACK:
```

The menus and submenus offered by the LC MARVEL Gopher will keep an information junkie busy (and supremely content) for days and days. You owe it to yourself to spend an evening exploring this resource—just to bring yourself up to speed on what's out there.

 # Scholarly Societies

The library at Canada's University of Waterloo has created a Gopher that provides links to Gophers and other servers of scholarly societies—societies like the American Philosophical Association, the Association for Computing Machinery (ACM), and Institute for Electrical and Electronics Engineers (IEEE).

Societies here isn't as stuffy as it sounds. The library uses the word to mean organizations in which membership is "determined by scholarly credentials, not by the existence of a contract of employment or of visitation rights, as in the case of a research centre." A society will typically have a word like *Society*, *Association*, *Union*, or *Institute* in its name.

You can use this feature via the World Wide Web. Simply load your Web browser and point it at **http://www.lib.uwaterloo.ca/**

society/overview.html. You will find the site interesting, to be sure, but you will probably find the Gopher implementation to be more useful.

 ## Waterloo via Gopher

To get to this feature via Gopher, specify the Gopher address **watserv2.uwaterloo.ca**. Then choose "Electronic Resources Around the World," then "Campus and other information systems (CWIS, gophers, BBS)," and then "Gophers of Scholarly Societies."

NET TIP

Other subject guides on the Web

The subject guides I've told you about in this chapter are just a few of the many attempts to bring some order to the vast amounts of information on the Internet. Here are several others you might want to explore with your Web browser. Find the one you like best and use it as your starting point when you need to find some specific piece of information.

- *Yahoo—A Guide to WWW*

  http://www.yahoo.com/
- *Virtual Library*

  http://www.w3.org/hypertext/DataSources/bySubject/Overview.html
- *ElNet Galaxy*

  http://www.einet.net/galaxy.html
- *PLANET Earth Home Page*

  http://white.nosc.mil/info.html
- *Special Internet Connections (Yanoff List)*

  http://www.uwm.edu/Mirror/inet.services.html
- *Internet Resources Meta-Index*

  http://www.ncsa.uiuc.edu/SDG/Software/Mosaic/MetaIndex.html

 # Conclusion

Take some time to simply explore the resources and sites I've highlighted in this chapter. They are truly among the best that the Internet has to offer—and I feel very strongly that it's important to identify the best. For the Internet is a vast, rolling tide, under which you can easily drown. I want to keep you afloat, of course. But I also want to help you bend the tides of information to your will. I hope this chapter has succeeded in doing that.

16
Foreign language practice

THE worldwide scope of the Internet is one of its most impressive and important features. It makes global e-mail nearly instantaneous and very, very cheap. And, regardless of where you live, it makes it easy to exchange views and to learn about people and issues in hundreds of locations.

But it also makes it possible for any student to practice foreign language skills, regardless of what that language may be. For our purposes here, we'll assume that *foreign* means all non-English languages, though, of course, English is "foreign" to the vast majority of the world.

 ## Real-time chat

Though it is only one of many foreign language-related resources, Internet Relay Chat (IRC) is an obvious place to begin. You'll find the key commands summarized in Chapter 12 of this book. When I checked into IRC recently, there were well-attended groups called #COLOMBIA, #CHINESE, #TAIWAN, and #JAPAN, among many others. And here is a quick sample from the #ESPANOL group:

```
(drago) Bajenle a sus HORMANES
(drago) HORMONES
(ATREVIDA) Aqui no pasa nada
(HOOK) CUALQUIER GENTE ENTRANDO HOOOOOOLLAAAAAAAAA!!!
(cisne) ikaro : siiiii chilena!!
```

```
(FanSchop) atrevida y que quieres accion ????
(GITANO) ASI SON POR ACA,MODESTAMENTE
(CLARK) QUIEN FUE EL ATREVIDO QUE DIJO QUE SOY MALO PARA LA PELOTA ????!
(v083py7k) Salut Ciao Hola Key Si Hey Tung Tin Marhaba Hola ciao
(tractor) bien atrevida....
(abel) hola
```

 # Taking pot luck

If I could read and write Spanish or some other language, I might
have a different opinion. But after spending some time in the
#ESPANOL and several other groups, I got the impression that not a
lot of real conversation goes on. It seemed to me that most
participants spent most of their time changing their handles, or
leaving and then rejoining the groups. In a word, English speakers
appear to have no monopoly on inane IRC and chat conversations.

On the other hand, with literally hundreds of IRC channels to choose
from, it is entirely possible that the members of some other Spanish
language channel were engaged in a deep discussion of Cervantes
and the true symbolism of the windmill. Or, if such a group did not
exist while I was online, it could have come into existence the
moment I signed off. One way or the other, I wouldn't know about it.

So you really do take pot luck. My advice is to open your comm
program's capture buffer (if you are not at a university computer
center terminal) and key in /list -min 10 to generate a list of channels
with 10 people or more. Then look at this list for likely places to
practice a given language. If you keep at it, you will undoubtedly
discover that there are really good foreign language IRC groups that
meet on a regular basis.

 # Wiretap language resources

As I've noted elsewhere in this book, the Wiretap Online Library is
one of the most interesting and intriguing of all Internet locations.
You can get there by Gophering to **wiretap.spies.com** and choosing
"Wiretap Online Library," then "Articles," and then "Language." But
you can also FTP to **ftp.spies.com**. Or visit Wiretap on the World
Wide Web at **http://www.spies.com**.

When you Gopher to Wiretap, you will see a menu like this:

```
Language
Page 1 of 1

1    College Slang Dictionary                    Text
2    Esperanto English Dictionary                Text
3    Glossary of Computer Terms in Vietnamese    Text
4    List of Hindu Names                         Text
5    Meihem in Ce Klasrum: GB Shaw's proposals   Text
6    Mnemonics                                   Text
7    Official English: A No Vote                 Text
8    Palindromes                                 Text
9    Qalam Arabic Transliteration                Text
10   Quick & Dirty Guide to Japanese Grammar     Text
11   Resources for Adult Learners of Welsh       Text
12   Small Urdu Dictionary                       Text
13   Spoonerisms and Malapropisms                Text
14   Study Guide to Wheelock Latin               Text
15   Taeis Languages (frp)                       Text
16   Top 100 Words used on Usenet                Text

Enter Item Number, SAVE, ?, or BACK:
```

It's eclectic. It's wild. It's fascinating. My knowledge of Japanese, for example, is limited to what I learned from the novel *Shogun*. But I found Tad Perry's "Quick and Dirty Guide to Japanese" so interesting that I'm convinced I could learn that language if only I had the right *sensei*!

 # Check the Clearinghouse

You will also want to check the University of Michigan Clearinghouse described in Chapter 15. The file to get is **acadlist.lang**. Prepared by Diane K. Kovacs and the Directory Team at Kent State University Libraries, this is a 23-page, single-spaced list of the Internet resources—mostly mailing lists—that are devoted to some aspect of language, foreign and otherwise.

Here's a brief excerpt from the Kovacs file. As you would expect, you'll find mailing lists and other Internet resources devoted to French, Greek, and Latin. But you might be surprised to see from these examples that there are also entries dealing with Gaelic, Iroquois, and Klingon (identified as "quite an active mailing list").

Again, keep in mind that the excerpts shown here represent only a small fraction of what you'll find in the complete file:

```
Discussion Name: CAUSERIE
Topic Information: "Causerie" means talk or chat.
That is what this list is all about.  Just for the fun
of it.  Everyone is welcome though you should be aware
of the fact that all the communication is in FRENCH.
Subscription Information: listserv@UQUEBEC.CA
Edited? No
Contact Address: Pierre Chenard
UQPSGEN@UQSS.UQUEBEC.CA - Pierre J.  Hamel
HAMEL@INRS-URB.UQUEBEC.CA
Submission Address: CAUSERIE@UQUEBEC.CA
Keywords: French Language
VR: 9th Revision 1/1/95

Discussion Name: CLASSICS
Topic Information: Classics and Latin discussion group.
Subscription Information: listproc@u.washington.edu
Edited? No
Archives: Yes
Contact Address: Linda Wright LWRIGHT@u.washington.edu
Submission Address: CLASSICS@u.washington.edu
Keywords: Greek Language (Classical) - Latin Language
VR: 9th Revision 1/1/95

Discussion Name: FRENCHTALK
Topic Information: French (FRENCHTALK) is not
restricted to linguistics; also for learners;
contributions in French preferred
Subscription Information: listproc@yukon.cren.org
Edited?
Archives:
Contact Address: Mike Krus frenchtalk-owner@yukon.cren.org
Submission Address: Keywords: French Language
VR: 9th Revision 1/1/95

Discussion Name: GAELIC-L
Topic Information: GAELIC-L is a multi-disciplinary
discussion list set up to facilitate the exchange of
news, views and information between speakers of
Scottish Gaelic, Irish and Manx.  It also provides
online tuition for people learning to speak Gaelic.
Subscription Information: listserv@irlearn.ucd.ie
Edited? Yes
Archives: Yes
Contact Address: Marion Gunn MGUNN@irlearn.ucd.ie -
Caoimhi/n P.  O/ Donnai/le caoimhin@smo.ac.uk - Craig
Cockburn craig@scot.demon.ac.uk
Submission Address: GAELIC-L@irlearn.ucd.ie
Keywords: Scottish Gaelic - Manx Gaelic - Irish Gaelic
VR: 9th Revision 1/1/95
```

```
Discussion Name: HELLAS
Topic Information: The goal of this e-conference is to
offer to all Greeks on Bitnet a way to Communicate.
The language, preferably, used in this e-conference is
Greek (with latin characters, 'Vlachofragika').
Subscription Information: listserv@uga.cc.uga.edu
Edited? Yes
Archives: Private
Contact Address: Spyros Liolis sliolis@utcvm.utc.edu -
Spyros Antoniou sda106@psuvm.psu.edu - Nikos George
george@pop.psu.edu - Nikos George nxg6@psuvm.psu.edu
Submission Address: HELLAS@american.edu
Keywords: Greek Language (Modern)
VR: 9th Revision 1/1/95

Discussion Name: IROQUOIS
TI Iroquois Language Discussion
Subscription Information: listserv@VM.UTCC.UTORONTO.CA
Edited? No
Archives: Yes
Contact Address: Carrie Dyck cdyck@epas.utoronto.ca
Submission Address: IROQUOIS@VM.UTCC.UTORONTO.CA
Keywords: Iroquois Language
VR: 9th Revision 1/1/95

Discussion Name: KLINGON
Topic Information: Klingon; not restricted to
linguistics; also for learners; contributions in the
Klingon language encouraged; this is quite an active listSubscription
Information: tlhIngan-Hol-request@village.boston.ma.us
Edited?
Archives:
Contact Address: tlhIngan-Hol@village.boston.ma.us
Submission Address: Keywords: Klingon Language
VR: 9th Revision 1/1/95
```

Other options & possibilities

Things are always changing and growing on the Net, so you will
definitely want to check the latest lists of newsgroups and mailing lists
for your languages of choice. Or try doing a Veronica or World Wide
Web search and see what you come up with. Here are a few specific
examples you might want to look into:

> ➤ Dictionary word lists. You'll find word lists on the Internet for
>   Dutch, German, Italian, Norwegian, Swedish, Finnish,
>   Japanese, and Polish—to name just a few. They can be a big
>   help when your English/Finnish (and vice versa) dictionary is in
>   the next room! FTP to **black.ox.ac.uk**, Path: /wordlists/.

Also try FTPing to **ftp.uu.net**; Path: /doc/dictionaries/DEC-collection/.

➤ Esperanto. For an Esperanto dictionary, check the aforementioned Wiretap Gopher (**wiretap.spies.com**). Or use your FTP skills to get a copy of said dictionary from **ftp.spies.com**, Path: /Library/Article/Language/esperant.eng.

➤ French practice. If French is of interest, you won't want to miss the newsgroup **k12.lang.francais**, a group specifically designed to encourage French practice with native speakers.

You can also get daily news briefings in French from the Yale University Gopher. Gopher to **yaleinfo.yale.edu** and select "The Internet," then "News and weather," then "France." Or you might try the Michigan State University Gopher. Gopher to **gopher.msu.edu** and choose "News & Weather," then "Electronic Newspapers," then "French Language Press Review."

➤ German, Japanese, Spanish, and Russian. If you have an interest in any of these languages, be sure to check out the corresponding newsgroup, listed below:

k12.lang.deutsch-eng	Bilingual German/English practice with native speakers.
sci.lang.japan	Japanese language, both spoken and written.
k12.lang.esp-eng	Bilingual Spanish/English practice with native speakers.
k12.lang.russian	Bilingual Russian/English practice with native speakers.

➤ Latin study guides. Latin is the one language I studied in high school and college. I will never forget hearing my professor read Catullus the way his contemporaries would have heard it. So help me, it sounded like French! In any event, I can't say that I ever heard of the book *Wheelock's Latin*. But apparently it's now the most widely used introductory text at colleges and universities—and a study guide for it is available at Wiretap. You'll find it on the Wiretap Gopher (**wiretap.spies.com**), or you can FTP to **ftp.spies.com**, Path: /Library/Article/Language/latin.stu.

17
Reference
works online

A tremendous amount of reference material is available—for free—via the Internet. However, while it's important to be aware of this fact, you may often find that it's a lot quicker to use non-Net sources like books and CD-ROMs. After all, when you want some fact, figure, or phone number, it's almost always faster and easier to pull a book off the shelf or pick up the telephone than it is to trundle down to the campus computer center or fire up your dorm room machine and go online to get access to some reference work.

As I'll show you in the next chapter, there is also an alternative that combines the convenience of a book with the speed of a computer. Many public domain reference works are available as disk files thanks to Project Gutenberg and similar efforts. You want to use Roget's Thesaurus? Download a copy of the whole thing, and search it any time you like on your hard drive—using your word processor or a program like Vernon Buerg's LIST. It's infinitely faster than going online to do the same thing.

In this chapter, I'm going to show you how to tap into some quick-reference sources—namely the Gopher Jewels and the RiceInfo Gopher. But you should keep in mind that the items you find there—like, for instance, *The CIA World Factbook*—are available from numerous other sites and sources as well. They may even be on your own campus Gopher. If you want a list of possible sites, use Veronica to do a search of Gopherspace.

 # General reference sources via Gopher

I don't know about you, but I make a distinction between *reference* and *research*. Research, to me, is a relatively involved process of exploring many different sources to develop a whole picture of a subject or question. Reference is a quick hit. Who did what to whom, where, when, and how? What's the number? What's the code? What's the time in Pago-Pago right now?

If your concept of reference tallies with mine, then you won't want to miss the "General Reference Resources" menu on the Gopher Jewels. As I explained in Chapter 15, you may very well find the Gopher Jewels on your local Gopher. If not, you can Gopher to **cwis.usc.edu**. Choose "Other Gophers and Information Resources," and then "Gopher Jewels."

From the Gopher Jewels menu, choose "Library, Reference, and News," and then choose "General Reference Resources." That will lead you to a series of menus with items like these:

```
Airlines Tollfree Phone Numbers
Airport Codes American English
Dictionary Daily Almanac (from UChicago)
Imperial College, Dictionary of Computing
Internet Glossaries and Definitions
Local Times Around the World
On-line Calendar for month/year
Roget's Thesaurus (1911 edition)
Telephone Area Codes: US and Canada
U.S. Zip Code Directory
Unit Conversion Table
Webster's Dictionary
World Phone Books
```

And that's just the beginning. The message is that, however you gain access, the Gopher Jewels feature is a prime source of ready reference information, and much else besides.

 # The RiceInfo Gopher, again

In Chapter 15, you learned about the fantastic Rice University RiceInfo Gopher. Well, it's back! Gopher to **riceinfo.rice.edu** to get started. Or visit the RiceInfo site on the World Wide Web at **http://riceinfo.rice.edu/**.

Choose "Information by Subject Area." Then look for a menu item called "Reference." That will take you to a submenu that looks like this:

```
Acronyms (from UK) American
English Dictionary (NIH)
CIA World Fact Book
Periodic Table of Elements
Phone Books
The Free On-line Dictionary of Computing - About
The Free On-line Dictionary of Computing - Search
U.S. Congressional directory
U.S. Geographic Names Database
U.S. Zip Code Directory
US State Department Travel Advisories
Weights & Measures
```

NET TIP

Don't forget mnemonics!

The secret to remembering things is to associate them—in some absurd (and memorable) way—with something familiar. Thus, scholars in the Middle Ages could memorize lists of over 1,000 things by mentally walking their way through a well-known cathedral. They would form mental pictures along the way consisting of the thing they knew—like the Lady Chapel—and associate it with what they wanted to remember—like one of the Seven Virtues.

*If you gopher to **wiretap.spies.com** and choose "Wiretap Online Library," "Articles," and then "Language," you will find an item devoted to mnemonics. Really neat ways to memorize things like taxonomic classifications or resistor color codes.*

Think I'm joking? Okay, how about these three ways to remember Kingdom Phylum Class Order Family Genus Species?

- *King Phillip came over for good soup.*
- *King Phillip come out for god sake.*
- *King Phillip calmly ordered five greasy steaks.*

Or this for remembering the geological ages (Cambrian Ordovician Sirillian Devonian Carboniferous Permian Triassic Jurassic Cretatious Paleocene Eocene Oligocene Myocene Pileocene Pleistocene Recent)?

Camels often sit down carefully. Perhaps their joints creak. Possibly early oiling might prevent premature rheumatism.

Mnemonics rule!

 # Government information on the Net

In the spirit of Thomas Jefferson, the United States Congress offers a service called Thomas: Legislative Information on the Internet. Thomas offers the full text of House and Senate bills, searchable by keyword or by bill number. You'll also find information on how our laws are made; directory information for House of Representatives members and committees; the yearly calendar; daily committee hearing schedules; the current week's House floor schedule; and more.

To access the Thomas home page, shown in Fig. 17-1, point your Web browser at **http://thomas.loc.gov**.

Not to be outdone by Congress, the Executive Branch also has a presence on the World Wide Web. You'll find the Whitehouse home page, shown in Fig. 17-2, at **http://www.whitehouse.gov**.

 # Offline CD-ROM reference

I'm a real fan of the concept of "appropriate technology." Which means, first, that just because something *can* be done doesn't *ipso facto* mean that it *should* be done. And second, that a technology that's dynamite in one area may very well prove totally useless in another.

Electronic reference is an excellent example. By all means, take a crack at the Internet reference resources discussed in this chapter. I would not have included them if I didn't think they were of value. But if you *really* want to use your computer to speed up routine reference

Figure 17-1

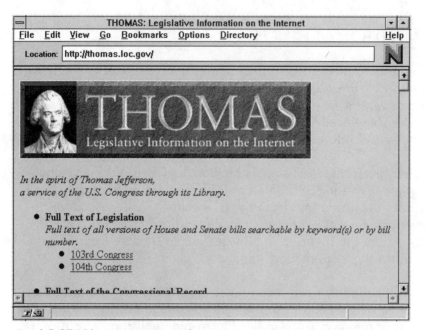

As if C-SPAN were not enough, you can now monitor your representatives to Congress via Thomas on the World Wide Web.

Figure 17-2

The Whitehouse home page on the World Wide Web

chores, make sure you've got a large, fast hard drive and a double-speed CD-ROM drive.

Use the hard drive to hold the full-text reference works you'll learn how to FTP in Chapter 18. With a dictionary or thesaurus on your hard drive, it's easy to search the whole thing for what you want. Use your double-speed CD-ROM drive to read and search CD-ROM archives and reference works.

Grolier Electronic Publishing's Multimedia CD-ROM Encyclopedia, for example, lists for $395. (Mail-order prices are considerably less.) It includes the entire text from the 21-volume *Grolier Academic American Encyclopedia*, with indexed information on 33,000 subjects. Not to mention the images, audio tracks—I particularly like the bird songs—animations, and video clips.

You will definitely need a computer that meets the Multimedia PC specification, version 2, to take full advantage of this product. But it truly is impressive. Call Grolier Electronic Publishing at 800-356-5590 for more information.

You may also want to consider the Microsoft Bookshelf. With a list price of $99, this product includes a collection of reference volumes ranging from the *Columbia Dictionary of Questions* to the *American Heritage Dictionary of the American Language* (which, if you have a sound card, pronounces more than 80,000 of its 350,000 words!) to *The Hammond World Atlas*, and lots more. For details, call Microsoft at 800-426-9400 or 206-939-8661.

18
Words & music

ONE of the most exciting things the Internet offers is instant access to a huge number of classic books. I'm not talking about some library card catalogue listing. I'm talking about the real thing—the full text of *Huckleberry Finn*, instantly whisked into your computer as a single file! And, while the music side of things is not quite as well developed, features to let you download sheet music as a series of graphic images are under construction. Meantime, scores are available in early music notation and as guitar tablatures. And there are tons of lyrics for songs, both popular and obscure.

Full text from Project Gutenberg

Project Gutenberg was started in 1971 by Michael Hart at the Materials Research Lab at the University of Illinois. Mr. Hart began by typing in the *Declaration of Independence*. He then tried to mail a copy to everyone on the Net. The Internet was much smaller then—in fact, it wasn't even called the Internet—but the mass mailing jammed the system.

That experience led directly to the development of Project Gutenberg, a project that enlists the aid of volunteers to key in the text of public domain works, which are then made available in central repositories around the Net. Hundreds of titles are already available, with thousands more planned by the year 2001.

Here's a quick sampling of titles to give you an idea of the kinds of things that are available from Project Gutenberg. Most are available in both plain text and compressed (zipped) format. Project

Gutenberg classifies items by the year each was added to the collection. The following list was compiled from several different years (and thus different "etext" directories):

Aesop's Fables
Alice in Wonderland, by Lewis Carroll
Amendments to the Constitution of the United States
Annapolis Convention, 1786
Articles of Confederation
Bill of Rights, 1791
Book of Mormon
CIA World Factbook
Charlotte Town Resolves, 1775
Civil Disobedience, by Thoreau
Constitution of United States of America
Constitution of Iroquois Nations
Declaration of Independence, 1776
Declaration of Rights of Man and of Citizen, 1789
Declaration and Resolves, First Continental Congress, 1777
Declaration and Resolves, First Continental Congress, 1775
Declaration of Independence
Descartes' A Discourse on Method
Emancipation Proclamation, 1862
Far From the Madding Crowd, by Thomas Hardy
Federalist Papers
First Thanksgiving Proclamation—June 20, 1676
Frankenstein by Mary Shelley
Huckleberry Finn by Twain/Clemens
Kennedy's Inaugural Address
King James Bible
Lincoln's Gettysburg Address
Mayflower Compact
Northwest Ordinance, 1787
O Pioneers!, by Willa Cather
Paradise Lost (Raben), by John Milton
Paris Peace Treaty, 1783
Red Badge of Courage by Stephen Crane
Roget's Thesaurus
Scarlet Letter, by Nathaniel Hawthorne
Song of Hiawatha, by Henry W. Longfellow
Sophocles' Oedipus Trilogy

Through the Looking Glass, by Lewis Carroll
Tom Sawyer, by Twain/Clemens
Washington's Farewell Address, 1796

To tap into Project Gutenberg, FTP to **mrcnext.cso.uiuc.edu** and look in the directories called /pub/etext/etext90/, /etext/etext91/, and so forth. Or Gopher to **gopher.tc.umn.edu** and choose "Libraries" and then "Electronic Books." At the Gopher site, you can do a keyword search for a particular author or title.

NET TIP

Project Gutenberg on CD-ROM

If you're seriously interested in the full-text files Project Gutenberg has to offer, you might want to consider getting the Project Gutenberg CD-ROM from Walnut Creek. It's updated twice a year, and an automatic updating subscription is available. The cost is $39.95, plus $5 shipping per order. California residents, add 8.25 percent sales tax.

You can order from Walnut Creek by calling 800-786-9907. Or send an e-mail message to **orders@cdrom.com**. *Or visit their Web site at* **http://www.cdrom.com**.

 # OBI: The Online Book Initiative

Full-text books and other documents are also available via the Online Book Initiative (OBI). In fact, if you'd like to help them expand their collection, they would love to hear from you. Just send electronic mail to **obi@world.std.com**. Or call them at Software Tool & Die, 617-739-0202. Or drop by their office if you're in the area: 1330 Beacon Street, Brookline, MA 02146.

But first, you'll want to explore their collection. OBI offers its wares via Gopher, so it is very, very easy to use. To tap in, Gopher to **world.std.com** and select "OBI The Online Book Initiative." You will see a menu like this:

```
Online Book Initiative at World.std.com
Page 1 of 1
```

```
1    About The Online Book Initiative    Text
2    The OBI FAQ                         Text
3    About The OBI Mailing Lists         Text
4    The Online Books                    Menu
Enter Item Number, SAVE, ?, or BACK:
```

Unlike Project Gutenberg, which categorizes items by the year they were added to the collection, the Online Book Initiative uses a Gopher menu on which each *author* (or sometimes, *general subject*) is a selection. When you select a given author, you are taken to a menu listing all of his or her works that are available to you for viewing or downloading.

When I selected item 4, "The Online Books," from the OBI Gopher recently, there were some 12 menus containing about 20 authors' names each. (There is even an entry to give you menu access to Project Gutenberg files.) Among the authors and subjects you will find on these menus are these:

A.E.Housman	Mark Twain
Algernon Charles Swinburne	Martin Luther King
Ambrose Bierce	Mary W.Shelley
Andrew Marvell	Melville
Anglo-Saxon	Nathaniel Hawthorne
Arthur Conan Doyle	Nerd Humor
Booker T.Washington	NetWeaver
Bram Stoker	Oscar Wilde
Charles Dickens	Percy Bysshe Shelley
Charles Hedrick	Plato
Charles Darwin	Recipes
Christopher Morley	Religion
David Hume	Robert Herrick
Edgar Allan Poe	Roget
Edgar Rice Burroughs	Rudyard Kipling
Emily Bronte	Samuel Clemens
Ezra Pound	Shakespeare
Fairy Tales	Sinclair Lewis
Founding Fathers	Soviet Archives
Francis Bacon	Standards
Geoffrey Chaucer	Star Trek Parodies
Gutenberg	Star Trek Stories
H.H.Munro	Tennyson

Henry David Thoreau
Hippocrates
Horatio.Alger.Jr
Hugo Awards
JFK
Jane Austen
Japanese
John Milton
John Donne
John Greenleaf Whittier
John Henry Newman
John Keats
John Stuart Mill
Joseph Conrad
Katherine Mansfield

Thomas More
Thomas Paine
Tommaso Campanella
U. S. Congress
United Nations
Unix
Vatican
Virgil
Walt Whitman
Walter Scott
William Blake
William Butler Yeats
William James
William Wordsworth
Winston Churchill

NET TIP

What's the use of full text?

Despite the Sony Data DiscMan and similar products, I doubt that people will ever read books on a computer screen. They will read something, to be sure, but that something is much more likely to be a multimedia document of some sort. So what's the use of being able to obtain, say, the full text of Milton's Paradise Lost *or the novels of Jane Austen?*

Probably you would not want to read these works on your desktop or notebook computer. But, as you know, works of fiction are not indexed. The only way to find a phrase, a scene, or a word in fiction is to page through the printed book. Put that same book on your computer, however, and you can instantly locate anything within its "pages."

That's great for research. And it sure makes it easy to incorporate quotations and extracts in your term papers and other projects. In fact, since most people have only recently become aware of the availability of electronic texts, the discoveries they make possible may just be starting.

There is also the fact that with a little bit of massaging, you can produce your own laser-printed editions of these public domain works. Paperback books are so cheap that there is probably not much money to be saved doing this. But imagine how tickled your younger sister would be to get Janie in Wonderland, *courtesy of Lewis Carroll, a little search-and-replace word processing magic, and the Online Book Initiative.*

Music, music, everywhere

There is, indeed, music everywhere on the Internet, but it's not the conceptual equivalent of the full-texts offered by Gutenberg and OBI. You'll find directories of sheet music, for example, but you can't yet download the full-text of sheet music that you could print out to play a song. (Moves are being made in that direction, but the time is not yet.)

Instead, there are newsgroups and mailing lists devoted to every aspect of every kind of music, its composition, and recording. Not to mention fan club-style discussions of leading popular performers, past and present.

There are also files containing the lyrics to songs from the present, the recent past, and the distant past. And there are *discographies* to give you bibliographical information on records and CDs, when they were published and by whom, the songs they contain, and so on.

Start with the University of Michigan Clearinghouse

When you are interested in exploring Net resources on any topic, it is really not a bad idea to get into the habit of making the University of Michigan's Clearinghouse your first stop. You'll want to see Chapter 15 for details on how to tap in and what you can expect to find. (You can start by FTPing to **una.hh.lib.umich.edu**, Path: /inetdirsstacks/.) There are two music resource files to get via FTP: **acadlist.music** (Music) and **music:rlmvcole** (Popular Music).

The first was compiled by Kara Robinson under the direction of Diane K. Kovacs and the Directory Team at Kent State University Libraries. Here are just a few of the dozens of topics on the list:

➤ Recordings of the pre-LP era

➤ Association for Chinese Music Research Discussion

➤ Any topic related to bagpipes

➤ Discussion about barbershop harmony, quartets, and choruses

➤ Discussion of issues related to International Bluegrass Music

➤ Discussion of blues music and its performers

➤ Forum for people interested in brass musical performance

➤ Medieval, Renaissance, and Baroque music

The second list, **music:rlmvcole**, is the Internet Guide to Popular Music, prepared by Rolaant McKenzie and Vicki Coleman. It covers not only mailing lists, but also newsgroups, FTP sites, general resources, an index by music category, CD purchasing, and much more. Blue Oyster Cult, Bowie, Mariah Carey, Miles Davis, the Grateful Dead—the McKenzie/Cole list, as its title implies, covers these and many other artists in depth.

I followed their instructions to tap the Jethro Tull archive at **remus.rutgers.edu**. And I found not only the file JT.GIF shown in Fig. 18-1, but also the guitar tabs for the song shown in Fig. 18-2.

Figure 18-1

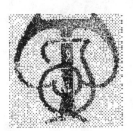

Aqualung, my friend . . .
Here's the Jethro Tull "JT"
logo from
remus.rutgers.edu.

Figure 18-2

```
AQUALUNG
heavy metal intro:

    888844                                4.8 2  P  8   4       2
e:!--------------!--------------------------!-4-4-4-!-----6---6-------6---
h:!--------------!--------------------------!-6-6-6-!-----8---8-------8---
g:!--------------!--------------------------!-6-6-6-!-----8---8-------8---
D:!--------------!--------------------------!-6-6-6-!-----8---8-------8---
A:!-5---1-3-4-3-!-5---------1--3-4----3-----!-4-4--6-!-----6---6-------6---
E:!---3---------!-----3-------------------!------------!

              Sit-ting on a park bench        eye-ing lit-tle girls
              snot is  runnig down his nose   greasy fingers smearing
              Drying in the cold sun          watching as the frilly
              Feeling like a dead duck        spitting out pieces of

        4.  8  4   8 8     88 4 2  88888  4   8 842
e:!------!-8---8--8--6--8-!-6-8---9--9-!-6-6-6-6-9---9-!-9--7-7-5-!---------
h:!------!-10---10-10--8--10!--8-10-11-9-!-8-8-8-8-9--11!-11-9-7-7-!---------
g:!------!-10---10-10--8--10!--8-10-11-10!-8-8-8-8-10-11!-11-9-8-7-!---------
D:!------!-10---10-10--8--10!--8-10-11-11!-8-8-8-8-11-11!-11-9-9-7-!---------
A:!------!-8---8--8--6--8-!-6-8--9--11!-6-6-6-6-11-9-!-9--7-9-5-!---------
E:!------!-----------------!---------9-!---------9----!----7---!---------
```

Guitar tabs for Aqualung. If you have a guitar and know how to read tablatures, with practice, you can sound like Ian Anderson, a.k.a. Jethro Tull. What you see here is only the first part of the file.

➯ RiceInfo, lyrics, & Wiretap!

In Chapter 15, you learned about the marvelous resources offered by the Rice University Gopher. Well, when it comes to music, it won't let you down. Your next step should be to Gopher to **riceinfo.rice.edu** and select "Information by Subject Area." Look for "Music" on the resulting menu.

That selection will take you to the first of five (!) Gopher menus, every item of which is concerned with music. It amounts to over 75 selections in all—and most of them are *menus* leading to yet more resources. Sample menu items include:

➤ AM/FM (British Radio)

➤ Acoustic Guitar Digest

➤ Adam Curry's Music Server

➤ Barbershop Quartet Gopher

➤ Baroque

➤ Beethoven Bibliography Database at San Jose State University

➤ Book of Metal (from UMN)

➤ Doing Research in Music (from U.Waterloo)

➤ Early Music: Archives of EARLYM-L & rec.music.early

➤ Folk music info (from nysernet.org)

➤ Guide to Buying Classical Recordings

➤ Guitar FTP archives from ftp.nevada.edu

➤ Listservs in Music

➤ Lyrics Search (from SFSU)

➤ Madonna's Revenge

➤ Making Sense of Seattle

➤ Music Gems

➤ Music Jokes

> Music Research Digest

> Music software (DOS)

> Musical FTP Sites

> Recommended CD Recordings of Early Chamber Music

> Rock and Roll Confidential

> Smashing Pumpkins Newsletter

> SoundBlaster Digest

NET TIP

Lyrics online

It's also possible to find copious files of song lyrics on the Internet. Start by FTPing to **ftp.sunet.se** *or* **ftp.uwp.edu**, *Path: /pub/music/lyrics/. When you key in* dir, *you will see a directory that includes a file called* **Index.songs.gz**. *Key in* binary; *then key in* get "Index.songs.gz".

At that point you may want to logoff and decompress the file using the instructions provided in Chapter 7 of this book. You can then sign back on again and, using the directory you will now possess, go directly to the correct directory, each of which, as you will see, is lettered A to Z. There simply isn't space to convey a sense of the sheer vastness of the lyrics files you will find here. All I can say is, explore and have a ball. Or a waltz. Or a hootenanny. Whatever!

If you have a Web browser, you might also try **http://vivarin.pc.cc.cmu.edu/lyrics.html**.

 # Wiretap for discographies

The Wiretap Gopher is the place to look for discographies. Gopher to **wiretap.spies.com** and select "Wiretap Online Library." Select "Music" from the resulting menu and then "Discographies" to find items like these:

> Alien Sex Fiend Discography

> Black Sabbath Discography

> Bauhaus Discography

> David Bowie Discography

> Beatles Discography

> Depeche Mode Discography (appendix)

- ➤ Frank Zappa Discography
- ➤ Queensryche Discography
- ➤ Grateful Dead Discography
- ➤ Renaissance Discography
- ➤ Guns & Roses Bootlegs
- ➤ Rolling Stones Discography
- ➤ Metallica Discography
- ➤ Tears For Fears Discography
- ➤ Nirvana Discography
- ➤ U2 Bootlegs

You won't want to miss the "Everything Else" selection on the Music menu, either. I just love the idea of translations of Enya's lyrics:

- ➤ American Pie Lyrics & Annotation
- ➤ Led Zeppelin FAQ
- ➤ Beatle's Novelty Items List
- ➤ Summary of the Beatles on Video
- ➤ Best 150 Jazz Records of All Time
- ➤ The AC/DC FAQ alt.rock-n-roll.acdc
- ➤ Dead Milkmen Lyrics
- ➤ Usenet MIDI Primer
- ➤ Enya Translations and Annotations
- ➤ Wagner's Ring Synopsis
- ➤ Grateful Dead 1992 Year in Review
- ➤ Wedding Song List
- ➤ Grunge Must-Have List

 # More music sites on the Web

If you can't find your favorite group or musical genre in the sites I've told you about so far, don't despair. I've truly only scratched the surface as far as music sites on the Internet are concerned. Use Veronica or one of the World Wide Web search techniques I told you about in Chapter 5 to find your particular favorites. Or check one of the many sites on the Web that are devoted to music. Here are some to get you started:

➤ Acid Jazz
   www.cmd.uu.se/AcidJazz/

➤ CD Databases/Clubs
   http://www.btg.com/~cknudsen/xmcd/query.html
   http://biogopher.wustl.edu:70/1/audio/bmg
   http://gemm.com/

➤ Celtic Music
   http://celtic.stanford.edu/ceolas.html

➤ Entertainment/Music (Comprehensive Guide)
   http://www.yahoo.com/Entertainment/Music/

➤ Music Calendar (Music events calendar, listing concerts by location)
   http://calendar.com/concerts/

➤ Music FAQs
   http://www.cis.ohio-state.edu/hypertext/faq/usenet/
   music/top.html

➤ Music Library
   http://www.music.indiana.edu/

➤ Music References
   http://www.art.net/Links/musicref.html

➤ Music Resources
   http://www.music.indiana.edu/misc/music_resources
   .html

➤ Music Reviews (Personal recommendations of musicians from other Internauts)
   http://jeeves.media.mit.edu/ringo/

➤ Music Samples
   http://actor.cs.vt.edu/~wentz/index.html;

➤ Nine-inch Nails Unofficial Home Page
   http://www.scri.fsu.edu/~patters/nin.html

➤ Underground Music Archives
   http://sunsite.unc.edu/ianc/index.html

➤ Web Wide World of Music (includes the Ultimate Band List and links to more than 150 bands)
   http://american.recordings.com/wwwofmusic/

19
Room & board

B ACK in the sexist Dark Ages when many of our parents went to school, *college* was defined as "four years of vacation between a man's mother and his wife." Today we all know that this simply isn't true. Today we know that college is four years of putting up with a roommate that you didn't choose, in preparation for living with someone that you *did* choose after you graduate. In a word: It's good training!

But you are not alone. The Net is the perfect place to commiserate with others who have similar complaints—whether it's about roommates, the meal plan food, or other issues dealing with room and board.

Alt.flame.roommate

One of the most active newsgroups on the Net, at least during the school year, is **alt.flame.roommate**. So fire up your newsreader and have a look. Here's what you're likely to see:

```
alt.flame.roommate
Page 1 of 1
[71 messages in 15 discussion threads]

  1   Help! My roommates are abusive in the mornings! (5 msgs)
  2   fluffchick roommate bitch for 1 whole yr.!!!!! (10 msgs)
  3   Straw poll (6 msgs)
  4   RFH article in "Reader"
  5   The adventures of the fluffchick sorority wannabe RFH pt.1 (3 msgs)
  6   As promised, hell roommate tale (2 msgs)
  7   Even the hall was hellish!!!! (4 msgs)
  8   Another hellish room-mate (2 msgs)
```

```
 9  sister (6 msgs)
10  AAAAAAAAAAAAA!!!!! (2 msgs)
11  stomp stomp stomp (7 msgs)
12  fun at baylor (3 msgs)
13  best friend turned bitchy (11 msgs)
14  Nocturnal roommate, please advise. (9 msgs)
15  Please, for the love of my sanity

Enter Thread Number, ADD, ?, or EXIT:
```

And a few choice remarks—cleaned up and expurgated to be publishable in a G-rated book like this:

> I've moved. :) Murder came to mind, but I wasn't willing to eat prison food.

> Melinda was, on a whim, the Fabulous Pop Tart! and will be gosh knows what next . . .

> Even the hall was hellish!!!! Jessica Fluffbitch was not the only one on the floor who was evil. My floor was HELL.

> Karen was known to burst into tears. Could not control floor. Mousy short-haired little dork.

> Me? I wear black often, listen to indie and alternative music, avoided frat scene, go to clubs and coffeehouses, liberal. Considered Dorm Freak #1.

> Chloe—like me. From San Francisco. My best friend at school. Considered Dorm Freak #2.

> Lahar. Known as "La Whore". Her room was a bordello.

> Colleen and Amy. Roommates, with screechy voices and evangelically Christian attitudes. Big poster of JC on the door. Went around the dorm knocking on the doors of the "pagans and existentialists" (Emily, Chloe, and I) trying to convert us.

> Larke-Anya's roommate. Super-rich. Fluent in French. Boyfriend is a 25-year-old model. Thought she was superior to the whole floor. Called Jessica's crew "Naive nouveau riche boring peons" and called Chloe, Emily, and me "the little hipster kiddies." Looked about 30 herself.

Uncle Ezra's there to help

When college life, roommates, and other things are getting you down, help is just a Telnet away. Telnet to the Cornell University system at **cuinfo.cornell.edu 300**, or Gopher to **gopher.cit.cornell.edu** and ask Uncle Ezra!

The Gopher menu looks like this. Just pick item 7, and help is on the way:

```
1    Search             (Find what you're looking for...)        Menu
2    About              (Info about CUINFO and Gopher, Updates..  Menu
3    Academic Life      (Grad School, Classes, Exams, Fin Aid...  Menu
4    Administration     (Directories, Jobs, Human Resources...)   Menu
5    Campus             (News, Buses, Dining, Housing, Alumni...  Menu
6    Computing/Networking(CIT, BBS, Dialup Access, User Groups...  Menu
7    Dialogs            (Mr. Chips, Uncle Ezra, Eunice, Nutrique  Menu
8    Ithaca and Environs (Entertainment, Transportation, Weather. Menu
9    Library            (CU Library, Electronic Books & Journals  Menu
10   Student Life       (Jobs, Career Info, Sports, Rides...)     Menu
11   World              (Other Gopher Servers, Items from Elsewh  Menu
12   Other CU Servers   (Reach other Cornell University Servers)  Menu

Enter Item Number, SAVE, ?, or BACK: 7
```

There are lots of good things here—in the Dialogs area, especially. But Uncle Ezra, is "the original CUINFO Q&A feature, sponsored by the Office of the Vice President of Academic Programs and Campus Affairs and by CIT." It offers personal counseling, advice for problems of all sorts, and general information. For example, here is the beginning of one Uncle Ezra letter:

> Dear Uncle Ezra,
>
> My roommate of three and a half years is suddenly changing very quickly. She has always been very quiet and reserved. Every weekend she went out with her boyfriend on both Friday and Saturday night, never out with her friends. They were engaged to be married in May of this year. (We graduate this year also). Suddenly at the end of January she decided to dump her fiance
>
> . . .

The letter—and Uncle Ezra's reply—went on for quite a few lines. Clearly the writer had a concern, and clearly the group of certified counselors who are "Uncle Ezra" took it seriously. And no one's

privacy is compromised, because the good Unc is scrupulous about changing names to protect anonymity. All kinds of legitimate problems are considered, and the questions and answers are posted for anyone to read and benefit from.

NET TIP

Pull an all-nighter at a cyber cafe

A coffee bar with an Internet link? That's the idea behind the Icon Byte Bar and Grill in San Francisco, the Red Light Cafe in Atlanta, and several other recently established "cyber cafes." Here's a recent posting to the newsgroup **rec.food.drink.coffee** *by a visitor to the Habit in Portland, Oregon:*

> The Portland, Oregon newspaper just reported on a place called The Habit at 21st and Clinton streets in Southeast Portland that has good espressos, lattes, etc., and five PCs with Internet access. Apparently you get so many minutes free if you buy coffee. If you just want to use the terminal, that's available for a buck or so. This idea sounds so good, I wonder why I didn't think of it myself. Come to think of it, it's an idea anybody could copy, once it's out there.

To find out if there's a cyber cafe near your campus, read the postings on the newsgroup **rec.food.drink.coffee***. Or check the Cyber Cafe Guide maintained by Mark Dz at* **http://www.easynet.co.uk/pages/ cafe/ccafe.html***.*

 # Food, glorious food—bleah!

Like "military intelligence," "college food" is an oxymoron. They may call it "food," but it's not. It's more like an experiment to confirm once again how very little nourishment is required to sustain the human body. And taste? What's taste got to do with it?

That's why you'll definitely want to check out the newsgroup **alt.college.food**. A few choice morsels:

> In Japanese universities we can hardly eat the good meal. It is a little bit cheaper, but the taste of it is terrible. I think it is better for the students in the world to be against the bad food in universities.

Of course! College food being bad is a worldwide struggle . . . even a universal struggle! If there were colleges on Mars the food would probably suck there too. . . .

At the university I was at previously (Ottawa), there was an acceptable level of vermin allowed in the food . . . :P

We've got a lake and lots of ducks on campus, so one evening when our cafeteria—which usually offers only 2 entrees—offered roast duck as a third, most people opted for the rancid macaroni and cheese. (The running joke was that the cafeteria workers must've laid out a trail of bread crumbs to their back door.)

There's something wrong with a place that charges $1 for a cup of Dannon Yogurt or 65 cents for a pint of milk when a QUART of milk can be had at the grocery store for 78 cents!

There was a tactic a friend of mine used to use to defend her food. She would cover her fries with gobs of ketchup, mustard, mayo, cheese, pepper, and tabasco sauce. Her plate was a nasty site. Needless to say, no one asked her for fries and she enjoyed her food in deliciously grotesque-looking peace.

 # For vegetarians only

If you're a vegetarian or are interested in becoming one, be sure to check out the newsgroup **rec.food.veg**. There you'll find coverage and comments on issues like these:

> ➤ Feminism and Vegetarianism

> ➤ Eggs in Food

> ➤ Adzuki and mung bean recipes?

> ➤ American Veterinarians for Animal Rights

> ➤ Vegetarian/Vegan Cheese

> ➤ Vivisection or Science: A choice to make

> ➤ Soy milk recommendations?

> ➤ How do I Keep Fresh Fruits From Rotting?

> ➤ Vegetarian Wedding Receptions

➢ Non-Leather S&M/Fetish Equipment

➢ Vegan Soy Cheese

➢ Vegans and Protein

➢ Vegan bagel topping

➢ RSPCA's Freedom Foods: Cruelty-free meat is here

➢ Vegan restaurants in Hawaii

➢ Soya milk vs soya drink?

➢ Nutritional Yeast—Bad For You?

➢ Plant Pain, part 1

➢ Plutarch on Vegetarianism

➢ REQUEST: Potato and spinach recipe

✳ **The Granola mailing list**

If you're interested in vegetarian-related issues, you will also want to subscribe to the Granola mailing list. On Bitnet, the address to use is **granola@vtvm2**, and on the Internet it's **granola@vtvm2.cc.vt .edu**. In the body of the message, key in sub granola your-full-name. The list owner describes the list like this:

> A place for the exchange of really cool recipes, discussion of the various types of vegetarianism, nutrition information, a supportive atmosphere, animal rights issues, cookbook recommendations, tips on surviving as a vegetarian while on a college meal plan, herbal remedies, ideas/support for those wanting to shift to a vegetarian diet, etc.

⇨ An electronic cookbook on the Net

The recipes on the Campbell's Soup labels get boring after a while. For some new and possibly more exotic ideas, point your Web browser at **http://www.deltanet.2way.egg** where you'll find the electronic Gourmet Guide—otherwise known as "the eGG." A recent issue included gourmet recipes for Super Bowl parties (salsa verde and twice-marinated steak hoagies) and suggestions for a Chinese New Year feast. See Fig. 19-1 for the eGG's "Welcome" screen.

Figure 19-1

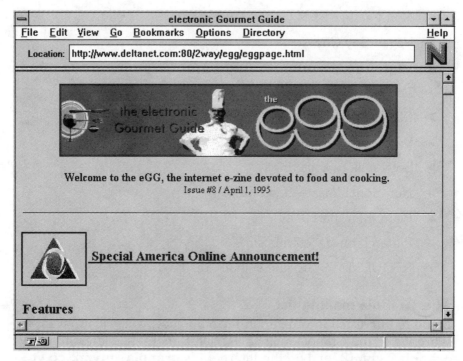

Welcome to the eGG, a Web site devoted to food and cooking

NET TIP

Gopher does recipes, too

*People from all over the world have contributed hundreds of favorite recipes to the newsgroup **rec.food.recipes**. If you're interested in cooking, you should definitely check it out. Only trouble is, since postings scroll off the group message board regularly, you'll have to take pot luck. If you're looking for ideas on novel ways to fix eggplant, the recipe you want may not be on the board. (Though, of course, you can post a request for such a recipe, and it will probably be answered within a few hours.)*

*That's why you should know about the recipe database that preserves postings to **rec.food.recipes** and makes them available on a Gopher menu. Gopher to **gopher.aecom.yu.edu** and choose "Internet Resources," then "Miscellaneous." On the Miscellaneous menu you will see "Search the Food Recipes Database." Select it, and then tell the system to search on some keyword like* zucchini *or* eggplant *or* Indian *and so on. The resulting menu will almost certainly contain a dozen or more recipes matching your search word.*

 # To your health with Healthline

If you've got non-threatening health-related questions but don't have time to visit your campus health services, you may want to Gopher to **selway.umt.edu**. This is the Healthline Gopher Server from the University of Montana.

Its goal is to offer many of the same types of information that you'd receive by going to any university health center, but to do so electronically. It is most definitely *not* designed to replace face-to-face consultation with a doctor or counselor. But it can help you learn about topics of general health interest.

Healthline includes "traditional" topics of physical and mental health (sexuality, drug & alcohol information, academic tips, and dietary facts), as well as pointers to information for the disabled, information about the effect of computers on health, health-related newsgroups, Gophers, and health-related information available from federal agencies.

These are just some of the topics covered:

➢ Anonymous HIV Testing

➢ Sexual Assault Recovery Service (SARS)

➢ Dietary Information

➢ Ankle Sprain Injuries

➢ Anorexia and Bulimia

➢ Antidepressants and Sleep Disorders

➢ Antioxidants: Why Do I Need Them?

➢ Asthma

➢ Cervical Dysplasia

➢ Depo Provera

➢ Do's and Don't's for Poor Sleepers

➢ Hay Fever (allergenic rhinitis)

Chapter 19

➢ Headache Questionnaire

➢ Health Information for International Travel

➢ Hypoglycemia

➢ Information About Measles, Mumps, and Rubella

➢ Instructions for Fasting Lab Work

➢ Lithium

➢ Migraine Headaches

➢ Mononucleosis

➢ Pinkeye

➢ Plantar Warts

➢ Prescription for Burnout

➢ Shaping Up Safely

➢ Stomach Flu

➢ When Your Diagnosis is Cystitis

➢ Women: Be Gentle To Yourself

20
Dating & mating: Love online

WELL, of course! The Internet offers a lot of information, but what it's really about is *people*! Given the widespread use of e-mail and the popularity of newsgroups, it's only natural that mechanisms would be created to make it easy to meet, date, and mate with others. There's even a feature to help you plan your wedding and select your wedding music.

Getting personal

The place to start your quest for love online is the newsgroup **alt.personals**, or its subgroup, **alt.personals.ads**. There *are* other newsgroups in the **alt.personals** hierarchy, but I'll leave you to explore them for yourself!

In fact, sorry to say, if you are at all sensitive to what might be called "frank language and words," you probably should avoid even the **alt.personals** group. Remember, anyone can post anything to any newsgroup. The personals are similar to those you'll find in a newspaper, but there is no editor to review and refuse to print the really awful stuff. Fortunately, most postings to **alt.personals** and **alt.personals.ads** are more like this:

```
Curious woman seeks...
Is there a man out there...
SWM Virgin Looking for SWF in Western PA!!
What do women see in men anyway?
SWF SEEKING BLACK MEN
GM looking for sex in Boston
Looking For Companion In Albany, NY
SJM seeks SJF for serious relationship in MA/NH Christian
SWM, 23, seeks Christian SWF in the South
Desperately seeking Lestat
Married couple seeks same
Seeking a codependent girlfriend in NC
Busty SWF ISO steamy e-mail
**BiF ISO BiF**
Bi-Females wanted
Seeking a Nubian Princess
Any female in London, UK reading this?
```

 # Personals on the Web

Naturally, there are World Wide Web sites devoted to personal ads as
well. If you'd like to click your way through hundreds of selections,
point your browser at one of these locations:

> ➤ Face to Face
>   **http://wwa.mall2000.com/**

> ➤ Personals
>   **http://www.public.com/personals/**

> ➤ Virtual MeetMarket
>   **http://wwa.com:1111/**

> ➤ Web Personals
>   **http://www.netmedia.com:80/date/**

Fans of the television show *Men Across America* may already know
about the show's Web site of the same name at **http://www
.interactive.line.com:80/men**. Each week, the Web site features
images and descriptions of 10 to 15 eligible bachelors, who,
according to the show's producers, are hoping to "find that one
special lady"—possibly on the Internet. For a sampling of one week's
lineup, see Fig. 20-1.

Figure 20-2

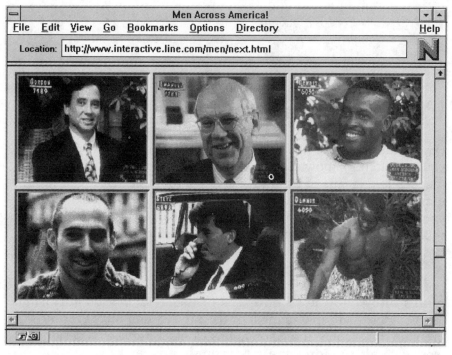

Men Across America, looking for love on the World Wide Web.

NET TIP

You're on your own

The line describing **alt.personals** in the David Lawrence list of active newsgroups reads: "alt.personals—Do you really want to meet someone this way? Only you can answer that question." If you're in school, you're an adult and you have at least an inkling that the world can be a wicked place. Proceed with extreme caution. End of lecture.

Except to say that whatever you do, it'll help if you speak the language. So here's a brief list of frequently used abbreviations. You'll find numerous variations, of course:

ISO	In Search Of	SBF	Single Black Female
SM	Single Male	SJF	Single Jewish Female
SWM	Single White Male	DWF	Divorced White Female
SBM	Single Black Male	GM	Gay Male
SJM	Single Jewish Male	GF	Gay Female

DWM	Divorced White Male	BM	Bisexual Male
SF	Single Female	BF	Bisexual Female
SWF	Single White Female		

 # Preserving anonymity

For obvious reasons, it is often desirable to remain anonymous until you've gotten to know someone better. That's impossible to do using the standard means of posting to a newsgroup, because your Internet e-mail address is automatically inserted in the "From:" field. But, as you may recall from Chapter 14, it's possible to post messages and replies anonymously, using what are referred to as *anonymous posting services*.

For details, send e-mail information requests to **help@anon.penet.fi** or **acs-info@chop.ucsd.edu**. The first address, located in Finland, lets you post and reply to most of the **alt.sex** and **alt.personals** groups. The second, the Anonymous Contact Service, is designed to work with **alt.personals**, **alt.personals.ads**, and **alt.personals.bi**.

When you get your automated e-mail reply to these queries, pay close attention to the first few lines, since they will contain the "alias" that has been assigned to you. This is followed by detailed instructions on how to use your alias and the service to post and reply to messages anonymously. As you will discover, you will also be able to send private e-mail to someone who has posted a message, without either of you knowing the other's actual e-mail address.

 # The EZ-Intro Contact Service (ECS)

Another option for anonymous posting is the EZ-Intro Contact Service (ECS), a service specifically aimed at the **alt.personals.ads** newsgroup. You will almost certainly find a message explaining the service posted to **alt.personals.ads**. But since you are likely to encounter literally thousands of postings the first time you read the group, here are the essential details about ECS:

> ECS is an automated, anonymous, double-blind, contact and matchmaking service for **alt.personals.ads**. It's a moderated service, and ECS advises potential users that "the moderator will not be making moral judgments, but will reject any article that is not in the scope of meeting other single compatibles or requesting the singles matchmaking service."

> The first step is to send an e-mail message to **ping@cupid.sai.com**. That will test the mail path and, if it works, automatically assign you an alias. (It might take several hours, or overnight, for this to happen.)

> Once you receive your alias, you can prepare your message, including a descriptive subject line. As long as your "From:" line contains your original "From:" e-mail address information, any posting or e-mail will appear to come from the alias assigned by the PING message.

> In the "To:" line, send your message to **[SM,SF,GM,GF,BM,BF]@cupid.sai.com**, selecting one of the six abbreviations (SM for "single male," and so on). To reply to a posting, send your mail to **user's-alias@cupid.sai.com**.

> Questions, complaints, and comments should be addressed via regular Internet mail to **admin@lemuria.sai.com**.

NET TIP

Getting scanned photos

Anyone using the ECS service may put a photo on file. Send a clear photo, maximum size 3" × 5", and a check for $10.00 (one-time handling charge per photo) to:

Shecora Associates, Inc.
P.O. Box 61
Brookline, NH 03033-0061

If you already have a photo scanned into a .GIF file and no larger than 40K bytes, you can mail it to **gif@sai.com**. *(Don't forget that you must convert binary files to text via UUENCODE before sending them to an Internet e-mail address. See Chapter 8 for instructions.) If you wish to restrict access to your picture, you must indicate that in the mail message with the .GIF file.*

> *Pictures in the database can be accessed in one of two ways. If the picture is marked "open to the world," the requester need only send mail to the database and the database will mail the .GIF file to the requester. If the picture is marked "restricted," the owner will have to authorize the database to send the picture to the requester.*

⇨ Romance is alive & well

All things are relative, of course, but have you ever wondered how men in the 1890s could get excited over catching sight of a woman's ankle? How could a "glimpse of stocking" ever have been something shocking? More to the point, in an age when men and women let it all hang out in shopping malls, on campus, and on TV, what is left to reveal?

If you want to know where love has gone, check out the **alt.romance** newsgroup. It may not have the answers, but it certainly has lots of ideas. And it's the ideal spot to find a shoulder to cry on or to offer your own in moral support. Typical postings include topics like these:

> ➤ What Should I Do?

> ➤ I didn't go to my prom!

> ➤ Why can't men commit?

> ➤ How to obtain the book "1001 ways to be Romantic"

> ➤ Smart Women

> ➤ Commitment, Children

> ➤ Keeping Romance Alive!!!!

> ➤ Dating Services

> ➤ Roomies from Hell . . . What to do?

> ➤ Does it ever get any easier?

⇨ True stories & support

I have long pointed out in print that one of the most wonderful things about online communication is that it is *plain communication*. When you can't hear someone's voice or see what they look like, when you have nothing but the verbal content of their messages, you really *can* communicate mind-to-mind and soul-to-soul. Here are just three message excerpts from the **alt.romance** group.

The man writing Message 1 decides to go out into the Net to find someone else. He does. It's great for him. And he posts to the group asking if anyone else has ever had a similar experience. Messages 2 and 3 are just two of the replies:

Message 1   Ok, here's my situation: I've been married for a little over two years. I dated my wife for about 3 years. Shortly after building our new dream home, she had/is having an affair. (Last 3 months). Our relationship deteriorated because she went from ugly duckling when I met her to a swan. Now she wants all the attention she can get. Anyway, after a few months of being hurt, I posted to alt.personals. Not really expecting much, I got several responses. One was from a girl who lived only a couple of hours drive away. Anyway, even though we both felt strange meeting the way we did, we really, really clicked. It was like we'd known each other all our lives. Has anyone else had a similar experience?

Message 2   Yes, yes, yes!!! I met my fiance on the Net. We clicked immediately and felt we'd known each other all our lives. It was to the point we would think the same things at the same time and even finish each other's thoughts and sentences. When we met "for real", I recognized him immediately, and it felt not as if we were meeting for the first time, but rather he was coming home after being away for a while. He felt the same too . . .

Message 3   I've had experiences where I really clicked with a woman in that eerie way, too. The first time was in a rebound situation, and in retrospect I see that I was clinging to her because she really seemed to like me, which assuaged my damaged ego; in addition, she seemed so amazingly great to me mainly because . . .

⇨ Wedding bells

Okay. So the two of you are committed. You want to get married. Next stop is clearly **alt.wedding**, where you will find message postings like these:

➤ Hyphenated names?

➤ Invitations . . . Ack!!!

➤ Wedding cake—servings per person?

➤ Bands in New Jersey—Recommendations?

➤ Who to include on invitation list

➤ What is the best way to store your wedding dress?

➤ Tipping

➤ Help! Im looking for a piece to read at a wedding next week.

➤ Interfaith ceremony

➤ Engagement Ring Customs

➤ DJ's in the Raleigh-Durham area

➤ Just engaged!

➤ Precious Moments Cake Topper

➤ Lazare Diamonds?

➤ Bras

➤ How to handle young flower girls...

➤ Mother's Dress Dilemma

➤ Wedding planning software

➤ Bridesmaid from hell?

➤ Broken engagement: Sue?

➤ Wedding humor

➤ Looking for caterer in Los Gatos/San Jose, CA

➤ MOB dress

 # And the band played on

For even more ideas and help regarding weddings, Gopher to **wiretap.spies.com** and choose "Wiretap Online Library," followed by "Music," followed by "Everything Else." That will lead you to a three-page menu. The item you want is "Wedding Song List" on the third page.

You will find two lists, one sorted by purpose (Prelude, Processional, etc.) and one sorted by title. Here's a *brief* sample from the first list. I wish I had known about it when Emily and I got married.

Song Title	Purpose
For His Bride (John Michael Talbot)	General
Be Thou My Vision	Hymn
Great is thy Faithfulness	Hymn
Hymn of Joy (Beethoven)	Hymn
Joyful, Joyful We Adore Thee	Hymn
Love Changes Everything (from *Aspects of Love*)	Prelude
Wind Beneath My Wings (Henry/Silbar)	Prelude
Air - Suite #3 (J.S. Bach)	Processional
Canon in D Major (Pachelbel)	Processional
Carillon (Sky - Sky 1)	Processional
Crown Him With Many Crowns	Processional
Jesu, Joy of Man's Desiring	Recessional
Joyful, Joyful We Adore Thee	Recessional
Praise the Lord (Handel - Judas Maccabeus)	Recessional
Trumpet Voluntary	Recessional
Wedding Song (There is Love) (Noel Paul Stookey)	Recessional
What a Wonderful World (Louis Armstrong)	Special
What God has Joined Together	Special

21
Thinking of transferring?

I N the end, it seems, almost everything comes down to money and to business. Even higher education. If you doubt it, just wait till you graduate and get the first of a lifetime's worth of letters and phone calls from your dear old alma mater importuning you for the long green. Give what you can; give till it hurts. But remember, unlike many tenured professors, you don't get a year off with full pay every seven years to take your family to Tuscany in quest of anything some obscure Italian poet may have scribbled before the age of 18.

But I digress. The fact is that, for whatever reasons, colleges and universities are in the business of attracting students, just like Proctor & Gamble, Lever Brothers, and Colgate are in the business of attracting customers to their soap and processed food products. It's just that colleges and universities don't call it *advertising* or *marketing*. God forbid!

But whatever it's called, any time one party is trying to attract another, misunderstandings (not to say "misrepresentations") can occur. That's at least one of the reasons why tens of thousands of students decide each year that if they're going to go into debt or otherwise spend all the money necessary for tuition, room, and board, they'd rather do it someplace they like. In a phrase: *transfer time*!

⇨ Checking it out

Here is yet another area of life where the Net can be of help—big time. There are all kinds of reasons for transferring and all kinds of reasons for picking a different school. But don't jump with a prayer and a promise. Come up with a list of schools and use the Internet connection at your present school to check them out.

It's as easy as using Gopher or the World Wide Web. For starters, run your local Gopher and search "All the Gophers in the World" for the name of a school of interest. Among your hits, you are certain to find a CWIS. Pronounced "kwiss," this is Net-talk for Campus Wide Information System. And it's your window into any college or university, since it's designed for the inmates, er, students, instead of prospective paying customers, I mean, students.

Pretending to be a dissatisfied undergrad at Harvard or Yale (and who can blame me, after all?), I did a Gopher search on *Princeton* just to check it out. I found 19 different Princeton Gopher servers—among them, the Princeton CWIS, known as the Princeton News Network. That particular Gopher led to a menu like this:

```
Princeton Univ, PNN [pucc.princeton.edu]
Page 1 of 1

1    HELP                                 Text
2    About PNN and Gopher                 Menu
3    Index to Information in PNN           Text
4    What's New on PNN                     Text
5    Calendars and Events                  Menu
6    Campus Organizations and Programs     Menu
7    Computing Resources                   Menu
8    Departments, Services & Facilities    Menu
9    Faculty & Staff Activities            Menu
10   Health/Family Care News               Menu
11   Library Information                    Text
12   Potpourri                             Menu
13   Safety Information                     Menu
14   Student/Grad Student Info/Activs.     Menu
15   Travel & Visitor Information           Menu
16   Univ. Employment Info:Staff/Student   Menu
17   Univ. Policies, Procedures, Reports   Menu
18   University Who's Who                   Menu
19   PNN Search                           Search

Enter Item Number, SAVE, ?, or BACK:
```

Exploring this CWIS, I found a write-up of the University Art Museum, including its hours, schedule, special lectures or "Gallery Talks," and exhibits. I found student job listings, complete with a table of pay grades and rates. (Top rate is $8.95 an hour. Bottom rate is $4.55 for a "sitting position," which presumably means you can study while you work.) The names and numbers of managers of Princeton's many Student Agencies were also online, as were the weekday and weekend train schedules to New York City.

There was much more besides. My point here is this: Old Nassau may indeed be "the best old place of all," but its CWIS is not unique. You can find information of equal depth and diversity by tapping almost any college or university CWIS. And you should—after all, how many times do you really want to transfer in your college career? When you were in high school, you probably didn't have access to the Net. Now that you do, you owe it to yourself to use its free resources to thoroughly check out the transfer site you have in mind before you make the big leap.

If you have a Web browser, you'll want to add two excellent Web sites to your Bookmarks list. The first is the American Universities directory maintained by Mike Conlan at the University of Florida. The second, College and University Home Pages by Christina DeMello at MIT, is international in scope. Here's where to find them:

➤ American Universities
  http://www.clas.ufl.edu/CLAS/american-universities.html

➤ College and University Home Pages (International)
  http://www.mit.edu:8001/people/cdemello/univ.html

These two lists provide great starting points for getting specific information as well as a general feel for a particular school. The home pages for Duke University (Fig. 21-1) and The Wharton School at the University of Pennsylvania (Fig. 21-2) are just two of the hundreds of pages you can check out with your Web browser.

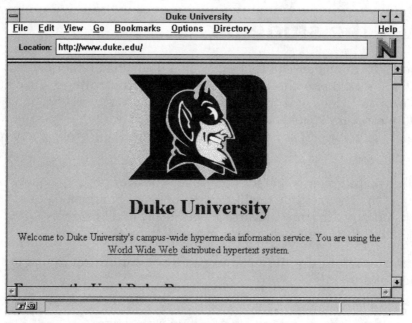

Figure 21-1

Duke University's "hypermedia information system" on the World Wide Web.

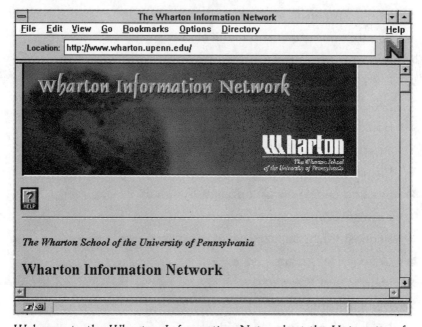

Figure 21-2

Welcome to the Wharton Information Network at the University of Pennsylvania's Wharton School!

 # Ask the students

The CWIS at any college is likely to be a goldmine of information. But you should also check out the newsgroup **soc.college**. Take an hour or so to look at it the first time. You may very well encounter 200 messages or more. When you're done, mark all the messages as "read" so you won't see them again. Then check the group every few days or so.

After you've gotten a feel for the group, consider posting a query of your own. The message might be as simple as "I'm thinking of transferring to Indiana University, but I really don't care for basketball. Is there any hope for me in Bloomington?"

In any case, here are the kinds to topics you can expect to find in **soc.college**:

➢ Tufts, Should I Go?

➢ Info Wanted on Pace University in Manhattan

➢ College Info Needed

➢ Yale information request

➢ Wanted: Information on Universities

➢ Info on China grad school aid

➢ For members of Lambda Chi Alpha only!

➢ School: Florida Institute of Technology

➢ Boulder—the Berkeley of the '90s?

➢ Apartment needed immediately near UC Berkeley

➢ Virginia Tech

➢ Seeking details on Champaign-Urbana!

➢ Eastern Oregon State College

➢ Request for hood/cap/gown makers

➢ College Democrats List

➢ Members of Kappa

➢ Delta Sorority

➢ Looking for Sigma Nu brothers

→ Read the campus newspaper

You probably won't be surprised to learn that many campus newspapers are now offered in online editions on the Internet, complete with feature articles, editorials, information on campus social events, and so on. Some, like Trinity College's *Trincoll Journal*, are multimedia extravaganzas that attract tens of thousands of readers each week to their site at **http://www.trincoll.edu/ tj/fasthome.html**.

You'll find a large collection of pointers to campus newspapers at **http://www.gnn.com/gnn/wic/news.09.html**, shown in Fig. 21-3. If there's a particular school you're considering, reading the campus paper can be an excellent way to get a feel for the students and life on campus.

Figure 21-3

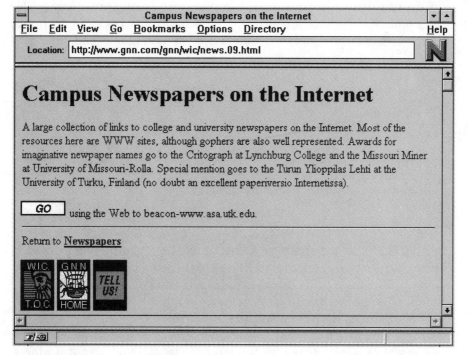

Get the straight scoop on campus life from student-run newspapers on the Internet

Third-party opinions

So far we've focused on information about colleges generated either by the colleges themselves or by students. But if you Gopher to **bloggs.review.com**, you can tap into the information assembled by The Princeton Review.

This organization has no connection with the university of the same name. It bills itself as "the nation's leader in test preparation." It further claims that "Each year, we help hundreds of thousands of students prepare for a variety of standardized tests through our courses, books, computer software, audio tapes, and videos . . . . We help students prepare for the following exams: SAT, SAT II, ACT, PSAT, SSAT, LSAT, GMAT, GRE, MCAT, TOEFL, and the Computerized GRE."

I have no idea whether these statements are true or not. All I know is that the company's Gopher is quite impressive. Among other things, it offers rankings of the best colleges, grad schools, b-schools, law schools, and med schools. Its Gopher Business School menu looks like this:

```
Business School
Page 1 of 1

1   Cracking The GMAT                                    Text
2   Financing Business School                            Text
3   GMAT Registration                                    Text
4   How The Admissions Criteria Are Weighted             Text
5   Rankings Of Selected Business Schools                Text
6   The GMAT Of January, 1995                            Text
7   The GMAT Of March, 1995                              Text
8   What Is The Graduate Management Admission Test (GMAT)? Text
9   What's New On The GMAT                                Text

Enter Item Number, SAVE, ?, or BACK:
```

But this is just an ice shaving on the tip of the iceberg. The Princeton Review Gopher is phenomenal. It has vast stores of information to offer—including candid comments about many colleges submitted by students—and all of it can be accessed via menus. Or visit their World Wide Web site at **http://www.review.com**.

Give it a shot, whether you're thinking of transferring or not. In fact, I'd recommend it as a way of checking out a given college for your younger brother or sister. This is a very impressive service.

22
What about grad school?

I think that I shall never see a sight as sad as a Ph.D. selling washing machines at Sears. Yet supply and demand will always rule, and there can be no doubt that many of us have spent too long in school, hoping to land in a cushy berth, but finding in the end that there's a serious dearth of good-paying jobs for those of an intellectual bent. So you end up selling washers—or cars or insurance—just to pay the rent.

Not long ago I read in the *Wall Street Journal* of attorneys in their thirties who graduated from top schools—with top grades, positions on the law review, and even clerkships at the Supreme Court—who can't find jobs. Here's the quote:

> ...good opportunities for attorneys in midcareer have become virtually nonexistent.
>
> "These people might as well be dead," says legal recruiter Lynn Mestel. "They might as well go back to school and start all over again. They'd have a much better time finding a job."
>
> *Wall Street Journal*, July 22, 1994, page B1

To me, that's frightening. In the law business, you're either a partner or a grunt. And of the classes of 35 to 45 freshly minted attorneys hired by the prestigious New York City firm of Paul, Weiss, Rifkind, Warton, & Garrison, "typically only five are elected to partner."

I'm a writer, so I don't profess to know the ways of professors. But I do know that the calculus is about the same. Only a tiny fraction of the graduate-student teaching assistants at a school are ever granted tenure as full professors. The only difference is that TAs don't have to work nearly as hard as law firm associates. But, then again, they don't get paid as much, either.

 # Is grad school right for you?

I'm sure some readers will think I'm being brutal. With all my heart, I hope they are right!

Heaven knows no one on campus is going to shake students out of the idyllic slumber of academe, for they're all in on the game. America's campuses, in my opinion, desperately need professors who can teach and enlighten and inspire. I know whereof I speak, for I had the great good fortune to have Kaufmann on Nietzsche, Seltzer on Shakespeare, Robertson on Chaucer, Kelly on Milton, and Carlos Baker on the Romantic Poets. (I only wish I'd been smart enough to take better advantage of the opportunity; but then, I was 20 or 21 at the time, so what did I know?)

We certainly need *some* grad students, and we desperately need good professors. But grad school should be like the ministry—go to it only if you have a genuine calling. Otherwise, you're likely to end up pushing 30, with a wonderful education and absolutely no job prospects. (I hear Sears has a great health care plan and generous— one week—vacation after 12 months of service.)

 # Info on the Net

But away with the grim. Let's assume that you feel you have the calling to seek out and enter grad school. Well, now that you have access to the Internet, checking out a school is pretty easy. In fact, the process is the same as the one I recommended in Chapter 21 for an undergrad checking out a transfer site.

To wit: Activate the Gopher on your campus computer and select the option that allows you to search by keyword. At the appropriate prompt, key in the name of the college or university you're considering. I did this recently and looked for Stanford. There was a brief pause and then the following Gopher menu page appeared:

```
1    Stanford Univ [gopher-server.stanford.edu]                     Menu
2    Stanford Univ, Academic Computing Support, Consulting Gopher   Menu
3    Stanford Univ, CAMIS (Center for Advanced Medical Info)        Menu
4    Stanford Univ, CSLI Gopher [kanpai.stanford.edu]               Menu
5    Stanford Univ, Dept of Genetics, Yeast Genome Information [g    Menu
6    Stanford Univ, Experimental Folio Gopher [lindy.stanford.edu   Menu
7    Stanford Univ, Gopher Gateway [gopher.stanford.edu]            Menu
8    Stanford Univ, Graduate School of Business [gsb-gopher.stanf   Menu
9    Stanford Univ, Heuristic Programming Project [hpp.stanford.e   Menu
10   Stanford Univ, Hungarian Gopher /HIX [andrea.stanford.edu]     Menu
11   Stanford Univ, Information Systems Group Gopher [medisg.stan    Menu
12   Stanford Univ (macharold.stanford.edu) [macharold.stanford.e   Menu
13   Stanford Univ, Medical Center [med-gopher.stanford.edu]        Menu
14   Stanford Univ, Medical Center Networking (SUMC Mednet) [medn    Menu
15   Stanford Univ (mordor.stanford.edu) [mordor.stanford.edu]      Menu
16   Stanford Univ (portfolio.stanford.edu) [portfolio.stanford.e   Menu
17   Stanford Univ, Project on People, Computers, and Design [pcd    Menu
18   Stanford Univ, Residential Computing Gopher [deathstar.stanf    Menu
19   Stanford Univ, Sumex-AIM Gopher [sumex.stanford.edu]           Menu

Enter Item Number, MORE, SAVE, ?, or BACK:
```

I could have looked for Stanford at these locations on the World Wide Web as well:

➢ American Universities
http://www.clas.ufl.edu/CLAS/american-universities.html

➢ College and University Home Pages (International)
http://www.mit.edu:8001/people/cdemello/univ.html

Exploring all the freely available information about Stanford will take you many hours and many pages of printouts. The key thing is that it's all there for you. And you will find similar riches for loads of other grad schools and universities throughout the world.

Be sure also to check out the Campus Newspapers Web site and the Princeton Review feature discussed in Chapter 21.

Grant$

Wouldn't it just kill you to work your way through grad school, only to discover on graduation day that there was a grant you could have gotten that would have considerably eased your burden?

That's why you owe it to yourself to tap into RiceInfo before you do anything about going to graduate school. Just visit the RiceInfo Web site at **http://riceinfo.rice.edu/**. Or Gopher to **riceinfo.rice.edu** and choose "Information by Subject Area," then "Grants, Scholarships, and Funding." That will take you to a menu like this one, full of funding sources and information:

```
Grants, Scholarships and Funding Information
Page 1 of 2
1    About this directory                                      Text
2    A Grant Getter's Guide to the Internet (U of Idaho)       Text
3    A Grant Getter's Guide to the Internet: Appendix A        Text
4    A Grant Getter's Guide to the Internet: Search            Search
5    ARPA Solicitations                                        Menu
6    Biomed Opportunities from Yale                            Menu
7    Canadian scholarships and grants from SchoolNet           Menu
8    Catalog of Federal Domestic Assistance—about              Text
9    Catalog of Federal Domestic Assistance—search             Search
10   Commerce Business Daily                                   Menu
11   DOE - Department of Energy                                Menu
12   Division of Engineering Research (Michigan State Univ)    Menu
13   FEDIX/MOLIS: Federal Information Exchange                 Menu
14   Federal Register (Access restricted to auth. participants) Menu
15   Federal Register via LEGI-SLATE (Rice University access only Menu
16   Fellowships & Grants from CUNY                            Menu
17   LegiSlate (requires login id & password)                 Telnet
18   NIH Guide to Grants and Contracts                        Menu
19   NIH Guide to Grants and Contracts                        Menu
20   NIH Guide to Grants and Programs                         Search
21   NSF Abstracts of Awards                                  Search
22   NSF Bulletin                                             Search
23   NSF Publications                                         Search
24   NSF Publications Overview                                Text
25   NTIS FedWorld (US government BBSs/online systems)        Telnet
26   National Science Foundation Gopher (STIS)                Menu
27   National Science Foundation STIS TOPICS system          Telnet
28   Other funding programs (from UWisc--probably out of date) Menu
29   Research Alerts: Texas Agricultural Experiment Station   Menu
30   Science and Technology Information System (NSF/STIS)     Menu
31   Texas Technology (from NASA Mid-Continent Tech. Transfer Menu
32   The NSF Bulletin                                         Menu
33   The Scientist (biweekly newspaper)                       Menu
Enter Item Number, PREV, SAVE, ?, or BACK:
```

The Chronicle of Higher Education

Anyone contemplating a career in academe—or simply curious about what's happening on college campuses—should Gopher to **chronicle.merit.edu** and check out the *Chronicle of Higher Education* feature called "Academe This Week." To access the World Wide Web version of this service, point your Web browser at **http://chronicle.merit.edu/.ads/.links.html**.

Figure 22-1 shows you what you can expect when going in via the Web. Here, however, we will focus on the Gopher version of this service.

The Gopher version

When you Gopher to **chronicle.merit.edu**, you will see a menu like the one shown here. If you are at all interested in the academic

Figure 22-1

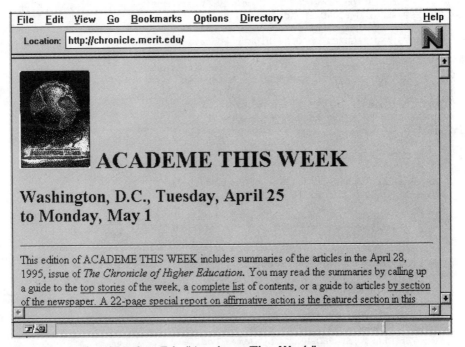

The Chronicle of Higher Eds "Academe This Week"

world, you will find this Gopher menu particularly enticing and will want to explore it further. The menu changes every week, but you can expect to see something like this menu from late April 1995.

Naturally, I was interested in seeing what people are reading on college campuses (other than *Internet 101*, of course). So I took the opportunity to check item 14, "Best-Selling Books in Academe."

```
chronicle.merit.edu Gopher
Page 1 of 1

1    NEW in "ACADEME THIS WEEK"                                    Text
2    A Special Report: AFFIRMATIVE ACTION ON THE LINE              Text
3    A GUIDE to The Chronicle of Higher Education, April 28, 1995  Menu
4    ORGANIZATIONS in Academe                                      Menu
5    -- News of Organizations                                      Text
6    -- Information provided by the Annenberg/CPB Project           Menu
7    INFORMATION TECHNOLOGY in Academe                             Menu
8    -- News of Information Technology                             Text
9    -- Information provided by Lotus Development Corporation      Menu
10   FINANCES AND PERSONAL PLANNING in Academe                     Menu
11   -- News of Finances and Personal Planning                     Text
12   -- Information provided by TIAA-CREF                          Menu
13   -- Information provided by Fidelity Investments               Menu
14   BEST-SELLING BOOKS in Academe: a new list                     Text
15   EVENTS AND DEADLINES in Academe                               Menu
16   FACTS AND FIGURES on U.S. higher education                    Menu
17   JOBS in and out of Academe: more than 600 openings            Menu
18   INFORMATION about The Chronicle's publications                Text
19   ABOUT "ACADEME THIS WEEK": search tips and more               Menu

Enter Item Number, SAVE, ?, or BACK: 14
BEST-SELLING BOOKS in Academe: a new list
Page 1 of 1

WHAT THEY'RE READING ON COLLEGE CAMPUSES

Best-selling books in college bookstores,
compiled by The Chronicle of Higher Education

                                                   Previous
                                                   Survey
                                                   --------
    1. TOM CLANCY'S OP-CENTER, created by
       Tom Clancy and Steve Pieczenik .............    1
    2. POLITICALLY CORRECT BEDTIME STORIES,
       by James Finn Garner ......................     2
    3. THE SHIPPING NEWS, by E. Annie Proulx .......    4
    4. THE CHAMBER, by John Grisham ...............     -
    5. THE ROBBER BRIDE, by Margaret Atwood ........    3
    6. THE CELESTINE PROPHECY, by James Redfield ...    6
```

```
 7. THE HOT ZONE, by Richard Preston ............    -
 8. THE BOOK OF VIRTUES,
    by William J. Bennett .....................    -
 9. COUPLEHOOD, by Paul Reiser .................    5
10. BREAKING THE SURFACE, by Greg Louganis
    with Eric Marcus ..........................    -
```

The Chronicle also offers job listings, searchable by job title or keyword. This is a wonderful resource which I encourage you to explore. Open your comm program's capture buffer and just poke around. You will not be sorry.

 # Tapping into newsgroups

As you undoubtedly know by now, there is a Usenet newsgroup for nearly every topic. Grad school is no exception. Currently, there are at least three groups you should check: **soc.college.grad**, **soc.college.gradinfo**, and **soc.college.teaching-asst**.

Here are some sample headlines from **soc.college.grad**:

➤ McGill Student in Biomedical Engr Grad Program?

➤ Looking for sources of Financial aid

➤ Questions about recommendation letters

➤ Finding Academic Papers on the Net

➤ My grad school "wish" list . . ..

➤ Political Science Funding Sources

➤ Info on Arizona State needed

➤ Need info about Lincoln Univ

➤ Asking about life on SUNY at Albany

➤ Ph.D. Fellowships in Robotics

➤ Creative Writing & Communications

➤ Choosing a graduate advisor

➤ Who Publishes Graduate School Rankings?

➤ Scholarships for Foreign Students

➤ Apartment near Northwestern?

➤ Info about grad programs in MIS

➤ Philosophy at Yale?

➤ Looking for advice in Santa Barbara

These are some recent discussion topics from **soc.college .gradinfo**:

➤ GRE question

➤ Studies in Computers and Human Communications

➤ Apartments near USC?

➤ Need Info on Grad Programs via Internet

➤ Computer Art Grad Programs

➤ Should I pursue MBA without working experience

➤ Duquesne (P-burgh) MBA any good? 98% placement!

➤ GRE or Undergraduate Record

➤ My grad school "wish" list . . ..

➤ Film Production at these institutions

➤ Political Science Funding Sources

➤ Info on Arizona State needed

➤ Ph.D. Fellowships in Robotics

➤ Apartment at College Park?

➤ History/American Rev/Loyalists

➤ Seattle Apt-Mate needed

➤ HELP: how to become a lecturer?

➤ Ph.D. Econ. ratings

➤ Rhodes Scholarship Info Wanted

➤ Need Financial Aid for College?

➢ Grad schools in Genetics/Molec Bio

➢ Georgia Tech

➢ Looking for Roommates at UT Knoxville

And from **soc.college.teaching-asst**:

➢ Creative Filmmaker Seeking Support

➢ Teaching in Hong-Kong

➢ Self-Evaluation?

➢ Asking about life on SUNY at Albany

➢ E-mail usage

➢ Grad. Life

➢ Office hours

➢ American and "English" academic positions

➢ Looking for a teaching-asst. position . . .

➢ Literature tests?

➢ Home study of MBA

Well, you get the idea. You can post a message on just about any aspect of graduate student life, and someone is almost certain to post a reply.

23
How to find a job on the Internet

WHO can keep track? One year jobs are hard to find, the next year employers complain that they have more openings than there are people to fill them. I know the state of the economy has something to do with it. That and population trends: baby bust; baby boomlet; baby, let's just take the summer off!

In this chapter I'll focus mainly on using Internet resources to find summer jobs, since that's likely to be of most interest to you as a college student. But I'll also tell about some of the places you can look for information on full-time employment.

I could write a whole book on the subject of finding a job on the Internet. In fact, I've done so. It's called, appropriately enough, *Finding a Job on the Internet* (co-authored by my wife, Emily). But you can hold off on that until, say, a couple of weeks before graduation.

The trick to getting a really good summer job is to start looking for it in the spring, while you're still in school. And the Internet is the ideal place to begin your search.

 ## Gopher & CWIS

Start by checking your local Gopher and Campus Wide Information System (CWIS). Searching Gopher on the keyword *summer* will probably give you something like this:

```
Search for: summer

Search Headings in this Section
Page 1 of 1

1    Internship and Summer Job Services                          Menu
2    Search Internship and Summer Job Services listings          Search
3    Internship and Summer Job Services - Federal Work Study     Menu
4    Internship and Summer Job Services - Non Work Study         Menu
5    Law\\Case Clerk (non-summer)                                Text
6    The Commons Free Summer Concert Series                      Text
7    Coal Bin Theatre Summer Schedule                            Text
8    The County Theater Summer Movie Schedule                    Text
9    Summer Research at Temple University                        Text
10   Summer Research at the U. of Michigan                       Text
11   Summer Urban Affairs Prog for Minority HS Students (SUAP)   Text
12   Student Employment Services (Semester and Summer Jobs)      Menu
13   Summer Off Campus Non Work Study (June)                     Menu
14   Summer Off Campus Work Study (June)                         Menu
15   Summer On Campus Non Work Study (June)                      Menu
16   Summer On Campus Work Study (June)                          Menu
17   Items Possibly Related to "summer"                          Menu

Enter Item Number, SAVE, ?, or BACK: 2
```

I picked item 2, "Search Internship and Summer Job Services listings," and responded to the resulting "Search for:" prompt with the keyword *architecture*. Here's what appeared:

```
Search Internship and Summer Job Services listings
Page 1 of 1

1    JOB TITLE : Architecture Intern                    Text
2    JOB TITLE : Architecture & Engineering             Text
3    JOB TITLE : Architecture Internships               Text
4    JOB TITLE : CAD/Computer Graphics Intern           Text
5    JOB TITLE : Junior Designer (architecture)         Text
6    JOB TITLE : Dept. of State Interns                 Text
7    JOB TITLE : Landscape Architect                    Text

Enter Item Number, SAVE, ?, or BACK: 7
```

Figure 23-1 shows the listing for the Landscape Architect summer job that appeared when I selected item 7 from the menu.

In addition to presenting a menu to let you look at job openings by location (Metro New York, Midwest, West Coast, etc.), this particular Gopher also had job listings like these:

```
Community Service Interns
Environmental Associates
Environmental/Lab Technician
```

```
Federal Law Enforcement Intern
Feminism & Public Policy Intern
Geology/Admin. Interns
Hostelling Internships
Logistics &/or Marketing Job
Mapping Internship
Olympic Committee Internship
Outward Bound Staff
Resource Asst.--Conservation
Specialty Advertising Rep
Various Community Service Internships
```

Figure 23-1

```
JOB TITLE : Landscape Architect                    Job#: 12341
Job Category: ISJS/Non Work Study/Midwest States
Employ. Dates: 06/01/95 - 09/05/95    Application deadline:03/24/95
Hrs/Week & Wage: 35    ***/       Work Schedule:
Number of Positions: 1            Transportation:
Worksite: Cleveland OH


Skills:        STANFORD STUDENTS ONLY. ARCHITECTURE/LANDSCAPE
               MAJORS. STRONG GRAPHIC & WRITING, WORK WELL
               W/TEAM

JOB DESCRIPTION:  PR Plans, Inc. is a professional consulting
               firm engaged in city planning, urban design,
               site planning, park/recreation planning and
               community development work as well as other
               related planning and development activities.
               Summer or semester internship, as well as full-
               time employment. Send resume & work samples to
               Johnathan Smith, AICP, AIA, 175 Shaker Blvd.,
               Cleveland, OH 44114. 216-555-1234.
```

A sample summer job listing via Gopher.

NET TIP

Pick your location

Clearly the best place to start looking for summer jobs is with your own college Gopher. But there's no reason why you can't search the Gophers at other schools as well. If you want to find a summer job in Maine, for example, find a college near your chosen location and see if it has a Gopher. (Use your own Gopher to track down the distant Gopher you want.)

You may find that some job listings on college Gophers are open only to students at that particular school. But if the Gopher at Whatsamatta U. reveals that the nearby R&B Construction Company has one or more job openings, there's nothing to stop you from applying, regardless of where you attend school.

 # Ask Veronica about summer jobs

The next step is to do a Veronica search on the phrase *summer jobs*. When I did that recently, I got four pages of Gopher menus. Here are just a few of the most interesting items, drawn from those four pages:

```
Summer Jobs for Engineers
Environmental Summer Jobs
Jobs for Engineering Students this summer!
Remarks at Summer Jobs Conference 4/14/95
Internships, Summer Jobs, & International Jobs
Internship, Co-Op And Summer Jobs
Summer Jobs in Forest Ecology
Summer Jobs--College of Agriculture
Summer Jobs--All Majors
Summer Jobs--College of Business
Summer Jobs--Camps & Resorts
Summer Jobs--College of Engineering
Summer Jobs--Federal Jobs
Summer Jobs--International Jobs
Summer Jobs--College of Liberal Arts
Summer Jobs--College of Science and Math
Summer Jobs--Center for Teacher Education
Summer Jobs--Sorted by College and Category
Ideas for student summer jobs
Summer_Camp_Jobs_in_the_US
DIRECTORY OF OVERSEAS SUMMER JOBS
CDC Directories of Summer Jobs
Resumes for Summer Jobs
Summer Jobs Advertised Through the Career Center
Navy Scholarships and Summer Jobs
PART TIME/FULL TIME SUMMER JOBS: LINGUISTICS
Summer jobs for C/C++ programmers--MD, USA
Guide to Summer Jobs
Summer Camp Jobs
```

Pretty impressive, huh? Remember, these listings come from Gophers located throughout Gopherspace. And, as you can see, not all of them involve actual job listings. "Resumes for Summer Jobs," for example, asks the question "Why prepare a resume for a summer job?" and then offers some excellent advice. It was written by Karen Towns at the Kenyon College Career Development Center.

Check the library reference area for key titles

Veronica also turned up a list of books dealing with summer jobs and internships. The information included only the titles and the call numbers at the college's reference desk. But it's certainly worth checking your college library's reference area for these:

Getting Work Experience: The College Students' Directory of Summer Internships that Lead to Careers

Summer Employment Directory of the United States

Directory of Summer Jobs in Britain

Directory of Internships, Work Experience Programs, and On-the-Job Training Opportunities

Internships

National Directory of Internships

Overseas Summer Jobs

Summer Jobs: Finding Them, Getting Them, Enjoying Them

America's Top 100 Internships

Mark Oldman and Samer Hamadeh have published a really neat book called America's Top 100 Internships. *Funny, well-written, and insightful, you will probably want to get your own copy. But you can get a really good look at the book by Gophering to* **bloggs.review.com***, the address of the Princeton Review. Pick "Career" in the menu that will appear, and you'll see another menu that includes selections dealing with internships: "Starting Early," "What 'They' Want," "Are Internships Worth It?"*

Here are two "Top Ten" lists from the book—the best internships to have, and then those that pay the best:

America's Top Ten Internships	Highest Compensation
Abbott Laboratories	Abbot Laboratories
Apple Computer	Apple Computers
Boeing	Arthur Andersen
The Coro Foundation	Boeing
Intel	Citibank
Lucasfilm	Frito-Lay
Microsoft	Hallmark Cards
Nat'l. Tropical Botanical Garden	Hewlett-Packard
TBWA	Inroads
The Washington Post	Intel

 # Check the Online Career Center

Though not specifically aimed at summer jobs, the Online Career Center (OCC) is an absolutely wonderful resource. You can search for jobs, and you can post your resume for searching by potential employers. All you have to do is Gopher to **occ.com** and select "Online Career Center" from the menu. Or visit the OCC site on the Web at **http://www.occ.com/occ/**. Figure 23-2 shows their opening screen.

Among the many selections you will find on various menus are these:

➤ Company Sponsors and Profiles

➤ Employment Events

➤ Career Assistance

➤ '95 College & University Resume Books/Diskettes

➤ Search Jobs

➤ Search Resumes

➤ Other Employment Databases/

➤ Recruitment Advertising Agencies

➤ "Online Career Center" On Campus

➤ How To Enter A Resume

➤ Help Wanted-USA/Gonyea and Associates, Inc.

➤ OCC Supports Recruiters' Networks World-Wide

➤ Auburn University MBA Resume Book

➤ UC Irvine—Graduate School of Management

➤ Hofstra MBA Resume Book

➤ University of Tennessee—Electronic Resume Book

➤ Washington University's Olin School of Business

Figure 23-2

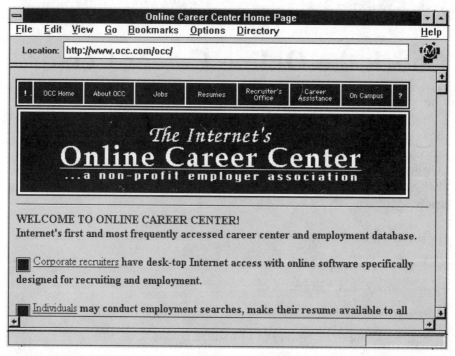

The Online Career Center on the World Wide Web

You can use OCC to search for jobs from just about any angle you can imagine: by company, by state, by city, by skill, by U.S. location (East, South, South Central, etc.), and by country. When I tried this recently, I picked France and came up with openings like these:

```
Civil Engineer-junior with 11 years experience looks for job
Translations agency seeking freelance translators
Trading Systems Development--Europe, Japan
Wineries (mostly from California, France, Germany)
Translator French/English
SGML--France (recruiter)
WINE SALESPEOPLE WANTED
UNIX System Admin. with C needed in Montreal
Designer/typographer needs contracts
Job Opening: Junior Sysadmin.
International Accountant--USR-IL
Trading, Quants--Europe
Positions available US/Canada/Europe--SHL Systemhouse
Government position for Research Epidemiologist
Parlez Vous Francais SQA/contract-recruiter
Sfw Localization in Paris, (Agency)
Soft. Eng. in Geometric Modeling Position
FRANCAIS/DEUTCH/contract-recruiter/So.Bay
```

NET TIP

Jobs-oriented newsgroups

In casting your net, don't forget about newsgroups. Here are some of the groups specifically devoted to job postings:

bionet.jobs	*Scientific Job opportunities.*
biz.jobs.offered	*Position announcements.*
hepnet.jobs	*Job announcements and discussions.*
misc.jobs.misc	*Discussion about employment, workplaces, careers.*
misc.jobs.offered	*Announcements of positions available.*
misc.jobs.offered.entry	*Job listings only for entry-level positions.*
misc.jobs.resumes	*Postings of resumes and "situation wanted" articles.*
relcom.commerce.jobs	*Jobs offered/wanted.*
sci.research.careers	*Issues relevant to careers in scientific research.*
vmsnet.employment	*Jobs sought/offered, workplace & employment related issues.*

 # Clearinghouse guides to Internet job resources

Among the many subject guides available from the University of Michigan Clearinghouse I told you about in Chapter 15, you'll find three that deal specifically with Internet job-search and employment-related features:

➤ **Employment Opportunities and Job Resources on the Internet** by Margaret F. Riley of the Gordon Library at Worcester Polytechnic Institute in Worcester, Massachusetts. This is the most comprehensive of the three. It's organized by Internet feature (newsgroups, Telnet, Gopher, mailing lists, and World Wide Web) and is updated periodically to include additional services. (Clearinghouse filename: **jobs:riley**)

➤ **Job Search and Employment Opportunities: Best Bets from the Net** by Philip Ray and Bradley Taylor of the University of Michigan. This guide takes a different approach. Rather than cover all the employment-related features and services on the Internet, the authors identify and describe only what they consider to be the "Best Bets" for job seekers in several broad areas—Education and Academe, Humanities and Social Science, Science and Technology, and so forth. The Net can be overwhelming, but this well-written and well-organized guide makes it seem almost manageable. (Clearinghouse filename: **employment:raytay**)

➤ **Finding Library Jobs and Library Employment: Navigating and Electronic Web** by John Fenner of the University of Western Ontario. If you're planning a job search for a traditional library position, you should definitely get this guide. Mr. Fenner, a graduate student himself, has assembled into a single 60-plus page document a wealth of information about newsgroups, mailing lists, Gophers, and other Internet resources of special interest to librarians or librarians-to-be. (Clearinghouse filename: **jobs:fenner**)

There are many ways to get to the Clearinghouse. Perhaps the easiest is to look for it on your local Gopher. Or Gopher to

gopher.lib.umich.edu and select "What's New and Featured Resources" and then "Clearinghouse. . . ." You can also use your Web browser to visit one of these sites (Note the tilde (~) before the letters *lou* in the second address):

http://www.lib.umich.edu/chhome.html
http://http2.sils.umich.edu/~lou/chhome.html

24
Travel information

AS befits a globe-girdling network, there is plenty of travel information on the Internet—whether you're planning a trip abroad or within the U.S. You may want to start by checking out some of the World Wide Web sites devoted to travel destinations.

Club Med, Daytona, & more

You can visit Club Med's home page, for example, and click your way through descriptions of all the various resorts and vacation packages they offer. (See Fig. 24-1.) And you'll find that Daytona Beach hotels are anxious for your Spring Break business—they've created a Web site specifically aimed at college students looking for a good time at the beach. But those are just two of the many Web sites offering travel information. Here are their addresses, along with several others you may want to try:

➤ City Net Maps and Travel Information
   http://www.city.net/

➤ Club Med
   http://www.clubmed.com/

➤ Cybertour of the USA
   http://www.std.com/NE/usatour.html

➤ Daytona Beach Springbreak Hotels and Activities
   http://www.america.com/mall/store/springbreak.html

➤ GORP (Great Outdoors Recreation Pages)
   http://www.gorp.com/

➢ Hawaii InfoWeb (Sponsored by Outrigger Hotels)
  www.outrigger.com/infoweb/Welcome.html

➢ Olympic Games 1996
  http://www.mindspring.com/~royal/olympic.html

➢ Net Travel Guide and Travel Resource Center
  **http://www.ora.com/gnn/meta/travel/res/nettravel
  .html**

➢ TravelWeb (Hyatt Hotels and Resorts, Best Western, Hampton
  Inn, etc.)
  http://www.travelweb.com/

Figure 24-1

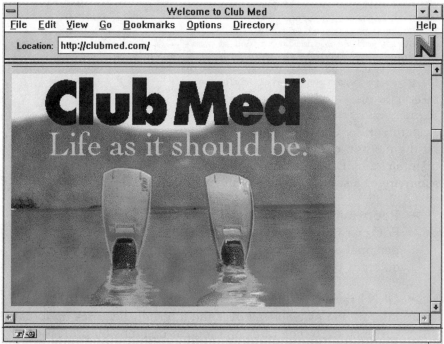

*When the snow starts falling, pack your snorkel and fins and head to Club
Med!*

 # Check out the RiceInfo Gopher

Another good source of travel information is the RiceInfo Gopher.
Gopher to **riceinfo.rice.edu** (or visit their Web site at **http://riceinfo.rice.edu**) and pick "Travel" off the main menu. That will
take you to a menu similar to this one:

```
1   About this directory                                  Text
2   Airlines: Tollfree Phone Numbers for Airlines         Text
3   Airport Codes                                         Text
4   Avalanche Warnings and Information                    Text
5   French Embassy in Washington, DC (French travel info) Menu
6   Green.Travel Mailing List                             Menu
7   Guide to online travel info (UManitoba)               Text
8   Moon Travel Handbooks                                 Menu
9   Omni-Cultural-Academic-Resource                       Menu
10  Road Reports, Colorado                                Text
11  State Dept. Travel Advisories                         Menu
12  Subway guides / Indicateur des metros                 Menu
13  Travel Information Library (University of Manitoba)    Menu
14  U.S. State Department Travel Advisories               Menu
15  US State Department Travel Advisories                 Menu

Enter Item Number, SAVE, ?, or BACK: 7
```

Select item 7, "Guide to online travel info," and you'll think you've
hit the mother lode of Internet travel resources. The material is
maintained by Brian Lucas. Here's a quick, drastically shortened
summary of just four of the resources described:

➤ **Rec.travel** Library. A collection of travelogues, guides, and
FAQs written by volunteers on the Net. Emphasis is on
personal advice, recommendations, and opinions, providing a
different perspective from that given by many travel books.

➤ GNN Travel Centre. A good collection of pointers to travel
information available all over the Internet. Features up-to-date
currency exchange rates and regular columns by professional
and amateur travel writers.

> ➤ Arctic Adventours. A Norwegian tour operator specializing in expeditions and explorations in the Arctic.

> ➤ Hotels Plus. A USA-based tour operator offering over 4,000 hotel locations throughout Europe, Asia, and Africa, and over 1,600 auto rental locations in 22 European countries. *Consumer Reports'* "Travel Letter" has named Hotels Plus a "Best Buy" for several years running.

Moon Travel Handbooks

One of the resources on the RiceInfo Gopher is "Moon Travel Handbooks." Based in Chico, California, Moon Publications has produced travel handbooks since 1983. The books are both cultural essays and consumer reports.

According to the company, "From the start, Moon Handbooks have been famously comprehensive, with more historical background, more outdoor recreation, more restaurants, hotels, and other practicalities—simply more information—than any other series of travel guidebooks. . . . Moon's recently established services on the Internet emerged from our desire to communicate directly with as many of our readers as possible. We're always working to improve our Handbooks, and appreciate any and all correspondence about price hikes, new hotels, closed restaurants, transportation tips, map errors, and anything else that may prove useful to the next traveler."

You can tap into Moon Travel via RiceInfo. But you can also access the company's Gopher directly by Gophering to **gopher.moon.com**. Or visit their Web site (shown in Fig. 24-2) at **http://www.moon .com:7000/**.

Figure 24-2

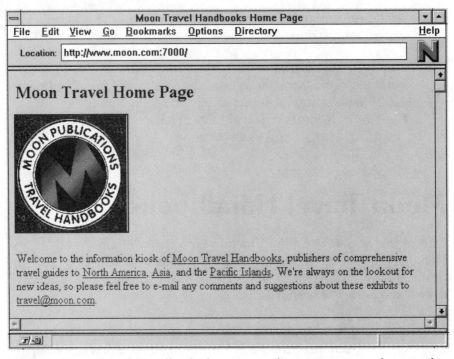

Visit the Moon Travel Handbooks home page for interesting and unusual travel guides for North America, Asia, and the Pacific Islands.

NET TIP

The Walt Disney World mailing list

Walt Disney World is the most popular tourist attraction in the world. So it is only fitting that there be a mailing list devoted to it. Here's the list and the write-up:

```
Walt Disney World
Contact: toddm@twain.ucs.umass.edu (Todd D. McCartney)
Purpose:
A comprehensive guide to Walt Disney World for the amateur or
veteran traveler. Some sections of the book include: Admissions,
Transportation, Resorts, The Magic Kingdom, EPCOT Center,
Disney/MGM Studios, Water parks, other attractions, night life,
fun facts and much more! The book is in its third year of
updating and continues to grow with each new revision.
Subscribers will receive the book through e-mail about 4-5 times
per year. Please note: Be sure to have disk space on your
account. The book is approximately 235,000 bytes and growing with
each version.
```

To subscribe to the list, send a message stating that you wish to subscribe to the WDW Guide Book mailing list. Send your message to **toddm@twain.ucs.umass.edu**.

The Subway Navigator

The Subway Navigator is based in Paris, France. But, thanks to the Internet, it might as well be based in the building next door. To tap in, simply Gopher to **gopher.jussieu.fr** and choose "Indicateur des metros" and then "Subway indicator. Or Telnet to **metro.jussieu.fr 10000**.

Most of the subway systems in the world are covered (Vienna, Montreal, Toulouse, Frankfurt, Munich, Hong Kong, Barcelona, Boston, New York, San Francisco, Washington, D.C., etc.). Pick one, then follow the prompts for departure and destination stations. The system will tell you exactly which line to take, what stops you will pass through along the way, and about how long it will take to reach your destination.

Guides to the Big Apple

At this period in human history, New York City is still the cultural and financial capital of the world. If you've got a lot of money to spend, it's easy to have a wonderful time. If you're on a budget, you'll have to be a bit creative. Either way, you'll need the right information. And the Internet feature, *The Net Person's Guide to New York City*, can supply it.

Just Gopher to **quartz.rutgers.edu** and choose "NYC-The Net Person's Guide to New York City" from the first menu. Or get the guide by FTP from **quartz.rutgers.edu**, Path: /pub/nyc/.

For New York City information on the World Wide Web, try one of these locations:

➢ **http://www.cs.columbia.edu/nyc/**

➢ **http://eMall.com/ExploreNY/NY1.html**

NET TIP

Travel-related newsgroups

Internet newsgroups can be a good source of travel information. Here are some of the groups that deal with travel-related matters:

alt.travel.canada	*All about travelling to Canada.*
alt.travel.road-trip	*Ever go to Montreal for pizza—from Albany?*
bit.listserv.travel-l	*Tourism discussions.*
rec.travel.air	*Airline travel around the world.*
rec.travel.asia	*Travel in Asia.*
rec.travel.cruises	*Travel by cruise ship.*
rec.travel.europe	*Travel in Europe.*
rec.travel.marketplace	Tickets and accommodations wanted and for sale.
rec.travel.misc	*Everything and anything about travel.*
rec.travel.usa-canada	*Travel in the United States and Canada.*

 # Nude beaches: the definitive guide

If you're interested in the best nude beaches in the world, FTP to
ftp.sunet.se, Path: /pub/usenet/news.answers/nude-faq/beaches/.
Key in dir and you will see a listing like this:

```
FTP> dir
200 PORT command successful.
150 Opening ASCII mode data connection for /bin/ls.
total 86
-r--r--r--    1 9500      9500         26370 Apr  3 00:22 Australasia
-r--r--r--    1 9500      9500          9430 Apr  3 00:23 Caribbean
-r--r--r--    1 9500      9500         23595 Apr  3 00:24 Europe
-r--r--r--    1 9500      9500         17831 Apr  3 00:25 Hawaii
drwxrwxr-x    2 1001      1100          8192 Apr  6 01:27 North-America
```

Maintained by Richard M. Mathews, each of the first four entries is a
file covering beaches in a particular part of the world. North America
is further divided into files for North, East, West, and California. The
reviews are thorough and authoritative. And, in addition to details and
impressions, they contain driving directions and addresses. Here's
how one volume on beaches in western North America begins:

```
This posting is a list of Clothing Optional beaches, hot springs,
and parks frequently mentioned in rec.nude. This list is far from
being a definitive list of Clothing Optional locales, and postings
to rec.nude asking about other such locales or presenting "trip
reports" to such locales are highly encouraged.
This is one of seven volumes of the "REC.NUDE FAQ: Naturist Site
Reports". These are posted on the first of each month.
This volume covers Western North America (except for California
and Tahoe).

In this issue:

WRECK BEACH, BC                    CONUNDRUM HOT SPRINGS, CO
MARSH ISLAND, WA                   SOUTH PADRE ISLAND, TX
THE EVERGREEN STATE COLLEGE, WA    HIPPIE HOLLOW, TX
ROOSTER ROCK, OR                   GRACY COVE, TX
SAUVIE ISLAND, OR                  FLAT ROCK, AR
```

If you are seriously interested in the clothing-optional lifestyle, move up to the directory /pub/usenet/news.answers/nude-faq. (The CDUP command should do it.) Then get all the files: **part1**, **part2**, etc. These files will tell you everything you want to know, including tons of addresses, publications, and a guide to using the newsgroup **rec.nude**.

The world's best roller coasters

Some people plan trips around bird watching and keep careful notes on the ones they see. For others, wineries or breweries supply a structure for the trip. And for some, it's the world's roller coasters. If roller coaster riding appeals to you, start by taking a look at the newsgroup **rec.roller-coaster**.

Then get the Roller Coaster FAQ by FTPing to **gboro.rowan.edu**, Path: /pub/Coasters/. There are several parts to the FAQ, so be sure to get all of them. Then check the list of image files that are available at the site. Figure 24-3 shows just one of dozens of roller coaster images you can download.

Figure 24-3

This is one of several gut-wrenching photos of the Kumba Coaster at Busch Gardens in Tampa, Florida. Please make sure that your seatbelt is fastened.

25
Studying abroad

IF you're interested in spending part of your college years studying in a foreign country, start by tapping the Internet. There's plenty of information, possibly even on your local Gopher.

The Gopher at Missouri University, for example, has an item called "Study Abroad Programs in a Nutshell." Programs are listed by country. Here are some sample listings for China and France:

CHINA

Xi'an Foreign Languages University, Xi'an—Study intensive Chinese language, history and culture. Academic year program (September 1–June 30). Earn 30–32 credit hours (complete area studies language requirement). Approximate cost: $6,690. Up to eight students participate each year. Requirements: 2.7 GPA, sophomore, junior or senior standing, strong desire to learn Chinese, and good academic standing at time of departure. Application deadline: February 15, 1996.

FRANCE

Universite Jean Moulin (Lyon III), Lyon—Study intensive French or a standard French university curriculum. Full year program (September to late June). Earn 24–30 credit hours. Approximate cost: $11,780. Up to four students participate each year. Requirements: 2.75 GPA, junior or senior standing, and French 106 or 126 or the equivalent. Application deadline: December 1, 1996.

Summer in France, Grenoble—Study intensive French language, civilization and literature. Six-week program (late June—end of July). Earn 7 credit hours. Approximate cost: $2,370. Usually 15–25 students participate each year. Requirements: 3.0 average in all French courses taken, completed at least French I and II or the equivalent, good health. Contact: Sylvana Escobar-Robertson, A&S 137, phone 882-3271. Application deadline for Summer 1996: February 15, 1996.

NET TIP

Don't leave home without the Money Abroad FAQ

Dealing with foreign currencies and other money matters can be a real problem for first-time overseas travelers. That's why Internaut Stephane Laveau created the Money Abroad FAQ. It offers all kinds of advice for travelers, and includes a handy country-by-country index with approximate exchange rates. You'll also find information on which form of payment (cash, check, or credit card) is best in each country.

The Money Abroad FAQ is on the menus of many travel-related features on the Internet. You'll also find it at this location on the Web:

http://www.inria.fr/robotvis/personnel/laveau/money-faq/ money-abroad.html

 # Ask Veronica...

Once you've reviewed the offerings on your local Gopher, you might want to try a Veronica search to broaden things beyond what's available on your own campus. Here are some of the items I found with a Veronica search on the phrase *study abroad*. Each item led to a text file or an additional menu with more information about specific programs.

```
Study Abroad
Graduate Study Abroad
Study Abroad Programs
Georgia State University Study Abroad Program
Study Abroad Center
```

```
Study Abroad! Culture Shock: Altering your mind set
Study Abroad! Home base: London afterwards, all Europe
Study Abroad! Shedding its rustic reputation: Yucatan
Study Abroad! The gem of northern Italy: Siena
Study Abroad! Ushered through London street by street
Environmental Study Abroad
SA-CKLIST      Study Abroad Procedures
SA-FINANCE     Study Abroad Financial Information
SA-SHARE       Study Abroad Shared Student Information
Jerusalem Center and Study Abroad
A Year Abroad: Study at the University of East Anglia
Study Abroad Resource Center
Study Abroad & Internships
Guide to All SUNY Study Abroad Programs
Study Abroad Programs By Country
Comments From Former Study Abroad Students
Study Abroad Publications/Resource Listing
Sample Resume Showing A Study Abroad Experience
STUDY ABROAD: Mexico
Grants Available For Study Abroad Advisers/1996 Conference
```

 # Search the Web with InfoSeek

Remember our discussion of InfoSeek in Chapter 5? To refresh your memory, InfoSeek is the Internet search tool I like so much. Specify a word, a phrase, or even a complete sentence and InfoSeek will search over 200,000 Web pages to find the ones that match your query. Why not try it for locating information on studying in a foreign country?

Start by going to the InfoSeek home page at **http://www .infoseek.com**. Click on the option for their free demo. Then key in your query—something like study abroad programs or study abroad europe or whatever. Within seconds, InfoSeek will present information on up to 10 Web sites that you can explore further.

One of the sites I discovered was the home page for an organization called the American Communication Association, shown in Fig. 25-1. In addition to dozens of listings for specific "Study Abroad Programs" sponsored by American colleges and universities, I also found lots of other great stuff on the menu: "Finding Jobs Abroad," "Foreign Language for Travellers," "Real Scholars' Pub Guides," "Travel Health Information." This site is definitely worth a visit. You'll find it at this address on the World Wide Web:

http://www.uark.edu/depts/comminfo/www/travel.html

Figure 25-1

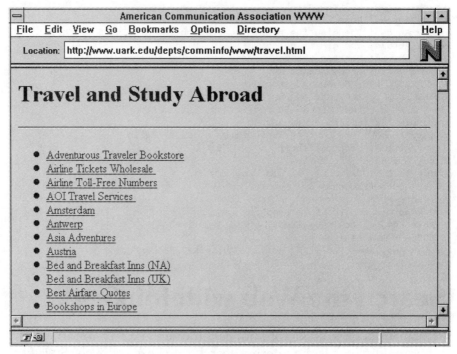

Check out the American Communication Association Web page for tons of information on traveling and studying in foreign countries.

My InfoSeek search also located the home page for the National Registration Center for Study Abroad (NRCSA). This organization collects information about thousands of schools—and maintains current information for the top 100 to 200. They also evaluate foreign language "immersion centers" and universities around the world and select the best programs for international visitors. To visit the NRCSA Web site, shown in Fig. 25-2, point your Web browser at this address:

http://execpc.com:80/~nrcsa/

NET TIP

Finding a Fulbright (or a Rhodes)

If money is a problem—and when isn't it?—you might explore the requirements for getting a Fulbright or Rhodes Scholarship. Just do a Veronica search on the phrase fulbright or rhodes. *Remember, Veronica lets you use ANDs and ORs in your searches.*

Here is the kind of thing you will find. Notice that this is just the first of 11 pages:

```
Search GopherSpace by Title word(s) (via University of Pisa)
Page 1 of 11

 1 09/27/95 FULBRIGHT GRADUATE STUDY ABROAD PROGRAM        Text
 2 Rhodes seeks faculty help in 'painful choices'          Text
 3 Fulbright-Hays US Government Predoctoral Grants          Text
 4 C14-82-488.0 James William Fulbright, 8pp               Text
 5 10/15/95 RHODES SCHOLARSHIPS:                           Text
 6 Fulbright grants for United States faculty and professionals Text
 7 Fulbright-Hays Dissertation Research Abroad             Text
 8 07/31/95 HUGH KELLY FELLOWSHIP AT RHODES UNIVERSITY:    Text
 9 President Rhodes announces he will step down            Text
10 Fulbright Scholar Awards Competition Open (NEW)         Text
11 FULBRIGHT SCHOLAR                                       Text
12 Fulbright scholarships                                  Text
13 Fundacion_Fulbright-Garcia_Robles                       Text
14 Fulbright-Hays US Government Predoctoral Grants         Text
15 Fulbright-Hays US Government Predoctoral Grants         Text
16 The Wooden Architecture of Little Poland Fulbright-Hays Text
17 Fulbright-Hays Fellowships Doctoral Dissertation Research Text
18 Fulbright Programs                                      Text
19 Fulbright-Hays Dissertation Research Abroad             Text

Enter Item Number, MORE, SAVE, ?, or BACK:
```

Figure 25-2

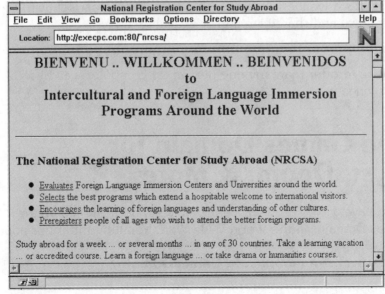

The National Registration Center for Study Abroad welcomes students to its home on the World Wide Web.

26
Games galore!

THOUGH I can't prove it, I'm certain that every computer that has ever existed has been used to play games of one sort or another. It's almost as if, like human beings, the machines need a little recreation now and then.

I'm sure the PC historians will quibble, and I know I'm leaving out CP/M, but from the consumer, end-user standpoint, one can pretty much date the real start of computer games from the introduction of Adventure as one of the four packages offered by IBM and Microsoft with the original IBM/PC in 1981. (The other three packages were DOS 1.0, BASIC, and VisiCalc.) Adventure is a text-based game that was developed by the Stanford Artificial Intelligence Lab (SAIL) in the 1970s. It's a wonderful game, but it pales in comparison with the commercial and shareware games available today.

The Internet, of course, has more game-related information and software to offer than any one person (or computer) can absorb. So let's plunge in.

The Games Domain for Myst, Doom, & more

If you have a Web browser, your first destination should be the Games Domain on the World Wide Web. You'll find it at this address:

http://wcl.rs.bham.ac.uk/GamesDomain/

Created and regularly updated by Dave Stanworth, this site provides links to hundreds of games-related resources on the Net. Myst, DOOM, Netrek, and countless other games are represented.

Here are just a few of the general categories you'll find on the Games Domain home page, shown in Fig. 26-1:

➤ Direct download of games and demos from FTP sites

➤ Games FAQs

➤ Games-related home pages

➤ Games-related magazines

➤ Games programming

➤ Commercial home pages (sites run by companies with game players in mind)

➤ Walkthroughs (for when you get stuck!)

Figure 26-1

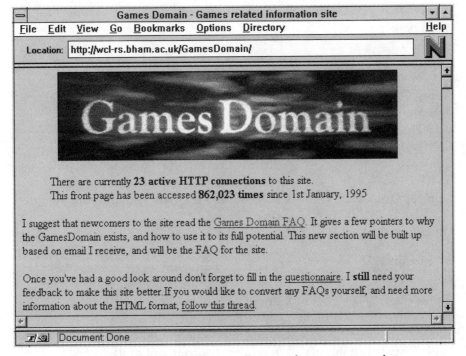

Serious gamers should add the Games Domain home page to their Bookmarks list.

 # The game center of the Internet universe

If it's PC games you're interested in, your next stop should be the University of Massachusetts at Lowell (UML), where you'll find the archives for the PC gaming community. To get there, FTP to **ftp.uml.edu**, Path: /msdos/Games/. The games offered are all public domain (PD) or shareware, and they are exclusively for DOS and Windows users.

Fortunately, this site makes no attempt to be all-inclusive. The reason this is good news is that there are thousands and thousands of DOS and Windows games out there, but, like everything else in life, the majority are mediocre. That's why I was especially pleased to learn that UML is the official Internet distribution site for games from Apogee, Epic MegaGames, MVP, and Id, as well as Game Bytes electronic magazine. (Apogee is the company that brought us Wolfenstein 3D, Duke Nukum, Word Rescue, and many other top-rated games.)

Here are the categories you will find in the PC games archives:

Apogee	Apogee-distributed games (official site)
Arcade	Arcade-style games
BBS Doors	Games suitable for BBS Doors
Cards	Various games based on playing cards
Demos	Demos of commercial games (playable and unplayable)
Editors	Game editors for free and commercial games
Education	Educational games
Epic	Epic MegaGames (official site)
Flight Simulator	Microsoft Flight Simulator accessories
FPS Football	Front Page Sports Football stuff
Game Bytes	Game Bytes Magazine (official site)
Game Dev	Game Development materials
Id	Games distributed by Id Software
Links 386 Tournament	Links 386 Tournament stuff

MahJongg	Various MahJongg games
Misc	Games not covered elsewhere
Moraff	Moraff games
MVP	MVP Software (official site)
Patches	Commercial patches
Program	Game programmer accessories/libraries
Puzzle	Puzzle-type games
Sports	Sports-related games
Tetris	Tetris/Columns-type games
Text Adventures	Text adventure games
Trivia	Trivia games
Utils	Games utilities
VGAPlanets	VGAPlanets multiplayer game and support files
Windows	Miscellaneous games for Windows 3.1

NET TIP

UML game site "mirrors"

For maximum distribution and network throughput, the UML PC games collection is "mirrored" (duplicated) on several other sites. Choose the site closest to you for best results. UML is located in Massachusetts. Other sites offering the collection include:

Location	Name	Directory
Missouri	**wuarchive.wustl.edu**	/systems/msdos/msdos-games
Wisconsin	**ftp.uwp.edu**	/pub/msdos/games/
Germany	**ftp.Uni-Paderborn.de**	/pcsoft/msdos/games
S. Africa	**ftp.sun.ac.za**	/pub/msdos/uml
Sweden	**ftp.sunet.se**	/pub/pc/mirror/games
Taiwan	**NCTUCCCA.edu.tw**	/PC/msdos
Thailand	**ftp.nectec.or.th**	/pub/mirrors/games
UK	**src.doc.ic.ac.uk**	/computing/systems/ibmpc/ msdos-games/Games

 # Rated EC: extreme carnage!

It's just possible that through my books and magazine articles on the subject, I've done more to turn people on to the wonders of shareware than anyone else. I don't know. I certainly hope so. In any case, I couldn't be more tickled to see the kind of quality demonstrated by companies like Apogee, Id Software, and Epic MegaGames. I've long maintained that the best shareware is every bit as good as the best commercial software. The products offered by these folks demonstrate that fact with a vengeance. (See Fig. 26-2 and Fig. 26-3 to get an idea of the quality of the graphics you'll encounter with two of Apogee's most popular games.)

Figure 26-2

Raptor: Call of the Shadows. The mega-hit airborne adventure from Apogee. You're a mercenary flying your high-tech fighter in this vertical-scrolling shooter. Requires 386+, 2MB+, VGA. Supports soundcards, mouse, and joystick.

Figure 26-3

Duke Nukum II. The Duke is back and blazing away in "neo-L.A."

Here's what *PC Magazine* (April 12, 1994) had to say about DOOM and Blake Stone, two games you can get from the UML site:

> If the U.S. Congress knew about Id Software's DOOM and Apogee Software's Blake Stone: Aliens of Gold, they'd be investigating violence in computer games, not video games. The first-person viewpoint and smooth movement in these successors to the shareware smash hit, Wolfenstein 3D, will have you peering sideways into the monitor to see if there's a monster around the corner. . . . The shareware versions of these games include one mission made up of numerous levels. The full, registered versions offer multiple missions.

> [W]here DOOM's advanced 3-D engine gives it more realistic visuals, including curved walls and outdoor scenes, Blake Stone's sound effects are better, with different sounds for each enemy, including a despairing "Not Meeeee!" if you shoot a helpful informant. . . . Fans of ultraviolent shoot-'em-up games will definitely want both of these games.

I should add that DOOM requires 4 megs of RAM and 10 megs of hard disk space (!), and Blake Stone requires 600K of free DOS memory and 8 megs of hard disk space. Both companies recommend using a sound board as well, and I heartily concur. I've played Wolfenstein 3D both with and without sound, and there is simply no comparison to the experience of playing it with a SoundBlaster or compatible.

NET TIP

Macintosh game software

If you have a Mac and are interested in PD and shareware games, try these two FTP sites:

1. FTP to **ftp.uu.net***, Path: /systems/mac/.*

2. FTP to **sumex-aim.stanford.edu***. Then key in* dir.

Games-oriented newsgroups

As always, it's a good idea to see if there are any newsgroups devoted to your topic of interest. Here are the names of the leading games-oriented newsgroups at this writing:

> **comp.sys.ibm.pc.games.announce** Check here for new release announcements, software publisher news, bug information, reviews, top 100 games, and Game Bytes information.

> **comp.sys.ibm.pc.games.action** Arcade-style games like DOOM, Mortal Kombat, and X-Wing.

> **comp.sys.ibm.pc.games.adventure** Continuing character games, puzzles, and so forth—like Hand of Fate, Judgment Rites, or King's Quest 6.

> **comp.sys.ibm.pc.games.flight-sim** Flight simulation games like Aces Over Europe, Air Warrior, and Falcon 3.0.

> **comp.sys.ibm.pc.games.misc** Sports and puzzle games; miscellaneous games.

> **comp.sys.ibm.pc.games.rpg** Role-playing games like Lands of Lore, Dark Sun, Shattered Lands, and Ultima VII: Part 2.

> **comp.sys.ibm.pc.games.strategic** Strategy games like Civilization, Master of Orion, and the V for Victory series.

⇨ Other, related, newsgroups

You will want to be sure to get the main PC Games FAQ, since it is an incredible resource of game-related sources and information on the Net (including game-specific FAQs and mailing lists). Check the newsgroup **comp.sys.ibm.pc.games.announce** for parts 1 and 2, since they are regularly posted there. You can also find an archive copy at the FTP site **rtfm.mit.edu**, Path: /pub/usenet/ comp.answers/PC-games-faq/. Or you can get it from Glossbrenner's Choice on the disk called Just the FAQs.

According to the FAQ, the following newsgroups often deal with topics of interest to game players. An asterisk (*) indicates that there are several subgroups that might be of interest.

alt.cd-rom
alt.games.*
alt.games.doom

alt.games.vga-planets
comp.sys.amiga.games
comp.sys.mac.games
comp.sys.ibm.pc.hardware.*
comp.sys.ibm.pc.hardware.cd-rom
comp.sys.ibm.pc.hardware.chips
comp.sys.ibm.pc.hardware.storage
comp.sys.ibm.pc.hardware.systems
comp.sys.ibm.pc.hardware.video
comp.sys.ibm.pc.soundcard.*
rec.arts.int-fiction
rec.aviation.simulators
rec.games.*
rec.games.corewar
rec.games.design
rec.games.empire
rec.games.hack
rec.games.int-fiction
rec.games.moria
rec.games.mud.*
rec.games.programmer

NET TIP

Game cheat sheets

Cheating on a game is no fun, but sometimes, when you're completely stumped, you have no choice. Should that time come to you, there are at least three places you can go. You will find text files containing hints, tips, and answers for most leading shareware and commercial games:

*1. FTP to **ftp.funet.fi**, Path: /pub/doc/games/solutions/*

*2. FTP to **ftp.gmd.de**, Path: /if-archive/solutions/.*

*3. FTP to **ftp.uwp.edu**, Path: /pub/msdos/games/romulus/cheats/ and /pub/msdos/games/romulus/hints/.*

*4. Gopher to **wiretap.spies.com** and choose "Wiretap Online Library," then "Mass Media," then "Games and Video Games." (You can also FTP to this site using the address **ftp.spies.com**, Path: /Library/Media/Games/.)*

 # Netrek!

If you haven't heard about Netrek, you will! Netrek is a 16-player, graphical, real-time battle simulation with a Star Trek theme. The game is divided into two teams of 8 (or fewer), which engage in dogfights and attempt to conquer each other's planets. There are several different types of ships, from fast, fragile scouts up to big, slow battleships. This allows a great deal of variance in play styles.

Netrek is set up as a client/server combination. If you want to play, you'll need the client binary for your machine (most are X-based). The graphics are strictly character-based, but the action can't be beat. To tap in, visit one of these sites on the World Wide Web:

http://obsidian.math.arizona.edu:8080/netrek.html
http://web.city.ac.uk/~cb165/netrekFAQ.html

You'll also want to check out the newsgroup **rec.games.netrek**. Here's a sample of the kinds of messages you'll see:

```
 1 rec.games.netrek FAQ List
 2 Netrek Server List
 3 Netrek FTP list.
 4 Theme nights on servers... (2 msgs)
 5 New Hours (2 msgs)
 6 sunscreamer -> MUCUS PIG (2 msgs)
 7 upgrade server (7 msgs)
 8 WANTED: Medium clue teams for scrimmage
 9 Who are better players...Paradise or Bronco? (13 msgs)
10 COW-Sound upgrade 11 CLASSIC BATTLES: suggestion (3 msgs)
12 tywong, man or myth? (3 msgs)
13 Home Field for playoffs (2 msgs)
14 Where is it?
15 INL Stats: suggestion (3 msgs)
16 World vs World
17 Sturgeon Update
18 INL servers and "BE QUIET" (9 msgs)
19 who's who - a hunk of code for YOU (4 msgs)
```

The Netrek FAQ, which you'll find at the Web sites or posted to the newsgroup, will tell you everything you need to know to get started. So, good luck, cadet. You'll need it.

MUDs & their relatives

Adventure, the text-based game I mentioned at the beginning of the chapter, gives you a paragraph telling you where you are as it starts. From that point, you enter commands like look, inventory (to check what you're holding), get, nw (to go northwest), or some other directional command.

Whatever you enter, the computer will have some reply. Thus, if you key in get food, the computer is likely to respond, "I don't see any food here." If you key in abracadabra, the computer might surprise you by saying "That is a very old magic word, and it doesn't work here." On the other hand, if you key in xyzzy, you can never be sure what will happen.

Multi-user everythings

The Internet MUDs you may have heard of—and their ilk—are all based on the Adventure model. The term *MUD* can be interpreted as Multi-User Dungeons, Multiple User Dimension, or Multi-User Dialogue. The key thing is that the term refers to text-based games that can be played on the Net by multiple users at the same time. Thus, MUDs and their variants, like Multi-User Shared Environments (MUSEs), use the Internet IRC chat feature to facilitate multi-user interactions.

In general, these are all live, role-playing games in which you assume a new identity and enter an alternate reality through your keyboard. To explore this world, you use a series of Adventure-like commands— like look, go, take, and so on. The big difference is that when you play the classic Adventure game, you are playing against the computer. But when you're in a MUD, you will run across other users, who may engage you in a friendly discussion, ask you to join or help them in some mythic quest—or try to kill you for no apparent reason.

 # How to get into the MUDs

Addictive? You bet. But your fun must be purchased at a price. Every MUD has its own personality and creator (or "God"). This is the person who was willing to put in the long hours required to establish the particular MUD's rules, laws of nature, and information databases.

In effect, when you enter a given MUD or MUSE or whatever, you are entering a world created by a single individual (or, at most, one or two individuals). They set the rules. They create the situation and the challenges you must overcome. If you don't like it, there are plenty of other games to choose from.

Trouble is, in order to find out about the game and to learn the rules of play, you've got to do a lot of reading. And there is no guarantee that, after you've learned the rules and are ready to play, you will like the MUD or whatever at all. On the other hand, if you've got time on you hands and a free Internet account, who cares?

 # Getting started

If you want to plug into MUD-like culture, the single most important document to get is Jennifer "Moira" Smith's MUDs FAQ. Ms. Smith has done an absolutely splendid job of distilling the essence of MUDs and online gaming culture. I simply cannot say enough for her FAQ.

You will find a copy on the Glossbrenner's Choice disk called Just the FAQs. But you can also get the file by checking the Usenet newsgroup **rec.games.mud.announce**. It will probably be in at least three parts.

MUD newsgroups & more

There are several Usenet newsgroups devoted to MUDs. These include:

rec.games.mud.admin — *Postings pertaining to the administrative side of MUDs.*

rec.games.mud.announce — *Announcements of MUDs that are opening, closing, moving, partying, etc.*

rec.games.mud.diku — *Postings pertaining to DikuMUDs.*

rec.games.mud.lp — *Postings pertaining to LPMUDs.*

rec.games.mud.misc — *Miscellaneous postings.*

rec.games.mud.tiny — *Postings pertaining to the Tiny* family of MUDs.*

And there are at least two Gopher sites and one FTP site you should visit if you decide that MUDs are for you:

- *Gopher to the University of Tuebingen.*
  Address: **nova.tat.physik.uni-tuebingen.de 4242**.
  Choose the menu selection "Documents and papers about MUDs."

- *Gopher to the University of Texas at Austin.*
  Address: **actlab.rtf.utexas.edu**.
  Look for the menu selection "Virtual Spaces:MUD."

- *To get a classified list of all available Internet MUDs, FTP to* **caisr2.caisr.cwru.edu**. *Path: /pub/mud/. Or check the newsgroup* **rec.games.mud.announce** *for the list that is uploaded every Friday.*

27
Movies, TV, & Comics

WHERE would the world be—particularly the world of academe—without movies, TV, and comics? And I'm not talking about all the learned monographs on popular culture and "films." I'm talking about pure, mindless recreation. The kind you need after your midterms are over. The kind you need, in measured quantities, every day.

Yahoo Entertainment

Start by visiting the Yahoo Entertainment page at this location on the World Wide Web: **http://www.yahoo.com/Entertainment/**. From the opening screen (shown in Fig. 27-1), you can scroll through dozens of topics, until you get to "Television."

Click on that and you'll be whisked to another page with links to all sorts of television-related Internet resources. All the most popular shows are represented—*Letterman*, *Seinfeld*, *Friends*, *Beavis and Butt-head*, and *Saturday Night Live*, to name just a few. And there's no telling what you'll find. The picture of the Seinfeld gang shown in Fig. 27-2 is a .GIF file made available by a company promoting its Seinfeld video clips and screen savers.

You'll have a great time exploring Yahoo's Entertainment offerings. One area not to miss is the "Deep Thoughts" section, featuring Deep Thoughts by Jack Handey of *Saturday Night Live* fame. There's

Figure 27-1

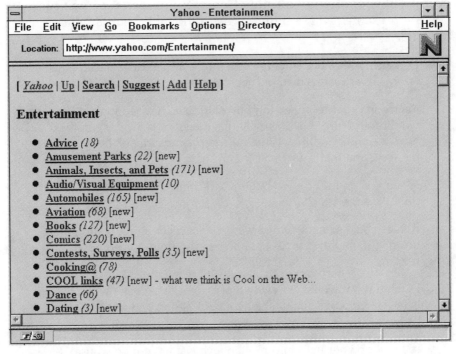

You'll be entertained for hours by the Yahoo Entertainment page on the Web.

Figure 27-2

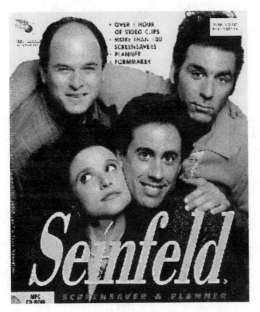

Jerry and the Seinfeld gang as a downloadable .GIF file.

even a "Random Deep Thoughts Generator"—each time you click, you are presented with a different deep thought! Here are just a few to ponder:

Dad always thought laughter was the best medicine, which I guess is why several of us died of tuberculosis.

Maybe in order to understand mankind, we have to look at the word itself: *Mankind.* Basically, it's made up of two separate words—*mank* and *ind.* What do these words mean? It's a mystery, and that's why so is mankind.

When you go in for a job interview, I think a good thing to ask is if they ever press charges.

If trees could scream, would we be so cavalier about cutting them down? We might, if they screamed all the time, for no good reason.

I wish a robot would get elected president. That way, when he came to town, we could all take a shot at him and not feel too bad.

If you drop your keys into molten lava just let 'em go 'cause, man, they're gone.

In weightlifting, I don't think sudden, uncontrolled urination should automatically disqualify you.

The old pool shooter has won many a game in his life. But now it was time to hang up the cue. When he did, all the other cues came crashing to the floor. "Sorry," he said with a smile.

If God dwells inside us, like some people say, I sure hope He likes enchiladas, because that's what He's getting!

NET TIP

The *Saturday Night Live!* FAQ

If you're an SNL fan, you might want to check out the SNL-FAQ, which you'll find in lots of places on the Net. Among other things, it will alert you to the existence of the newsgroup **alt.tv.snl***. And it will answer questions like these:*

- *What is SNL?*
- *Is it really live?*
- *Is there an episode guide?*
- *Where is the show broadcast from?*
- *Wasn't Steve Martin a player?*
- *What is a "Five Timer"?*
- *How do I get tickets for SNL?*
- *How can I contact Lorne Michaels?*
- *Which star has been on the show the longest?*
- *Who were the youngest and oldest hosts?*
- *It's only x weeks into the season. Why are they showing reruns?*
- *How can I learn more about SNL?*

NET TIP

The Official David Letterman Songbook

Ever since he moved to CBS, David Letterman has been hard not to like. He always seems to be having so much fun up there. To get the lyrics for such immortal classics aired on the show as "The Viewer Mail Theme," "The Strong Guy, the Fat Guy, the Genius," and "Late Night World of Love," FTP the official songbook file from **rtfm.mit.edu** *Path: /pub/usenet/news.answers/letterman/songbook.*

 # TV episode guides & more

Another good source of television information on the Net is the Wiretap Gopher. Gopher to the address **wiretap.spies.com** and choose "Wiretap Online Library," then "Mass Media," to get to this menu:

```
Mass Media
Page 1 of 1

1 Books                      Menu
2 Comics and Japanese Anime  Menu
3 Film and Movies            Menu
4 Games and Video Games      Menu
5 Miscellaneous              Menu
6 Science Fiction and Fantasy Menu
7 Star Trek                  Menu
8 Television                 Menu

Enter Item Number, SAVE, ?, or BACK:
```

When you select "Television," you will be taken to a series of menus containing items like these:

Alf Episode Guide
All in the Family Episode Guide
Amazing Stories Episode Guide
Avengers Episode List
Battlestar Galactica Episode Guide
Blake's 7 Abbreviated Program Guide
Cheers Mega List of Episodes
Cheers Trivia
Doctor Who Episode List
Doctor Who's Canonical List of Sluts
Fawlty Towers Episode Guide
Highlander Episode Guide (Season 1)
Interview with Peter Chung (MTV Liquid TV)
Lost In Space Episode Guide
MASH Episode Guide
Married With Children Episode Guide
Moonlighting Episodes
Northern Exposure Episode Guide
Outer Limits Episode Guide
Parker Lewis Episode Guide Supplement
Red Dwarf Episode Guide
Seinfeld Episode Guide
Twilight Zone Episode Guide
Twin Peaks Allusions
Twin Peaks Cast
Twin Peaks Pilot—every second of it
Twin Peaks Symbolism
Twin Peaks Timeline
Twin Peaks Timeline (extended)
WKRP in Cincinnati Episodes

The Trek!

The Wiretap Gopher also has what must be the definitive collection of information about *Star Trek*. Gopher to **wiretap.spies.com** and choose "Wiretap Online Library," then "Mass Media," then "Star Trek," and you'll find this incredible collection of stuff:

Deep Space 9 Episode Guide
Discussion of Star Trek Cloaking Devices
Klingon Vocabulary
Location of Vulcan: The Final Word
Music of Star Trek
Star Trek (original) Episode Guide
Star Trek Drinking Game
Star Trek Novels Year In Review
Star Trek Ship Names
Star Trek TNG Episode Guide
Star Trek Top Ten Lists p.1
Star Trek TNG List of Lists
Star Trek TOS Romance/Love List
Star Trek Stardates

Tardis Television Database & Archives

If you have a Web browser, you can take advantage of yet another great collection of TV episode guides and related information—the Tardis Television Database and Archives, shown in Fig. 27-3. To get there, point your Web browser at this address:

http://www.tardis.ed.ac.uk/~dave/guides/index.html.

NET TIP

Tap the Movie Database Server!

Ever wonder who directed some movie you've just heard about? And what other movies has this actor or actress appeared in? Not even the leading movie reference books can give you the kind of information, sliced so many different ways, that you can get from a computer.

Just ask the Movie Database Server. To find out about it, send e-mail to **movie@ibmpcug.co.uk**, *making sure to include the single word* help *as your message. Soon you will find a help file in your mailbox telling you how to frame other requests to search the Movie Database—by title, director, cinematographer, actor, writer, and more. You can even call up a list of every movie a given actor has appeared in. Multiple requests may be submitted in a single message.*

Figure 27-3

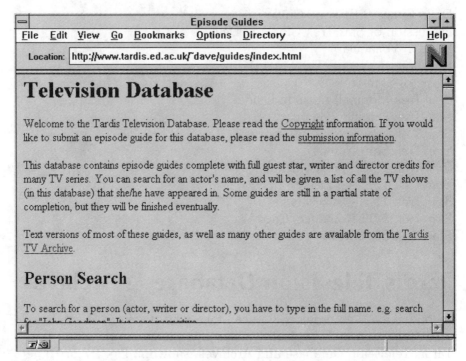

You can search the Tardis Television Database and Archives for your favorite TV show, or for a particular actor, writer, or director.

Transcripts from Journal Graphics

In recent years Journal Graphics has pretty well gotten a lock on the transcript business. And it has expanded its scope well beyond the Sunday morning political programs with all their talking heads. Radio and television programs are all included.

One of the great things about the Journal Graphics feature on the Internet is that you can *search* for transcripts by specifying a person's name or other keyword. You will find this to be truly impressive. But, while the information about who appeared where and when is free, the actual transcript is not. Costs range from $20 for fax delivery to $15 for overnight delivery to $10 for delivery by regular mail. Visa, MasterCard, and American Express are accepted, so you can place your order while you are online.

To tap in, Telnet to **database.carl.org** and select "Other Information and Article Databases" from the menu that will then appear. As you will learn, the Journal Graphics database "contains more than 75,000 records that refer to broadcasts that appeared on CNN, ABC, CBS, PBS, and National Public Radio since 1981. Included are the story's headline, the program name, an abstract, the names of guests, and the program's anchor. Subject terms are assigned to each record by Journal Graphics, Inc."

When I searched for actor Liam Neeson recently, the system gave me a list of appearances. I chose to get more information about an appearance on the PBS TV show *Charlie Rose*. Here's what appeared, finishing with a prompt at the end that I could have used to place an order for this transcript right away:

```
Host/Reporter: Correspondent
Headline:          A Tribute to Those Who Make Movies Magical
Program name:      Charlie Rose
Network:           WNET

Summary:           Rose presents interview excerpts with actors and
                   others who were involved in films nominated for
                   Oscar awards, and discusses the making of movies
                   and the roles played by actor, director, writer,
                   et al.

Show topics: Movies & Moviemaking; Performing Arts

Guests:            ANTHONY HOPKINS, Actor; LIAM NEESON, Actor;
                   LAURENCE FISHBURNE, Actor; STOCKARD CHANNING,
                   Actress; RALPH FIENNES, Actor; JIM SHERIDAN,
                   Director; GERRY CONLON, former Political
                   Prisoner; CHEN KAIGE, Director; TOM HANKS,
                   Actor; NORA EPHRON, Director; MARTIN SCORSESE,
                   Director

Air date:          03/18/1994 Show #:        1076 Segment:0
```

 # Comics on the Net? You bet!

Finally, how about some Internet sites for cartoon and comic-book fans? You'll need a graphical Web browser, of course, to follow the antics of Aaron A. Aardvark, Doctor Fun, Netboy, and the others. Assuming you have such, here are some of the most popular "comic destinations" on the Net:

➤ **Aaron A. Aardvark**   The blue-skinned aardvark who redefines naïveté, both digital and otherwise.
http://www.cts.com/~aardvark/abstract.html

➤ **Doctor Fun**   If you're a "Far Side" fan, you'll like Doctor Fun. See Fig. 27-4 for the Doctor Fun Page on the Web.
http://sunsite.unc.edu/Dave/drfun.html

➤ **Eden Matrix**   The home of Fantagraphics and Rip-Off Press and other underground publishers.
http://www.eden.com/comics/comics.html

➤ **Fun.Com**   All sorts of fun stuff, including a link to the "Comics 'n' Stuff" page, where you'll find Calvin and Hobbes, Krazy Kat, and other favorites.
http://vo.com/fun/

➤ **Netboy**   The wildly popular stick figure whose adventures have earned him the title of "King of the Internet Comic Universe."
http://www.interaccess.com/netboy.html

Figure 27-4

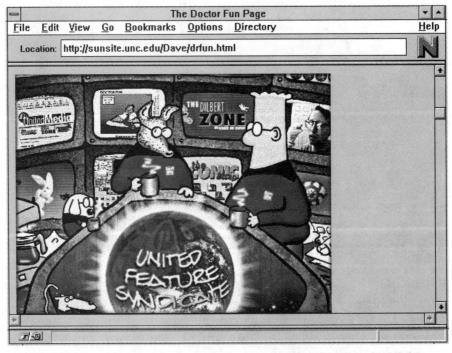

"Far Side" fans will want to visit the the Doctor Fun Page on the Web.

28
Articles of amusement

Joke collections, limericks, drinking games, & more online

I'VE got a friend named Jack who works at a store nearby. Every time I go in, he's got a joke for me. In fact, five jokes. Or a dozen. The guy could be a stand-up comic. And, amazingly, I don't think I've ever heard him tell the same joke twice. I, on the other hand, have trouble remembering Jack's best jokes by the time I get home. They are genuinely funny, but, for some reason, they just never stick.

I've been debating about whether to tell Jack about the Internet. I think it would be kind of like telling someone you knew was the lost Dauphin of France that you had absolute proof of his heritage. With Jack's eidetic memory and practiced delivery, and the vast joke and humor resources of the Internet, he could rule the world. Or at least become President of the United States.

 # "Humorous" newsgroups

At this writing, my friend Jack doesn't even own a computer, so the country is safe for the time being. But if he did have access to the Net, the first place I would tell him to check would be the various humor- or joke-related newsgroups. Here's a sampling:

alt.comedy.air-farce	Royal Canadian Air Farce.
alt.comedy.british	Discussion of British comedy in a variety of media.
alt.comedy.british.blackadder	The Black Adder program.
alt.comedy.firesgn-thtre	Firesign Theatre in all its flaming glory.
alt.comedy.improvisation	Group improvisational comedies.
alt.comedy.slapstick	Slapstick: comedy stressing farce and horseplay.
alt.comedy.slapstick.3-stooges	Hey, Mo!
alt.comedy.standup	Discussion of stand-up comedy and comedians.
alt.fan.dave_barry	Electronic fan club for humorist Dave Barry.
alt.fan.letterman	One of the top 10 reasons to get the alt groups.
alt.fan.letterman.top-ten	Top Ten lists from the Letterman show. (Moderated)
alt.fan.monty-python	Electronic fan club for those wacky Brits.
alt.fan.wodehouse	Discussion of the works of humor author P.G. Wodehouse.
alt.fan.woody-allen	The diminutive neurotic.
alt.fan.penn-n-teller	The magicians Penn Jillette & Teller.
alt.folklore.college	Collegiate humor.
alt.folklore.computers	Stories & anecdotes about computers (some true!).

alt.folklore.info	Current urban legends and other folklore. (Moderated)
alt.folklore.military	Military-oriented 'urban legends' and folklore.
alt.folklore.science	The folklore of science, not the science of folklore.
alt.folklore.urban	Urban legends, ala Jan Harold Brunvand.
alt.humor.best-of-usenet	What the moderator thinks is funniest. (Moderated)
alt.humor.puns	Not here.
alt.tasteless	Truly disgusting.
alt.tasteless.jokes	Sometimes insulting rather than disgusting or humorous.
alt.tv.comedy-central	Just what the hell is going on here?
alt.jokes.pentium	Playing with the problems plaguing Pentium.
alt.shenanigans	Practical jokes, pranks, randomness, etc.
rec.humor	Jokes and the like. May be somewhat offensive.
rec.humor.funny	Jokes that are funny (in the moderator's opinion) (Moderated).

NET TIP

Shenanigans!

What a wonderful word. Sure sounds Irish, but Webster's says "origin unknown" and pegs its first use at 1855. Well, never mind. You won't want to miss the **alt.shenanigans** *newsgroup.*

The FAQ alone is packed with information about books you can get detailing practical jokes and companies that supply joke items—even real police equipment. (Just think of the possibilities!) It's all quite harmless and funny. To get the FAQ, check **alt.shenanigans** *or* **alt.answers** *or* **news.answers**.

NET TIP

Rot-13 and coded jokes

*The group **rec.humor.funny** is one of the most popular groups on the Net. It accepts jokes from everywhere, but only those judged to be truly funny are posted to the group by the moderator, Brad Templeton, the fellow who runs Clari-Net. Inevitably, some jokes are bound to offend some people. To guard against such sensitive souls unexpectedly encountering something distasteful, some jokes are encoded like this:*

Gurfr ner gur gvzrf gung gel zra'f fbhyf...

The technique used to encode some jokes and other items on the Net is called Rot-13. This simply means that the alphabet is rotated 13 characters so that an A appears as an N, a B as an O, and so on.

The easiest way to decode this kind of text is to capture the encoded joke as a text file and then run ROT13.EXE against it. The file will be displayed on the screen, with all encoded text now readable (and all formerly readable text now encoded). ROT13.EXE is widely available on the Net in versions for every computer.

You'll find a copy of the DOS version and C source code on the Newsgroup Essentials disk from Glossbrenner's Choice. To use it to encode text, use a command like rot13 plain.txt > coded.txt *to redirect ROT13.EXE output to a file instead of the screen.*

*The other way to decode Rot-13 files is to use the commands built into the newsreader. If you are using the **nn** newsreader, for example, select the encoded article and then key in ZD. The capital Z tells **nn** that you want to look at the article right now, and the capital D tells **nn** to decode it.*

Here are the commands to use with each major newsreader:

Newsreader Program	Decryption Command
nn	*D*
rn	*Ctrl-X*
trn	*Ctrl-X*
tin	*d*

 The humor adventure begins!

As always, one of the best ways to track down information on the Net is to do a search of your local Gopher and then do a Veronica search of Gopherspace. The words *jokes* and *humor* would be very good search terms. But if you need a laugh in a hurry, try these Gopher and FTP sites:

➤ FTP to **cathouse.org**, Path: /pub/cathouse/. This is one of the main humor collection points on the Net. So you might want to start here.

➤ Gopher to **gopher.fct.unl.ptb** and select "Public info," then "Humor," then "Funny Texts."

➤ FTP to **donau.et.tudelft.nl**, Path: /pub/humor/.

➤ Gopher to **uts.mcc.ac.uk** and select "Gopher Services," then "The Joke File."

➤ FTP to **ftp.spies.com**, Path: /Library/Humor/Jokes/. Or gopher to **wiretap.spies.com** and choose "Wiretap Online Library," then "Humor," then "Jokes." (No matter who you are, you are guaranteed to be both amused and offended!)

➤ FTP to **nic.funet.fi**, Path: /pub/culture/tv+film/series/MontyPython.

➤ FTP to **ocf.berkeley.edu**, Path: /pub/Library/Monty_Python.

Yahoo humor, jokes, & fun

For one-stop joke shopping with your Web browser, try the Yahoo Entertainment page at this address:

http://www.yahoo.com/Entertainment/

Click on "Humor, Jokes, and Fun" for an incredible collection of pointers that goes on for several pages, starting with the one shown in Fig. 28-1. You'll find College Humor, Top 10 Lists, Barney the Dinosaur—you name it. Be sure to try the Excuse Generator ("I, your evil little brother, can get you out of anything") and Dave's Problem Solver (Fig. 28-2).

Figure 28-1

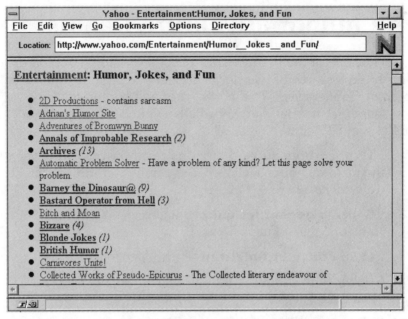

Yahoo Entertainment's collection of humor, jokes, and fun.

Figure 28-2

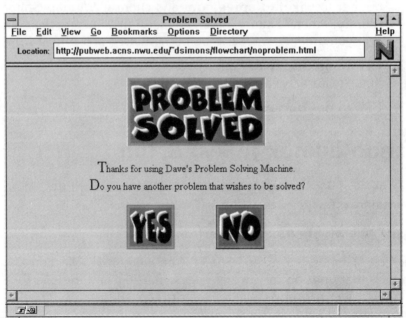

No problem is too large for Dave's Problem Solver on the World Wide Web.

→ Drinking songs, games, & recipes

I want to tell you about some really neat drinking-related features that you will find on the Net. Still, don't let all this fun and humor make you take drinking lightly.

I think it's unrealistic to assume that college students won't drink. You and I both know that sometime, somewhere during your college career, you are going to test the waters. And you probably should. Far better to make a fool of yourself now, among friends, than to have the experience in later life.

Drink if you will, but don't ever, ever, ever get into the driver's seat of a car when you're blasted. Have someone else drive you back to campus or call a cab or sleep it off on the cold, grassy ground, for heaven's sake! I refuse to believe that you're stupid.

And when and if you drink, don't drink without eating. I don't mean just a few peanuts when you walk in the door. You've got to have something substantial to sop up the beer, the wine, the vodka, or whatever, or you'll be taking á ride on the porcelain bus later in the evening.

Now, with all of those caveats and conditions stated, here are some newsgroups and FTP sites that you may want to check out:

> Newsgroups: **alt.beer**, **alt.zima**, and **rec.crafts.brewing**.

> FTP to **ftp.cwru.edu**, Path: /pub/alt.beer/. Here you will find the FAQ for **alt.beer**, plus lists of beer magazines, and information about the Campaign for Real Ale.

> FTP to **ocf.berkeley.edu**, Path: pub/Library/Recreation/big-drink-list. Try this site for mixing hints, tips, and recipes for nearly *every* drink anyone is *ever* likely to ask you to make. At this same site, check the path /pub/Library/Recreation/Booze_Cookbook for even *more* mixed drink recipes.

➤ FTP to **mthvax.cs.miami.edu**, Path: /pub/homebrew/. All about homebrewing beer, mead, and ale. You might also want to subscribe to a mailing list by sending your request to the subscription address **homebrew-request@hpfcmi.fc.hp .com**. And try FTPing to **nic.funet.fi**, Path: /pub/culture/ beer/, for more information on homebrewing.

➤ To get information on how to make your own alcoholic beverages, Gopher to **wiretap.spies.com**. Then pick "Wiretap Online Library," "Questionables," and "How To Make Alcohol." If you pick "Wiretap Online Library," "Articles," "Food and Drink," and then "Mead Recipes," you'll learn how to make the drink of Beowulf. From honey, of course.

⇨ Drinking games

Let's be Frank. Or Mabel. Or whatever. Drinking games are designed to get you drunk. So it is with some trepidation that I tell you to FTP to **sauna.cs.hut.fi**, Path: /pub/drinking_games/, for over 100 beer-drinking games. One of the classics is "Strange Brew," played as follows:

```
One of the all-time classics, a beer lovers "movie of a lifetime." What
you need to do is get A LOT of beer and a copy of the movie "Strange
Brew," starring Bob and Doug McKenzie, those whacked-out Canadian beer
hounds.

Version 1: Watch it. Anytime somebody says "eh" (pronounced like the
letter 'A'), drink. For example, "Get me a beer, eh?"

Version 2: Watch it. Anytime somebody says "hoser," drink. For example,
"You're a hoser."

Version 3: Watch it. Anytime somebody says "eh" or "hoser," drink. It's
all that simple.
```

Many of the other games you will find at this site are not nearly as simple. (Check out the file called "Simpsons" if you doubt me.) Still, it's all in good fun.

➡️ Limericks & other jokes

A really good limerick's not easy to find. (Because dirty words are so easy to rhyme?) But if you gopher to **quartz.rutgers.edu** and select "Humor," then "Limericks," you will find poems like these:

> A bather whose clothing was strewed
> By breezes that left her quite nude,
>   Saw a man come along
>   And, unless I'm quite wrong,
> You expected this line to be lewd.

If you go back to the Humor menu and select "gashlycrumb," you will meet Edward Gorey. Mr. Gorey is a longtime favorite of mine. But, I'm afraid the ASCII printed word does not do him justice. To get the full experience, you must see his drawings, which, indeed, you may have seen if you watch *Mystery* on PBS. (I recommend the books *Amphigorey* and *Amphigorey Too*.) In any case, here, with no illustrations, are "The Gashlycrumb Tinies" by Edward Gorey. I think you'll agree that Beavis and Butt-head would think them cool:

A is for Amy who fell down the stairs,
B is for Basil assaulted by bears.
C is for Clair who wasted away,
D is for Desmond thrown out of the sleigh.
E is for Ernest who choked on a peach,
F is for Fanny, sucked dry by a leech.
G is for George, smothered under a rug,
H is for Hector, done in by a thug.
I is for Ida who drowned in the lake,
J is for James who took lye, by mistake.
K is for Kate who was struck with an axe,
L is for Leo who swallowed some tacks.
M is for Maud who was swept out to sea,
N is for Nevil who died of ennui.
O is for Olive, run through with an awl,
P is for Prue, trampled flat in a brawl.
Q is for Quinton who sank in a mire,
R is for Rhoda, consumed by a fire.
S is for Susan who perished of fits,

T is for Titus who flew into bits.
U is for Una who slipped down a drain,
V is for Victor, squashed under a train.
W is for Winnie, embedded in ice,
X is for Xerxes, devoured by mice.
Y is for Yorick whose head was bashed in,
Z is for Zillah who drank too much gin.

⇨ Steven Wright

The FTP site at **cathouse.org** is a laugh a minute. Among other things, it's got what appears to be a complete transcript of everything comedian Steven Wright ever said. (Check the directory /pub/cathouse/humor/standup/steven.wright.) I have to say that the printed word can in no way substitute for Mr. Wright's deadpan delivery, but you can almost hear him saying:

> I got into an elevator at work and this man followed in after me . . . I pushed "1" and he just stood there . . . I said, "Hi, where you going?" He said, "Phoenix." So I pushed Phoenix. A few seconds later the doors opened, two tumbleweeds blew in . . . we were in downtown Phoenix. I looked at him and said, "You know, you're the kind of guy I want to hang around with."

> We got into his car and drove out to his shack in the desert. Then the phone rang. He said, "You get it." I picked it up and said, "Hello?". . . The other side said, "Is this Steven Wright?". . . I said, "Yes . . ." The guy said, "Hi, I'm Mr. Jones, the student loan director from your bank. It seems you have missed your last 17 payments, and the university you attended said that they received none of the $17,000 we loaned you. We would just like to know what happened to the money?" I said, "Mr. Jones, I'll give it to you straight. I gave all of the money to my friend Slick, and with it he built a nuclear weapon . . . and I would appreciate it if you never called me again."

Heh, heh, I got a million of 'em. Well, I don't exactly. But the Internet does. If you take the time to tap into even one tenth of the resources cited in this chapter, you'll be rolling in the aisles. And if you print the stuff out, you'll have your friends in stitches as well. It's all in knowing where to look. And now you do. Sorry. I gotta go. Say "hi" to Ian Shoals next time he's on the air.

Appendix

Glossbrenner's Choice

COMPUTERS and the Internet aren't really all that difficult to use, provided you've got two things—the right instructions and the right software. In the chapters of this book, I have done my very best to give you the right instructions. This appendix addresses the other need—the right software.

Through years of experience, I've become something of an expert on public domain and shareware software for DOS/Windows machines. I've even written several books on the subject. I know exactly what utilities and tools you need to make using your computer easier than you've ever imagined, and as a convenience to my readers, I have long made them available on disk as part of a collection I call Glossbrenner's Choice.

In addition to the software, however, I have also assembled a series of disks called the Internet Toolkit. These disks contain the FAQ files, the best directories, and other information you'll want to have as you get deeper into the Net. With two exceptions (Internet 3 and Internet 6), these disks can be used on both DOS and Macintosh systems.

If you have a Macintosh . . .

The PowerPC chip notwithstanding, it is likely to be a while before Macintoshes and PCs can share the same software. But the two systems have long been able to share text files, thanks to Apple's SuperDrive 3.5-inch disk-drive technology. If your Mac was manufactured after August 1989, it is almost certainly equipped with one or more SuperDrives.

Check your Reference manual for an appendix titled "Exchanging Disks and Files with MS-DOS Computers" or words to that effect. As you will discover, the necessary Apple File Exchange software is supplied on one of the Utility disks provided with your Mac system software.

Follow the Apple File Exchange instructions and you will be able to copy the files on the Internet Toolkit disks onto your hard drive. Since most of the files are plain ASCII text files, you can read and search them with your favorite word processor as easily as if you had created them yourself. There is no need to worry with any of the "translator" modules supplied with the Apple File Exchange software.

 # Costs & convenience

I want to emphasize that all of the files on the Internet Toolkit disks, as well as the programs in the DOS/Windows collection, can be found on the Internet itself and on BBSs, CompuServe, America Online, and other online systems. I urge you to use the file-finding, searching, and downloading techniques you've learned in this book to go online and get what you want.

What I offer here, for readers who want to take advantage of it, is selection and convenience. In the course of writing books about the Internet and online services, I am online many times a day, and I use the same files and programs you will find described here. In my opinion, they represent the very best of what's available on the Net. And since I have located and downloaded all of them, why not offer them to readers who would prefer not to do the legwork themselves?

NET TIP

Glossbrenner's Choice disks

Here's a list of the disks discussed in this appendix.

The Internet Toolkit

Internet 1	*Internet Must-Have Files*
Internet 2	*FTP Essentials*
Internet 3	*Telnet Essentials (DOS/Windows only)*
Internet 4	*Newsgroup Essentials*
Internet 5	*Mailing List Essentials*
Internet 6	*Compression & Conversion Tools (DOS/Windows only)*
Internet 7	*Just the FAQs*
Internet 8	*World Wide Web Essentials*
Internet 9	*Making Money on the Internet*

DOS/Windows Tools & Utilities

Animation Tools
Communicator's Toolchest
CommWin Communications Package
Encryption Tools
FANSI & LIST
GhostScript
Graphic Workshop
Graphic Workshop for Windows
Instant File Management: QFILER, QEDIT, & Associates
Newkey Keyboard Macroing Program
Paint Shop Pro for Windows
Qmodem Communications Program
Sound Tools
System Configuration Tools
Text Treaters
Visual BASIC Runtime (VBRUN) Libraries

 # The Internet Toolkit

The disks in the Internet Toolkit collection contain key FAQs, directories, guides, lists, and other information about using various features of the Internet. To make it easy to search these files, I've included a copy of Vernon Buerg's famous shareware LIST program

for DOS users on each disk. Any word processing program can be used to search the files as well.

 # Internet 1—Internet Must-Have Files

This disk includes the latest versions of several key files every Internet user should have. The files are described in Chapter 6, where you will also find instructions on where to find them on the Net. But you may find it more convenient to get them in one neat package:

> ➤ *Special Internet Connections* by Scott Yanoff (text file)

> ➤ John December's *Internet-CMC List* (text and PostScript versions)

> ➤ John December's *Internet Tools Summary* (text and PostScript versions)

> ➤ The Clearinghouse List of Subject-Oriented Internet Resource Guides (text file)

> ➤ *The Unofficial Internet Book List* by Kevin Savetz

The disk also includes an excellent tutorial for DOS/Windows users called *The Beginner's Guide to the Internet* by Patrick J. Suarez.

 # Internet 2—FTP Essentials

As you know from Chapter 6, Internaut Perry Rovers maintains a list of FTP sites that's about as comprehensive as one can imagine. And he has also written the definitive FAQ file on anonymous FTP. Both the site list and FAQ file are supplied on this disk. You'll find them to be invaluable in tracking down FTP site addresses, file archives, special collections, mirror sites for the most popular FTP locations, and so forth.

 # Internet 3—Telnet Essentials (DOS/Windows only)

This disk contains Peter Scott's remarkable Hytelnet package for DOS users. The program contains a gigantic database of Telnet locations that includes at least one screen per location describing what you'll find there. It is, in effect, a gigantic, computerized directory of Telnet sites.

For ease of use, the entire thing is organized as a hypertext-style menu system. Also on this disk is Bruce Clouette's optional Subject Guide for the main Hytelnet menu, as well as a Windows front-end program, WINHytelnet.

 # Internet 4—Newsgroup Essentials

This disk contains the Spafford/Lawrence lists of Internet newsgroups, organized by newsgroup category (alternative, computer, recreation, science, etc.):

> ➢ The List of Active Newsgroups—This list includes newsgroups for all categories except **alt** (alternative), which has its own list.

> ➢ The List of Alternative Newsgroups—This list includes *only* newsgroups in the **alt** category.

You'll also find the DOS version of the Rot-13 program, which you'll need if you want to be able to decode the coded jokes and messages posted in some newsgroups. You can use the same program to encode text in the Rot-13 format.

 # Internet 5—Mailing List Essentials

This disk contains two gigantic lists of Internet and Bitnet mailing lists, plus the LISTSERV REFCARD command summary to help you communicate with mailing lists.

➤ The SRI List of Lists—Covers both Internet and Bitnet lists.

➤ Publicly Accessible Mailing Lists—Mainly Internet lists, with about a dozen or so Bitnet lists.

 # Internet 6—Compression & Conversion Tools (DOS/ Windows only)

This disk contains all of the programs DOS/Windows users need to uncompress or unarchive or decode the various files you will find on the Net. Plus a Glossbrenner-written quick-start manual to show you how to use each one. Most of these programs come with on-disk manuals as well, but you probably won't need to read them. Here are the programs:

File extension	Required program name
.arc	ARCE
.arj	ARJ
.btoa	ATOB
.cpio	PAX2EXE
.gz or .z	GZIP
.hqx	XBIN
.lzh	LHA
.pak	PAK
.pit	UNPACKIT
.shar	TOADSHR
.sit	UNSIT
.tar	TAR
.uue	UUEXE (Richard Marks)
.Z	U16
.zip	PKZIP
.zoo	ZOO

Internet 7—Just the FAQs

On this disk you will find three kinds of things. First, there is the gigantic 100-plus page FAQ Index listing all of the FAQs currently available on the Internet. Second, there are the key FAQ files dealing with topics discussed in the chapters of this book. And third, there are additional FAQs, tutorials, and files I think you'll find of interest.

➤ FAQ Index—A list of all the FAQs currently available on the Internet. Includes precise file name to help you locate the file via Archie.

➤ Compression FAQ

➤ College E-Mail FAQ

➤ Finding-Addresses FAQ

➤ Gopher FAQ

➤ IRC FAQ, Primer, & Tutorial

➤ MUD FAQ

➤ PC Games FAQ

➤ Pictures FAQ

Internet 8—World Wide Web Essentials

This disk contains a huge amount of information about the World Wide Web. The Web is white hot! Hypertext, hypermedia, and all that other good stuff is here to stay. There is no better place to start than with the files on this disk. These include:

➤ *Entering the World Wide Web: A Guide to Cyberspace* by Kevin Hughes

➤ *A Beginner's Guide to HTML* from the National Center for Supercomputing Applications (NCSA)

> ➤ *A Beginner's Guide to URLs* from NCSA

> ➤ *The URL FAQ* by Alan Coopersmith

> ➤ *The List of WWW Service Providers* by Mary E. S. Morris

> ➤ *Interesting Business Sites on the Web* by Bob O'Keefe

> ➤ *The World Wide Web FAQ* by Thomas Boutell

The disk also includes a DOS program called DE-HTML. You can use this program to quickly and easily strip out the coding from HTML files you download from Web sites.

 # Internet 9—Making Money on the Internet

I created this disk while researching and writing a book called *Making Money on the Internet* (McGraw-Hill, 1995). The book and the disk address the needs of people interested in advertising or marketing goods and services on the Net.

Among the text files on this disk are the POCIA (Providers of Commercial Internet Access) Directory by the Celestin Company. This is a comprehensive and regularly updated list of companies that offer Internet connections and other services to individuals and businesses.

The disk also includes:

> ➤ *Advertising on the Internet FAQ* by Michael Strangelove

> ➤ *International Connectivity* by Larry Landweber

> ➤ *FAQ: International E-mail Accessibility* by Olivier M.J. Crepin-Leblond

> ➤ *The Internet Mall* by Dave Taylor (excerpts)

> ➤ *The Internet Press: A Guide to Electronic Journals about the Internet* by Kevin Savetz

> ➤ *Internet Pearls* by William Hogg of SoloTech Software

➤ *Guide to Network Resource Tools* by EARN Associates

➤ *A Primer on How to Work with the Usenet Community* by Chuq Von Rospach

Also on this disk, for DOS/Windows users, is a program called Internet Acronyms from William Hogg's SoloTech software. Searchable, viewable, printable, or accessible as a TSR, Internet Acronyms gives you close to 200 pages of Net acronyms and file extensions and their meanings. DOS and Windows users will also find a program called NetDemo from Rick Hower that serves as an interactive tutorial for using many of the Internet's main features.

DOS/Windows tools & utilities

It's been my experience over the years that, whatever computing task you want to accomplish, there's almost always a program that can easily do it. In fact, there are often several programs that fill the bill. The trick is in finding the programs and picking the very best one. That's what the Glossbrenner's Choice collection is all about.

All of the programs on these disks are fully functional, and most are extensively documented in ready-to-print manuals. The software itself is either *public domain* (PD) or *shareware*. Public domain programs are yours to do with as you please. But if you like and regularly use a *shareware* program, you are honor-bound to send the programmer the requested registration fee, typically $15 to $25. No one can force you to do this, of course. But when you see a really good piece of software, supporting its creator's efforts is something you will sincerely want to do.

Animation Tools

Windows 3.1 includes the software you need to both run and embed animation files in documents. But Microsoft does not include any of the animation files you might want to use to exercise this capability. This disk fills that gap. Here you will find everything you need to immediately begin taking advantage of the animation capabilities built

into Windows 3.1—and the pre-programmed animation files you need as animation fodder.

This disk also includes the Autodesk Animation driver for Windows (MCIAAP.DRV) and the DOS version of the AAPLAY program you'll need to play .FLI ("flick") files.

 # Communicator's Toolchest

If the comm program you use doesn't have the Zmodem protocol, you can use the tools provided on this disk to add it. Zmodem is quite simply the best download protocol, and *every* online communicator should have access to it.

The disk also includes a program for adding support for CompuServe's B+ (Quick B) protocol to virtually any comm program. Plus several other extremely useful utility programs to make life online easier.

 # CommWin Communications Program

My current favorite comm program for Windows users is Gerard E. Bernor's CommWin program. It's quick, clean, intuitive, and beats the Windows Terminal program all hollow.

Encryption Tools

You have to assume that if your e-mail *can* be read it *will* be. Thus, it is always a good idea to encrypt sensitive information before sending it electronically. The programs on this disk can so thoroughly encrypt a binary or text file that cipher experts from the National Security Agency or CIA would have a tough time decoding the results. If you have the key, however, you can decrypt files in an instant.

Among other things, this disk includes Philip Zimmermann's famous *Pretty Good Privacy* (PGP) public key RSA encryption program. For more on Mr. Zimmermann, see the Steven Levy cover story "The

Cypherpunks vs. Uncle Sam" in the June 12, 1994, issue of the *New York Times Sunday Magazine*.

 # FANSI & LIST

FANSI stands for Fast ANSI, and it's a program that everyone who ever uses the DOS command line, even from within Windows, ought to have. FANSI not only dramatically speeds up your system's display and keyboard, it gives you *complete* control over both. The feature you will find most crucial, however, is *scroll-recall*. This lets you use your arrow and paging keys to scroll back through screen after screen of previously displayed text. You can clip out portions of what you see or write the entire screen buffer to a disk file with DEJAVU.EXE.

I've spoken of Vernon Buerg's LIST program before. So here I will simply say that it is probably among the top five best DOS shareware programs of all time. I refuse to use a computer without FANSI and LIST at my fingertips. They are that crucial.

 # GhostScript (2 disks)

GhostScript lets you view and print PostScript files—even if you don't have a PostScript-compatible program or printer. The main program file, compressed, is over 1.2 megabytes. And the add-on utilities and font files take up a couple of megabytes more. Nevertheless, if you've got the space on your hard drive and you don't have PostScript, you might want to give GhostScript a try.

 # Graphic Workshop

Graphic Workshop (GWS) by Steven Rimmer, founder of Alchemy Mindworks, is designed to help IBM-compatible users deal with nearly any kind of graphics file. GWS lets you quickly view, print, crop, scale, and convert to and from virtually every graphics file format going, including ART, BMP, CUT, EPS, EXE, GEM/IMG, GIF, HRZ, JPG, JFIF, JPEG, IFF/LBM, MAC, MSP, PIC, PCX, RAS, RLE TGA, TIFF, TXT, and WPG.

 # Graphic Workshop for Windows

Steven Rimmer's Graphic Workshop for Windows does everything GWS for DOS does, and more. Including presenting you with a "thumbnail" screen showing you quick renditions of each graphic file on your disk. This saves time since it ensures that you will always load just the image you want.

 # Instant File Management: QFILER, QEDIT, & Associates

QFILER (Quick Filer) by Kenn Flee gives you *complete* control over your files and disk directories. You can tag a group of dissimilar files for deletion or for copying to another disk or directory. You can easily move up and down your directory trees, altering the date and time stamps of files, changing their attributes, compressing, uncompressing, and peering into archives.

Also on this disk is WHEREIS, a lightning fast Archie-like file finder. And QEDIT, the famous DOS text-editing program. QEDIT specializes in creating plain text of the sort you must use on the Net, yet it gives you many of the convenience features of a full-blown word processor.

 # Newkey Keyboard Macroing Program

Frank A. Bell's Newkey is a keyboard macroing program for DOS users that offers an easy way to repeat long FTP and Telnet site addresses. With Newkey loaded into memory, you can type an FTP address once and, should the site be unavailable, retype it to try again with a single key combination. The program has tons of features that easily put it on a par with commercial products like ProKey and SmartKey.

 # Paint Shop Pro for Windows

Paint Shop Pro (PSP) is the award-winning image conversion program for Windows. PSP lets you both convert and edit graphic images, though you may find it easier to use PSP as your conversion

tool, and Paintbrush or an equivalent program as your editing tool. In any case, PSP is an enormously impressive program with the ability to accept and save to—that is, to convert among—the following graphics file formats: BMP, CLP, CUT, DIB, EPS, GIF, IFF, IBM, JIF, JPG, LBM, MAC, MSP, PCX, PIC, RAS, RLE, TGA, TIFF, WPG.

Qmodem Communications Program

Here's what *Computer Shopper* had to say about Qmodem from Mustang Software: "This is simply the best DOS-based shareware communications package you can find . . . simple to set up and use, and it features about every bell and whistle you expect from a communications package . . . a true powerhouse. . . ." I heartily agree. If you don't have a first-class comm program yet, try Qmodem.

Sound Tools

Here are some of the most interesting sound files and sound utility programs available. (You will need a SoundBlaster or equivalent sound board.) Among other things, you can set things up so that you will hear Clint Eastwood say, as you exit Windows, "Well, we're not just gonna let you walk out of here . . ." Guaranteed to break the ice at parties.

Also included is the Microsoft driver for your PC's speaker (SPEAKER.DRV), which will allow you to hear .WAV and other sound files without installing a soundboard. And SOX, the "SOund eXchange" program that can convert sound files from one format to another.

System Configuration Tools

This disk includes the UARTTOOLS package mentioned in Chapter 3. It allows you to find out whether any of your COM ports have the 16550A National Semiconductor UART, and if so, what interrupts they are using. The disk also includes a number of other useful configuration tools for DOS users.

 # Text Treaters

This disk contains some 45 programs to manipulate, filter, and prepare a text file in virtually any way you can imagine. For example, CHOP will cut a file into the number of pieces you specify. TEXT lets you remove all leading white space on each line of a file, remove all trailing blanks, or convert all white space into the number of spaces you specify. CRLF makes sure that every line in a text file ends with a carriage return and a linefeed so it can be displayed and edited properly.

 # Visual BASIC Runtime (VBRUN) Libraries

Many of the programs you will find on the Net are written in Visual BASIC and require that a runtime library file be present on your disk. You are expected to have the necessary dynamic link library file, since most programmers don't include it in their packages. This disk gives you what you need: VBRUN100.DLL, VBRUN200.DLL, and VBRN300.DLL.

 # Order form

You can use the order form on the next page (or a photocopy) to order Glossbrenner's Choice disks. Or you may simply write your request on a piece of paper and send it to us. All disks are 3.5-inch, high-density (1.44MB), DOS formatted. The cost is $5.00 per disk, plus $3.00 for shipping by U.S. Mail ($5.00 to addresses outside the U.S.).

We accept Visa and MasterCard, as well as checks or money orders made payable to Glossbrenner's Choice. (U.S. funds drawn on a U.S. bank or international money orders.) Please allow one to two weeks for delivery. For additional information, write or call:

Glossbrenner's Choice
699 River Road
Yardley, PA 19067-1965
215-736-1213 (voice), 215-736-1031 (fax)
E-mail: **alfred@delphi.com**

Glossbrenner's Choice Order Form for Readers of **Internet 101**

Name _____

Address _____

City _____ State _____ ZIP _____

Province/Country _____ Phone _____

Payment [ ] Check or Money Order payable to **Glossbrenner's Choice**

        [ ] Visa/MC/AMEx_____ Exp __ / __

Signature _____

Send to: Glossbrenner's Choice   215-736-1213 (voice)
            699 River Road   215-736-1031 (fax)
            Yardley, PA 19067-1965   **alfred@delphi.com**

The Internet Toolkit

____ Internet 1 Internet Must-Have Files
____ Internet 2 FTP Essentials
____ Internet 3 Telnet Essentials
____ Internet 4 Newsgroup Essentials
____ Internet 5 Mailing List Essentials
____ Internet 6 Compression & Conversion Tools
____ Internet 7 Just the FAQs
____ Internet 8 World Wide Web Essentials
____ Internet 9 Making Money on the Internet

DOS/Windows Tools & Utilities

____ Animation Tools
____ Communicator's Toolchest
____ CommWin Communications Program
____ Encryption Tools
____ FANSI & LIST
____ GhostScript 1—Program Files
____ GhostScript 2—Fonts & Supplementary Files
____ Graphic Workshop
____ Graphic Workshop for Windows
____ Instant File Management: QFILER, QEDIT, & Associates
____ Newkey Keyboard Macroing Program
____ Paint Shop Pro for Windows
____ Qmodem Communications Program
____ Sound Tools
____ System Configuration Tools
____ Text Treaters
____ Visual BASIC Runtime (VBRUN) Libraries
____ Total number of disks, 3.5-inch HD ($5 per disk)   _____

Other Glossbrenner Books (Book prices include $3 for Book Rate shipping.)

____ The Little Online Book, Peachpit Press ($21)   _____
____ Making Money on the Internet, McGraw-Hill ($23)   _____
____ Finding a Job on the Internet, McGraw-Hill ($19)   _____
____ The Information Broker's Handbook, McGraw-Hill ($38)   _____

                                     TOTAL   _____

Pennsylvania residents, please add 6% Sales Tax.   _____

Shipping Charge ($3.00 for shipment to U.S. addresses
   and $5.00 for shipment outside the U.S.)   _____

              GRAND TOTAL ENCLOSED   _____

Index

Illustrations are in **boldface**

X

XBIN decompression, 82, 85
Xmodem, 43
xtoa and xxe files, 84

Y

Yahoo guides on WWW, 115-116, 189,
    284-286, **285**, 297, **298**
Yanoff List, 47, 74, 189
Yanoff, Scott, 74, 306
Ymodem, 43

Z

z files, 84, 85, 86
Ziff Davis home page for hardware
    information, 38, **38**
Zimmermann, Philip, 123, 312
zip files, 84, 85, 86
ZipIt, 86
Zmodem, 43, 45, 312
zones, 124-125
ZOO files/decompression, 79, 84, 85,
    86

About the Author

Alfred Glossbrenner is the author of more than 30 books on personal computers, online services, the Internet, and other topics. Hailed as "The Great Communicator" by the *New York Times*, he has been a freelance writer, editor, and book packager since graduating from Princeton in 1972. The best known of his non-computer-related books are *The Art of Hitting .300* (Hawthorn, 1980) and *The Winning Hitter* (Hearst, 1984), both written with the late, great Charley Lau. The thread that unites these books with his computer titles is an uncanny knack for explaining complex subjects in a way that anyone can understand.

Mr. Glossbrenner lives with his wife, Emily, in a 1790s farmhouse on the Delaware River in Bucks County, Pennsylvania.